The Beginner's Cow

The Beginner's Cow

MEMORIES of a VOLGA GERMAN from KANSAS

LOREN SCHMIDTBERGER

Donella Press
Kirksville, Missouri

Library of Congress Cataloging-in-Publication Data
(for 2016 edition)

Names: Schmidtberger, Loren F., 1928-
Title: The beginner's cow : memories of a Volga German from Kansas / by Loren Schmidtberger
Description: Kirksville, Missouri : Truman State University Press, [2016] | Series: American
Midwest series | Includes bibliographical references.
Identifiers: LCCN 2016009118 (print) | LCCN 2016015175 (ebook) | ISBN
9781612481685 (pbk. : alk. paper) | ISBN 9781612481692 (ebook)
    Subjects: LCSH: Schmidtberger, Loren F., 1928- | Russian
        Germans—Kansas—Biography. | German Americans—Kansas—Biography. | Farm
        life—Kansas—Ellis County—History—20th century. | Community life—Kansas—Ellis
        County—History—20th century. | Kansas—Social life and customs—20th century. | Elli1
        County (Kan.)—Social life and customs—20th century. | Ellis County (Kan.)—Biograph1
        | College teachers—New Jersey—Jersey City—Biography. | Saint Peter's College (Jersey
        City, N.J.)—Faculty—Biography.
Classification: LCC F690.R85 S36 2016 (print) | LCC F690.R85 (ebook) | DDC
    978.1/19--dc23
LC record available at https://lccn.loc.gov/2016009118

Reprint edition:
ISBN (paper): 978-1-955068-03-1
ISBN (ebook): 978-1-955068-04-8

In loving memory of my wife,
Mary

Hwaet is ðeos run?

—MPS

Contents

Part 2: Grade School Years

Part 3: Hays Junior-Senior High School

Part 7: The Senior Years, and the End of an Era

Part 8: Life Today

Part 9: Thoughts, Scattered and Otherwise, on Literature, Verve, and Verse

Acknowledgments

The many people I am indebted to from this book's inception to its completion appear in chronological order. The level of gratitude in all instances is deep.

I began *The Beginner's Cow* as a journal entry I showed to a bereavement professional at Hospice of Rockland County, New York. Mary, my wife of forty-seven years, had unexpectedly died. I had just retired from fifty-one years of teaching and we had moved some distance away from the college into a community relatively new to us. So I was decidedly at loose ends, and the woman I spoke with suggested that a constructive way of passing the time would be to flesh out the journal entry I showed her.

What happened next by chance could not have happened any better by design. After a meeting of the Widows and Widowers Club of Rockland County, Bob Harkin, retired deputy chief, FDNY, invited me to join a group of retirees who wrote for the fun of it. I was the first new addition in five years. The group's leader is Lynn Lauber, a novelist and freelance writer, who assigns a weekly prompt. We meet for an hour and a half or so at Joan Gussow's home in Piermont, New York, overlooking her famed garden on the banks of the Hudson River. A celebrated nutritionist, Joan's books include *Growing, Older* and *This Organic Life*. We take turns reading, and the camaraderie I have come to feel there is akin to what I imagine it to be with an enduring athletic team. So let me applaud the entire lineup now. In addition to Lynn, Joan, and Bob, there are Elliott

Eichler, Sylvia Glick, Joan O'Malley, Diane Raider, Marvin Penney, and Toby Hindin.

I sent a copy of my first essay to an avid reader and fellow member of Widows and Widowers, Pat McLaughlin. Her enthusiastic response emboldened me to ask other friends to read, and they have humored me along: Charles Castrovinci, Kathy Monahan, Charlotte Bast, Angela Caiati, Natalie Arner, Anne Serra, and Mary Mullane. Pat Salvesen's friendship has been sunshine that lightens up even the most discouraging moments.

Supportive and helpful, too, have been my siblings: Georgine, Alvin, Alvina, Armella, Virgil, and Janice. All of them read, fact-checked, and otherwise commented on at least those essays they outlived, Jan being the only one to have survived to the book's completion and who gave it a good cleaning of errata and infelicities of phrasing. This may be as good a place as any to mention that on this page I have not distinguished between the quick and the dead, acting on the belief that gratitude does not know these boundaries.

My children are all indisputably alive and have conscientiously urged me on. They are Mike, John, Ann, Paul, James, and Mary Frances, who gave me the advantage of her sound advice throughout the writing. Paul took time away from his own writing to assemble the essays into their final order and then edit them into coherence. In the course of this onerous, time-consuming task, he managed to add patience to his many preexisting virtues.

I am grateful to my sons- and daughters-in-law: Margie Sung, Corinne Lalin, Bob Pagano, James Masten, and Robin Samuels. And my grandchildren are a constant delight. They are Rebecca and Aidan Schmidtberger, Emily and Catherine Pagano, and Calee and Mollie Schmidtberger.

Finally, I would like to express my sincere gratitude to the wonderful people at Truman State University and Truman State University Press, with particular thanks to Barbara Smith-Mandell, whose steady and steadying hand led me from start to finish.

Introduction

Chants going forth from the centre from Kansas.

—Walt Whitman

I am sitting at my computer in Rockland County, New York—about twenty miles north of New York City—on a cold January evening. Just a few minutes earlier, I finished mixing a solution of rubbing alcohol and water for cleaning my windshield and the windshield wipers against the snow promised for the next day. The smell of my homemade antifreeze stirs a distant memory. It's like watching the curtain go up on a play.

In this memory—my earliest, in fact—I am sitting beside my grandmother on a brown, imitation-leather davenport. She has her arm around me, pulling me close against her blue and gray, paisley-print dress. It is 1931, and we are inside a farmhouse on the dusty, windswept plains of western Kansas. I am not quite three years old.

We are watching my father and Uncle Nick lifting Grandfather back onto his bed. Behind them is a white table. On it are a washbasin, a washcloth, and a bottle of liniment. Beyond the table is a large window, the frame shiny from a coat of pale yellow enamel paint, and on the wide windowsill are a water pitcher and some little bottles. Off to the side are a tobacco pouch and a pipe, but the room smells of alcohol and disinfectant, not tobacco. Daddy is tight-lipped, straining very hard. Grandfather is moaning loudly and refusing to cooperate—or unable to cooperate—with something Daddy and Uncle Nick are trying to do.

1

Grandmother's arm tightens around me. She leans over me, smiling sadly, and whispers, "*Gella Er ist frech.*" He's being naughty, isn't he?

•••

My grandparents (and parents too) were immigrants from Russia, where their forebears lived for over a hundred years. Yet the language they spoke after coming here to America was not Russian, but German. The explanation for this linguistic oddity takes us all the way back to the 1760s when Catherine the Great, Empress of Russia, recruited Germans to farm vast stretches of land along the Volga River. Newly crowned and ethnically German herself, Catherine the Great hoped to tame her empire's wild and lawless southeastern frontier by populating it with productive, permanent settlers.

Many German families answered her call. Exhausted by the strife of the Seven Years' War and enticed by the promise of free land as well as a "perpetual" exemption from military service, the Volga Germans, as they came to be called, created thriving farming communities on the once-barren fields along the Volga River. These colonies were located in the present-day Russian Federation, near the city of Saratov, not far from the border with Kazakhstan. The Volga Germans did not mix with their Russian hosts, however, nor did they learn Russian, maintaining instead their native language and customs for the next hundred years.

Relations eventually soured, and the Volga German exemption from military service was abruptly withdrawn in 1871. At the same time, the colonists were experiencing a land crisis: unable to acquire more land from the Russian authorities, their expanding population found itself in a slowly tightening vise. These two factors—the betrayed promise of a military exemption and the strangulating land squeeze—prompted a large-scale emigration from Russia beginning in the mid-1870s.

Historically speaking, the timing couldn't have been better for these immigrants because in 1862 President Abraham Lincoln had signed the Homestead Act into law. This legislation allocated 160 acres of undeveloped land in the western territories to eligible applicants. In addition, low-cost land was available through America's expanding railroads who had themselves received land grants from the government. The United States was thus offering nearly the same deal that Russia once offered: untilled land, free or at a very low price, to those willing to farm it. The Volga Germans streamed out of Russia and into the Great Plains of North America.

My father, Michael Schmidtberger, was born in 1885 in Herzog, Russia, one of the German settlements along the Volga River. My mother, Catherine Meier, was born in Kamenka, Russia, a similar settlement. My father was seven years old when he and his family left Russia, arriving in the United States in 1892. My mother was just three when she and her family made the journey in 1898. Both families arrived at Ellis Island in the shadow of the Statue of Liberty. From there, they traveled by train to join fellow Volga Germans in western Kansas, where colonies had been established as early as 1875.

I was born in 1928, and my earliest years coincided with a period of time that was harsh on Americans in general, but unduly so on Kansans and others in neighboring states. The Great Depression was a shared experience throughout the land, but Kansas was also hit by successive droughts that precipitated the devastating storms in the area that came to be called the Dust Bowl. An additional and recurring calamity was the locust plague. It presented the final test of the indomitability—or simple, mule-headed stubbornness, it might be thought—of the farmers who had not already left for California, like the fictional Joads in *The Grapes of Wrath*.

But all of these visitations of hardship converged in a short period of time, one atop the other, as it were, instead of sequentially. So focusing on my earliest memories produces a somewhat distorted view of the region where I grew up. For there are happy memories too. Regular rainfall did finally soak the parched prairie, and bountiful harvests followed; and all along were the pleasures (and occasional pains) of family life with my parents and six brothers and sisters. Then there followed the ways and byways fortuitously leading from the pastures of Kansas to the groves of academe. Next came the founding of my own family with Mary, who would be my wife for forty-seven years until her death ten years ago.

Ever a procrastinator, I didn't buy a burial plot for Mary's ashes until four years after her death. Our six children and I then interred the ashes in a ceremony the following spring, burying them in a cemetery near the house where the children grew up. When my own interment comes due, I'll no longer be in any condition to ponder the question, How did I get here? That is, How did I get to this graveyard in the lush, rolling hills along the East Coast from the place of my birth on a farm in Kansas?

These essays tell that story: from the beginner's cow, that gentle Hereford assigned to the newest, youngest milker in the family, to our one-room schoolhouse, to the storm cellar where we hid during tornadoes—but on whose cool bottom steps we, the youngest two, sometimes sat through the hottest hours of the summer afternoon, a wide-eyed audience to our oldest sister's reading of stories and poems by Robert Louis Stevenson. Then came five years of seminary in faraway Pennsylvania before returning to Kansas to finish college. Service in the Army during the Korean War would follow, then on to graduate school in New York where a temporary assignment at a local college would eventually stretch into fifty-one years there as a professor of English.

Much of the world I speak of in these essays no longer exists. The Volga German communities in Kansas have long since been fully assimilated into American life. Cows are milked by machines these days, and family farms are giving way to agribusiness. Seminaries for boys of high school age like the one I attended are largely things of the past. But the greatest change from the world of yesterday, perhaps, is that today's world is ultra-connected—and that is good, I think. Still, it is useful to revisit a time when we were so isolated out on the prairie that the arrival of our first radio in 1935—plus a windmill to charge it—marked a major turning point in our family's sense of connection to the larger world.

William Faulkner once wrote that "The past is never dead. It's not even past," a truth I felt deeply on my last visit to Kansas. That was four years ago when both of my brothers were still alive. I was heading west on I-70, nearing Ellsworth, when there arose on the distant horizon a number of gigantic wind turbines. As I drew closer, more and more of them drifted into view, until a panorama of turbines filled all the prairie north of I-70, their enormous blades revolving slowly in unhurried, regal grandeur. An awesome scene for sure it was, but after the last of the turbines receded from my rearview mirror and I turned off toward the farm where I grew up, there came to mind the wind charger my father erected there to power our first radio. That image is powerful too—that lone windmill against the prairie sky—and that memory stays with me today.

This book is a collection of memories that stay with me. In their particulars, some of them may appear to be novel, almost exotic to today's readers, most of whom have probably not experienced a dust storm, or milked a cow—be it a gentle, beginner's cow or a normally willful one. Most people have never watched, astonished, as a B-17 accidentally bombed the family farm. Or dozed through a lecture on the poetry of the Scottish Chaucerians. Yet experiences like these, if looked at closely, have a way of illuminating things that matter. Sharing my memories now, as I near my journey's end, seems a good way of connecting past and present in this ever-changing, glorious world.

• • •

A detailed account of the Volga German people—and my family's specific place in their history—can be found in the afterword, which covers the historical pressures behind the original move from Germany to the lonely Russian steppe, the circumstances and economics of migration to America a century later, the specifics of where the immigrants settled in America and why, the slow path toward assimilation in the United States, and the tragic fate of those who stayed behind in Russia at the hands of Joseph Stalin. In addition, a select bibliography of some of the excellent resources available for further inquiry is provided.

A final note: the German quoted throughout this book is a dialect specific to the Volga Germans of Ellis County, Kansas.

Part 1

Early Memories, and a Dose of Local History

The great advantage of living in a large family is the early lesson of life's essential unfairness.

—Nancy Mitford

Fick-door-y

When they arrived in the United States, the Volga Germans often gave their towns the same name as the place they left behind in Russia. That place, in turn, was frequently named for their long-distant village in Germany.

But the town in Kansas where my father was raised was called Victoria, a name that honored the reigning British queen. So what went wrong? Why would Volga Germans from Herzog, Russia, choose a name like Victoria for their new community in Kansas?

The answer is that they didn't. Victoria had actually been founded by Scottish immigrants—a mere thirty-eight of them—some three years prior to the arrival of the first Volga Germans. But the Scots' hope of bringing a genteel British way of life to the Kansas prairie—tallyho, the fox, and all that—failed within a few years, and those who survived the wind-driven winters and the summer heat returned to Scotland, abandoning Victoria.

Meanwhile, in 1875, the first families of Volga Germans from Herzog, Russia, were establishing a town adjacent to Victoria. Naturally enough, they called their new town Herzog. Within a few years, as additional German immigrants continued to arrive in Herzog, the adjoining area of Victoria—now completely emptied of Scots—was repopulated by Germans. But the name Victoria survived. It was Victoria that remained in the railroad listings, and it was Victoria that remained in the United States postal system. And the Germans, when speaking English, came to call their town Victoria too, though they pronounced it *Fick-door-y.*

Settling in Fick-door-y was no accident, and the historical forces leading to the choice of that particular land date back as far as the 1860s. At that time, a certain Reverend Wilhelm Staerkel, a Reformed minister in the Volga German colonies, traveled to Missouri and Kansas as a missionary, returning to the Volga in 1869. There, by all accounts, he sang the praises of America's Homestead Act.

As conditions in the Volga declined—the betrayal of conscription coupled with the suffocating effect of the land shortage—a meeting was held in the Herzog colony in 1874. A handful of emissaries were selected to journey to the United States and return with grain and soil samples. Even more important, they brought back enthusiastic, promotional literature from the American railroad companies who had vast swaths of cheap land-grant land to sell. The Volga Germans did not repeat the mistake they had made a century earlier when they blindly moved to Russia only to face terrible hardships ranging from blizzards to wolf attacks to marauding Kirghiz tribes. This time, they did their research first.

Following the emissaries' favorable reports, the first five emigrant families left Katharinenstadt in 1875 and reached Topeka, Kansas, establishing that city as a hub for Catholic Volga German immigrants. As for the founding of Herzog itself in 1876, the immigrant families who settled it stayed in Topeka while the men scouted for land. They took the Atchison, Topeka & Santa Fe Railroad out toward Great Bend, Kansas, but thought the price of the land there, $5 per acre, was too high. They returned to Topeka, and this time took the Kansas Pacific Railway to the Hays area, guided by some of the railroad's agents. And there—for the much more reasonable price of $2 to $2.50 an acre—farmland was purchased and the village of Herzog was reborn, this time in the United States.

Fick-door-y, then, is where it is largely thanks to a talkative nineteenth-century clergyman and a $3-per-acre discount.

The Land

My paternal grandfather, John Schmidtberger, built a house in the middle of Victoria, then homesteaded a quarter—and bought the adjoining quarter—on land some thirteen miles south on the fringes of Ellis County. For those unfamiliar with the term *quarter*, throughout most of the American heartland, the basic unit for buying and selling land is the section, a unit of land a mile long and a mile wide, containing 640 acres. Its subunits are, of course, the half section (320 acres) and the quarter (160 acres).

My grandfather built a farmhouse on this land thirteen miles away from Victoria. Why did he settle so far away from the rest of the community? Because by the time John came to Victoria, all the land closer to town had been taken. Still, this farmhouse was just the beginning of John's dreams for the future. He already had three sons and would probably have more. He would give each one of them a house on a half section, or even a full section, if not in Ellis County, then across the border in Russell County—never dreaming that Russell County would become one day the home of two senators, Bob Dole and Arlen Specter. Nor did John's dreams include the stroke that would leave him almost impoverished and a semi-invalid for the remaining nineteen years of his life.

They had just finished building the farmhouse when the stroke laid Grandfather low. But they moved out to the farm anyway. There my own father, then sixteen, and his brother Joe, age fourteen, were the men in the family now, responsible for working a 320-acre farm. Aided by Grandfather's instructions, which he issued from his chair or from his bed, the boys actually made a go of it. (Uncle Nick and Uncle Frank were much too young then to play a major part in the venture.)

Though far from Victoria, Grandfather's farm was actually fairly close to Pfeifer, Kansas, another town of Volga Germans from, of course, Pfeifer, Russia. That is where my mother's family had settled, and the rest is easily guessed. My father, Mike Schmidtberger, met my mother, Catherine Meier, and the two married in 1916.

Wedding photo of my parents, Michael and Catherine (Meier) Schmidt-berger, 1916.

In keeping with Volga German custom, my father and his bride moved in with his parents. In fact, their first four children—Georgine, then twins Alvin and Alvina, and then Armella—were born in that farmhouse. In 1924, my parents finally moved out of Grandfather's house into one of their own that they built on a section of rented land a mile away. That's where Virgil and I, and eventually our youngest sister, Janice, would be born.

Although this was a lateral move geographically, the move onto rented land was downward on the social ladder. Now my father was a sharecropper. That designation is not an elegant one, but it does deserve an explanation. A sharecropper is a farmer who tills some-one else's land for a share of the crop. In Kansas, the sharecropper received two-thirds of the annual yield while the landowner received one-third. Actually, since the sharecropper had to pay the consider-able expense of raising a crop, it really becomes more of a three-way split: one-third to the landowner, one-third for expenses, and one-third to the tenant farmer.

But I exaggerate the fall in social status. Dad was still a landowner too, because he retained his partial share in the family's original 320 acres. He also purchased a half section just four miles from Victoria, where my brother Alvin would eventually build a farmhouse. In any event, much of the land Dad farmed was our own, though our house and farmyard were on rented land, which we younger children none-theless thought of as our own.

Memories of My Father

I was born in October 1928, five months after my father's near-fatal accident. He was preparing a forty-acre strip for spring planting when the tractor he was driving overturned in a freak accident.

"The tractor," Alvina told me, "was unable to pull the planter up a steep incline and tipped over backwards, falling on Daddy and pinning him underneath it. Uncle Frank reached him first, but he could not budge the tractor off Daddy, who lost consciousness. Uncle Frank then rushed to our house, where Mother phoned the doctor. Neighbors who had been listening in on the party line hurried to the site of the accident, and together they managed to lift the tractor off Daddy, who remained unconscious. They were afraid to move him because of the severity of his injuries, so they waited until Dr. Anderson came from Victoria, thirteen miles away."

"They didn't wait long," Alvina continued. "Dr. Anderson's Model T Ford made good time." The doctor said my father had serious internal injuries, plus burns from the boiling radiator water that had spilled onto him. His chest was crushed. He would not survive the twenty-three-mile ride to the hospital. So, very, very carefully they brought him home. "If he makes it through the night," the doctor said, "there would be hope." During the night he regained consciousness, and two days later he was moved to Hays, twenty-three miles away, to St. Anthony's Hospital, where he would remain for the following three months.

Alvina always finished her account of my father's accident by describing the family's relief and happiness when Daddy finally came home. Then she'd add a postscript to the effect that shortly after Daddy's return, there was additional joy over the arrival of a healthy, happy baby they named Loren.

Alas, neither adjective—healthy nor happy—remained operative very long. A couple of months after my first birthday, I came down with pneumonia. A winter snowstorm left the dirt roads impassable by car. So it was off by team and wagon to the doctor in Victoria. A mattress on the wagon bed and some goose down quilts made the wagon as comfortable as a modern ambulance, I should think, though of course I have no memory of it.

As to being happy, my early memories generally are not. The very earliest one is Grandfather on his deathbed. There was also the Great Depression, which began in 1929, the year after my birth, and that would cast its pall over us through the mid-1930s. Memories of the Depression linger with me still. I'm thinking in particular of the time I overheard my father tell my mother that he was "down to his last nickel." I imagined further hardships to come and thought we might escape them by moving to California, as so many others did, before I learned that Daddy had only been down to the last nickel in his pocket when he finished the week's shopping at the Farmers' Co-op in Victoria.

There were also the tornadoes that sent us scurrying to the cellar, where we huddled around my oldest brother, Alvin, ten years older than I, as he stood holding fast to the rope that kept the cellar doors from sailing away. This was the exact same spot where my oldest sister, Georgine (more often called Jean), read to us younger children from a collection of books shelved there. On really hot days, she would take us—little Virgil and Loren, and then a couple of years later just little Loren—into the cool of the cellar while less fortunate older folks had to continue toiling the long afternoon through in the hot Kansas sun. Lest these memories descend into unremitting gloom, I am letting it be known now that I cherish to this day Georgine's reading, which ranged from Robert Louis Stevenson to the adventures of Chunky, the Happy Hippo.

I also remember the grasshopper plagues that denuded everything in sight. No, the stories of grasshoppers eating the clothes off the washline are not exaggerations. A swarm of grasshoppers was always a scourge to us farmers, but was manna from heaven for our chickens.

On one occasion, I remember seeing the chickens, fat with grasshoppers, clucking happily around the yard when the sky suddenly darkened. Dad called us to the cellar, and the chickens, responding instinctively to the darkening sky, returned to roost in the safety of the henhouse. I remember Daddy hooking the henhouse door after the last chicken was in, then racing to our cellar with his peculiar way of running without bending his knees, perhaps an aftereffect of his accident. He had just made it through the open doors and handed Alvin the rope to hold the doors closed when we heard a deafening sound, like a train roaring through our farmyard. But that couldn't be, since the nearest railroad tracks were ten miles away.

In about a minute the roaring stopped. Then we heard the wind dying down. After about five minutes, Dad told Alvin to let go of the rope. Alvin climbed up the steps and lifted up the cellar doors. One by one we stepped out into a gray, strangely calm day. The house was still there—intact, thank God. So were the barn, the cattle shed, the granary, and the washhouse.

But where the chicken house once stood lay splinters of wood twisted every which way, scattered hither and thither, this way and that. It'd been smashed to pieces. Amid the wreckage and for yards beyond lay chickens, lifeless now. Mother started to finger her rosary again, murmuring, when Georgine suddenly pointed at something next to the wrecked chicken house—something that seemed slightly out of place. Then I saw it. The tornado had lifted our outhouse from its place close to the chicken house and had set it down again, upside down.

Perched atop the two-holer, as if on a pedestal, stood our fierce rooster, not looking at all fierce now. Mighty Chanticleer, who used to strut around his harem so haughtily, looked rather subdued now— so bewildered and bedraggled he was. Georgine, still pointing to our rooster ridiculously astride the upside-down outhouse, started to laugh. Then Armella. Then Alvin. Then we were all laughing, even Mom and Dad.

Drought, Dust Storms, Depression

My earliest years—1928 to 1936—overlap with the era of dust storms that devastated a portion of the Great Plains. Known as the Dust Bowl, this area encompassed the panhandle regions of Texas and Oklahoma, southeastern Colorado and western Kansas. Our farm in Ellis County was not in the bull's-eye of this region, but lay in its northeastern periphery.

My early years also overlap with the Great Depression, so my earliest memories feature an intertwining of drought, deprivation, and dust storms—but dust storms especially. They frightened me, these gigantic clouds that came rolling across the prairie, leaving drab, grayish drifts of dust in their wake, covering and sometimes even burying whatever lay in the wind's way.

Dust storms were a terrible thing to witness: grim, ugly affairs. They rolled down from above and blotted out the light. "When the dust fell," writes Timothy Egan, in *The Worst Hard Time*, "it penetrated everything: hair, nose, throat, kitchen, bedroom, well." Yes, even the water we pumped from our ten-foot-deep well was dust-flavored after a storm. My parents and the older children would seal off our windows and doors with wet towels and sheets to keep out the dust. So after the storm passed and we stopped holding wet handkerchiefs to our faces, we needed only a broom, not a shovel, to sweep up the dust. In our one-room schoolhouse, though, after the particularly heavy storm of April 14, 1935, we had to use a wheat scoop the next morning to remove the dust that lay in scalloped heaps across the floor. That dust storm is remembered as Black Sunday; it darkened the skies as far away as New York and served as a very unwelcome grand finale to the dust storm era.

The next year brought rain, ending the drought, which of course ended the dust storms too, simultaneously relieving us of both afflictions. As of that point, though, our wheat farm had yielded no wheat to speak of for a biblical-sounding seven years. But we, like our neighbors in Freedom Township, eked out a living from other sources of income, primarily from our cows, pigs, and chickens. "We lived on those cream checks," was a refrain heard in much of the reminiscing about the "dirty thirties."

My own memories include the wooden egg crates we filled and delivered weekly to the Farmers' Co-op in Victoria. I also recall the chickens that we butchered and dressed to pay for an appendectomy—whose, I can't remember—at St. Anthony's Hospital in Hays. I don't think we ever sold our smoked hams or the pork sausage we made; they were for our large family's home consumption, especially through the long winter. But I do remember scraping the pigs' small intestines clean and then washing them before they were put to use as casing for the ground pork mixture that would be squeezed into them, making one long sausage that was coiled into a glass jar. I remember, too, of course, helping to lug the five-gallon cream cans into our Model A Ford for delivery to the railroad depot. Eventually there would come in the mail one of those cream checks that would see our family through the worst of the worst times.

Of course, my family and I weren't the only ones who needed to eat on our farm: cows need food too. Quite a few farmers, lacking the means to provide forage, were forced to sell or butcher their herds as the only alternatives to watching them starve. So how did our family get the forage for our herd of twenty-five or so milk cows, calves, and steers? Over half of the acreage we farmed at that time was pastureland—the terrain too uneven or stone-strewn for raising wheat. Passed over as undesirable by the first settlers, it was acquired by latecomers like my grandfather. The buffalo grass on these untilled acres held the soil in place during the dust storms and provided grazing for our herd. We were also able to supplement grazing, especially in winter, with forage from drought-resistant sorghum developed by government agencies as the drought crisis dragged on.

Still, how hard were times on our farm, as compared with farms farther south in the heart of the Dust Bowl? We had relatives in Dodge City, some eighty or so miles southeast. On returning from a visit to them in 1935, one of my uncles gave a sympathetic shake of his head. "They have it worse there," was all he would say. And he was right. Indeed, the strategies people employed to survive—some that worked and many that did not—put me in mind of Faulkner's remark in his Nobel Prize acceptance speech: "I believe that man will not merely endure; he will prevail."

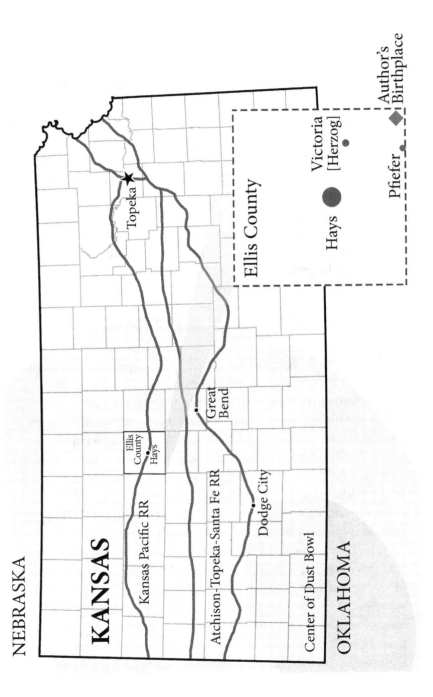

Regeneration

Memories of the dust storms inevitably lead to thoughts about the Joads in John Steinbeck's famous novel *The Grapes of Wrath*. After I read Steinbeck's description of the hardships that befell the Joads on their journey to California, and the tribulations and disappointments they suffered at their journey's end, I felt great relief and gratitude that my family did not take to the road, but stayed put on our farm in Ellis County, Kansas, where we waited out the drought, the dust storms, and the Depression.

In 1936, rain fell again, ending the seven-year drought. That September, the month when winter wheat is planted, there was enough moisture in the ground for the seeds to germinate. So in October, the newly planted fields, mostly barren for seven years now, showed all green again. These sprouts of winter wheat would lie dormant under the snow and then revive in the spring, sending up stalks three or more feet high.

From the top of the stems would emerge spears of wheat, first green, then a greenish gold, then, when ripe for harvesting, amber (if Turkey Red) or pale brown (if durum)—a wonder to behold.

In late spring, visitors from our country's coasts would invariably compare these vast fields of wheat undulating in the wind to ocean waves. In 1893, Katharine Lee Bates, traveling from Massachusetts to Denver, beheld the endless stretch of ripening grain in the Kansas wheat fields. "The wonder of the sea-like expanse," she wrote in her diary, inspired the opening lines of "America the Beautiful": "O beautiful for spacious skies / for amber waves of grain."

Photos have captured the amber color of a field of ripe Turkey Red well enough, but they can not reproduce the undulating motion of "amber waves." Modern motion photography can, of course, record wavelike movements, but alas, there are no longer any wavelike movements in wheat fields to be photographed—at least not in the wheat fields I have seen in recent years. The long—up to five feet tall—stalks that used to sway so picturesquely in the wind could also be flattened by rain into the mud, where they lay unharvestable. So varieties with shorter and sturdier stems were developed without altering the quality of the harvested kernels. The wheat harvested these days is only about two feet high and highly uniform. Not only does being shorter make standing upright easier, the uniformity of height enables the combine to cut all the heads while taking in a minimum of stalks, that is, straw. So the picturesque and poetic has given way to the practical in wheat farming.

To return to my parents' time: when the drought ended, not every acre of the prairie perked up right away. Here and there, in the midst of the greening landscape, lay the untilled fields of abandoned farms. Where nothing had been planted, now grew a tangle of unsightly vegetation: cockleburs, thistles, and the like. They interrupted the landscape, these abandoned fields, as if bearing silent witness to how sadly a farmer's toiling finally ended.

Abandoned fields did not remain abandoned very long. Their owners found new tenants, especially when normal rainfall returned. One of these abandoned fields lay only a mile south of our farm, but on the south side of the Smoky Hill River in Rush County, a faraway land to us Volga Germans in Ellis County. The prior farmer, Sy Montgomery, had not been able to make a go of it, but he had not left for California. After losing his only son in an excavating accident, he lost his health and died in Rush County's rest home for the indigent.

As a result, Sy's farm became available for renting, and in 1936 my father signed the lease, thus adding to our farm the land that to this day we still call Across the River. I was only eight years old in 1936, but I remember acquiring Across the River as a major turning point in our family's fortunes.

Even before 1936, it had become clear to Dad that the quarter section he owned would never yield enough to provide more than a marginal subsistence. He saw that the way to prosperity lay in farming more acreage. The money from selling wheat had to offset the high cost of the machinery used for raising it. But the tractor and implements for tilling a mere 160 acres could till many more. So by 1936, our McCormick Deering Model 15-30 tractor was tilling 480 acres, and Dad was looking for still more land to farm. The Great Depression and the lengthy drought had left him without the means for buying more land, so sharecropping was how we enlarged our farm.

The arable portion of the half section, Across the River, was about 180 acres, the remaining 140 acres being taken up by the river and the pastureland on the encircling hills. When Dad took it over, Across the River had not been worked for a couple of years. Viewed from a hillside, this dust-duned, weed-choked, forsaken land looked singularly unpromising.

Getting our tractor and implements onto this land was a bit daunting. Ed Hollandsworth's ranch lay between our farm and the river, so we had to drive through his pasture. Getting his permission was no problem: it was Ed, in fact, who had alerted Dad to the possibility of renting the land we now needed to get to.

There was no bridge, so we simply drove across the river. At the point where we crossed the Smoky Hill River, its bed of gray-orange sand was about 150 feet wide. But the actual stream itself, which meandered eastward in the Smoky's spacious bed, was generally only a few yards wide and perhaps a foot deep. So driving our tractor and our truck across was not an issue most of the time. If the stream was too high after a rain, we crossed with a team and wagon. When the water rose even higher, we detoured to the Gorham Road Bridge and then through two farms on the other side, a total distance of about seven miles.

I was too little in 1936 to help with restoring the land Across the River. This was mostly a matter of leveling the dunes of topsoil and getting rid of the massive tangles of weeds. Dad, Alvin, and Virgil first leveled the land, then they used a lister to create ridges, then a cultivator to cut away weeds and shore up the stalks of the young plants.

Alas, a cultivator could not kill cockleburs. These pesky weeds had to be literally extirpated—pulled up by the roots—which only the human hand could do. I was not too little to be pressed into this tiring service. So for the first year, Dad, Alvin, Virgil, and I went up and down the field, row after row, uprooting the young cocklebur plants before they could mature into the ugly seed balls they become.

(A popular Kansas joke has an enterprising farmer set up a road stand to sell cockleburs to tourists as porcupine eggs.)

Over time, water has been diverted from the Smoky Hill River for irrigation, reducing the river's flow to a rivulet. When I last saw the Smoky a few years ago, its bed was completely dry. The land we knew as Across the River is across no such thing anymore. Semantically obsolete, it is still the rich, productive piece of farmland that my father once saw in a weed-choked, abandoned homestead.

Mother's Story

My mother was pulled out of school at the beginning of third grade. It was the great disappointment of her life. The event seems a variation of the cruel stepmother motif, and resentment at having been so ill-served remained a part of Mother's life. But the experience did not leave her embittered, at least not in my perception of the matter.

When she talked to me about her early years, Mother would sometimes include her regret over the untimely end of her formal education, but it was usually not the focal point of her stories. Happy episodes were much more numerous than sad ones, and when she came to the story of her truncated schooling, she did not go into the details of how and why this happened. I learned much more about the event from my five older siblings than from her.

Catherine, my mother, was born in Kamenka, Russia, in 1895. In 1898, when my mother was three years old, her parents, George and Maria Meier, immigrated to America, joining relatives in Pfeifer, Kansas. Shortly after Catherine turned four, her mother died in childbirth along with the baby. Despite her young age, Catherine had distinct memories of her mother. When she read and sang to us children, she often talked about her own mother's beautiful singing voice and how she used to read stories from the two books they'd brought with them from Russia. My older siblings remember seeing these books that my mother treasured, but alas, they are no longer anywhere to be found.

When Catherine was five, her father married a widow, Katerina Apfelhans, who already had two children, ten-year-old Mary and eight-year-old Johnny. By all accounts, these two new siblings accepted my mother with lasting affection as their little sister. It was the stepmother from whom Mother felt emotionally distant from their first meeting on. Katerina—the stepmother—had no schooling at all and was, in fact, illiterate. My mother's real mother, on the other hand, not only cherished her two books, but had actually been a letter-writer back in Russia. By that I don't mean she was someone who dashed off cheery missives to friends far and near—she was someone who wrote letters for those who could not write. The mother and the stepmother were simply very different people.

Just when it was time for Catherine to start third grade, Katerina and her husband had their first baby. Katerina didn't feel well, was excessively tired, and insisted that Catherine stay home, along with her stepsister, Mary, to help care for the new baby. Mary had been taken out of school after only one year, but she had not liked school anyway, so she actually preferred staying at home.

But Catherine loved school, did especially well, and was well liked by peers and teachers. According to my sister Alvina's account, "Mother fussed and cried, begged to go to school, but to no avail." The nuns talked to her stepmother and her father, insisting that Catherine be allowed to return to school. Even the parish priest came out to the farm to persuade them to let Catherine continue with her schooling. "It is wrong to keep such an intelligent child home," he argued, but his words went unheeded. Catherine had to stay home to care for little baby Elizabeth; then her stay was prolonged with the arrival of the next baby, Regina, then with George, and finally Boniface over the next ten years.

Mother never blamed her father. She would say that he had to go along with his new wife's wishes to keep peace in the family. To spare her father, Catherine tried her best to be a dutiful daughter to Katerina. And here I do not have to rely on Alvina or my other siblings' accounts, because I heard it from the source myself. Die Pfeifer Grossmutter, as we called Katerina, once told me—it was at a birthday party for Grandpa—what a good child my mother had always been.

Nor did I ever hear Mother say a bad word about Die Pfeifer Grossmutter. So I was oblivious of any resentment Mother bore her until after Grossmutter died. I was about ten years old as we were driving home from the burial, with Alvin at the wheel, Dad and I in front, Mom, Georgine, and little Janice in back. I remarked, in wonderment, that "Momma didn't cry." That silenced everyone in the car. Then Daddy said to me, *"Mir braucha net immer weina"* (We don't always need to be crying). Then, in English, speaking louder, he commented on the weather and the state of the crops in the fields alongside the road while Mother, in the backseat, really did cry now into Georgine's shielding embrace.

Mother remained close to her half-sisters and brothers, and we children always thoroughly enjoyed our cousins' company when the families got together. One of the last times that happened was in 1947 when Grandpa Meier died. As we gathered for the burial, few would have noticed the single grave with only a marker on it a few rows down and off to the side from the grave where my mother's father and stepmother were now buried together, side by side.

On one of my frequent visits back to Kansas in much more recent years, Alvin, Armie, Virgil, Janice, and I visited the Pfeifer cemetery. We paused a few moments at Grandpa's and Die Pfeifer Grossmutter's grave, and I murmured the names on the tombstone: George Meier—Katerina Apfelhans Meier.

Then my sister Janice tugged on my arm and I followed her a few rows down, with Virgil, Armie, and Alvin following. Now, where there had once been just a plain marker, stood a tombstone. On it was inscribed, quite simply, "Mother. Maria Meier, 1867–1898."

"Mother put that up," Janice softly explained, "but she waited until after Grandpa died."

Tools of the Trade

An Inventory of Stock Phrases

My father was as competent a man as I have ever known. He could do just about anything, from butchering a pig to building a house. He was truly a jack-of-all-trades in the saying's original sense, without the pejorative phrase added.

To be sure, back in Dad's time and place, many farmers did things for themselves that nowadays are done by specialists—by carpenters, masons, machinists, shoemakers, and repairmen. But I'd venture to say that Dad did more of such things than other farmers in our area. So if I try to recall a product my father used, there float through my memory an endless procession of implements and tools my father wielded.

I see the manual hair clippers Dad used Saturday evenings, not just for giving haircuts to his three sons, but to a few other youths, and their elders too. Next I see his shoe last, and alongside it a dozen iron shoes ranging in size from six to twelve inches. He slides one of these in place on top of the last, and then fits the shoe that needs repairing over the appropriately sized iron, thus making sure the resoled shoe will fit whoever wears it.

But Dad does not stick to his last, so memory takes me to our work shed. Inside it, I see Dad with a pair of tongs in his left hand, lifting a ploughshare from the burning coal in the middle of the forge. Quickly he lays the white-hot ploughshare on an anvil, hammer in his right hand already uplifted, ready to strike while the iron is hot, hammering the ploughshare until it is as sharp as a sword.

Now I see myself seated on our grindstone, parked just outside the work shed. It is for sharpening lighter tools: axes, hatchets, knives, and the like. As if riding a bicycle, I pump the pedals that turn the sandstone wheel. In front, facing me, is my father. He is holding a hatchet against the revolving wheel. He leans over it, peering closely at the hatchet's edge, making sure he holds it at just the correct angle, keeping his nose close to the grindstone.

The hatchet sharpened, Dad hands it to me. So I bury the hatchet in the chopping block, there being no butchering of chickens today. Actually, for beheading chickens we used a knife, and I remember our butchering twenty-five chickens in one day to pay a hospital bill. After Dad sharpened the knife, he handed it to Virgil. I held the chicken's legs and wings together while Virgil did the beheading. That done, I set the chicken down, whereupon it would run every which way, headless, heedless, zigzagging, helter-skelter, this way and that like, well, like a chicken with its head cut off, until it finally flopped down, wherever.

That chicken's hapless meandering may well describe how this essay is proceeding, I fear, so let me retreat back to where our chickens still have their heads on straight and are clucking happily back to their boxes where they proceed to lay their eggs. One of my chores was to gather the eggs. So I would reach carefully under Biddy Hen, remove her egg, hoping all the while that she would not peck me, and then I would place the egg in the basket I was carrying. More than once I had the joy of feeling Biddy actually lay an egg, of squeezing the warm, damp egg into my palm. I placed it gently in the basket with the other eggs and continued gathering eggs until I reached the last of the boxes. Then, walking carefully, carrying all my eggs in one basket, I made my way past the dog and the cats to where mother was waiting for me at the washhouse.

Suitably Open to Suggestions

I made a fool of myself once by trying something that my older brother Virgil conned me into doing.

Many years ago, Montgomery Ward and Sears Roebuck attached little swatches of cloth, about a square inch, to pictures of slipcovers and articles of clothing in their catalogs. I must have been about five or six years old at the time when Virgil told me that if I heated one of the swatches in a frying pan, it would enlarge into the size and shape of whatever it was illustrating.

He pointed to a swatch beneath the picture of a man's suit. "That would become a real suit," he explained, then left. I thought of how grateful my father would be if I gave him a new suit. There were two suits to choose from, a gray one and a blue. I pulled off the blue swatch from its place beneath the picture of a blue suit and placed it in our frying pan, always there, ready for use, on our coal-oil stove.

I took a match from the box we kept in a drawer. We did not have one of those match dispensers that hung high up on a wall, out of the reach of children but in plain sight. I wonder now if my parents didn't think it was better to keep temptation out of sight, though within reach. In any event, I struck the match, lit the burner, and started frying a nice blue suit for my father.

But nothing happened. The pan got hotter and hotter. The handle was getting too hot to hold, even with a potholder, but the blue swatch wasn't changing shape at all. Suddenly I felt an awakening—a disenchantment. It was as if my eyes had just opened to see the shocking stupidity of what I was doing. Trembling, I turned the burner off, thankful that no one had seen me. I don't remember how I got rid of the incriminating evidence of my failed experiment in gift-giving— the burnt match, the scorched swatch, and the stain, if there was one, in the pan.

My parents never found out. Had they, I would surely remember the punishment for having committed the absolute worst of childhood sins—lighting a match. Nor did I complain to Virgil for having misled me so. I imagine I did not want to let him celebrate his success in duping me. Though when I think about it carefully, it finally dawns on me that he was probably hiding nearby, watching the whole thing and laughing—but with a pail of water ready. We didn't have running water back then. We carried it in pails from our well a few yards away, so there usually was a pail or two of water on the kitchen floor.

Nobody ever noticed that a blue swatch was missing from the new catalog. Probably no one looked at the blue suits for sale. This was during the Great Depression when my parents were too poor to order much of anything displayed on the pages of the Montgomery Ward catalog. Soon enough it would be put to a different use altogether, replacing the old catalog in the *nooshnick* (the Russian word for outhouse)—after the last of its pages were torn out.

Nooshnick was one of only a few words that the Volga Germans borrowed from Russia in their century-long stay along the Volga River. Perhaps because of the harsh, uncouth sound of *nooshnick,* my older sisters coined the more genteel, lightly humorous word, *donniker,* and *donniker* came to be what we always called our outdoor library.

Another Russian word that the Volga Germans brought with them was *arbus* (we pronounced it "*ehrbus*"), which means watermelon. It was only when I took a required course in German much later at St. Fidelis Seminary in faraway Pennsylvania, that I learned that the German word for watermelon is actually *wassermelone,* not *ehrbus.* I got a good piece of advice too, at the time.

In a conversation outside German class during recess one day, the word for watermelon came up, and I insisted that it was *ehrbus,* not *wassermelone,* as our young teacher maintained. Nothing would do but that we consult a dictionary. Would you believe it? No *ehrbus* was to be found there, only *wassermelone.* Young Father Jerry suggested that I add *wassermelone* to my obviously deficient German vocabulary. Then he icily advised me to try to learn German from the textbook instead of relying on my natural dialect, which, he suspected, was spoken nowhere in the world outside my own family farm back in Kansas.

Memory begets memory. The Russian word *ehrbus* takes me back to the same general time period when I tried frying a swatch of cloth into a suit. This time I was refusing to eat some peas, *erbsen* in German. My quick-witted mother, knowing how fond I was of watermelon, seized the opportunity that lay in the similar sounds of *erbsen* and *ehrbus*. After a day or two had gone by she assured me, her gullible youngest son, that the little green globes, *erbsen*, heaped alongside my mashed potatoes, were really baby *ehrbus*. "Yum, yum," she said, smacking her lips around a spoonful of these baby watermelons. "Just taste them and see." So I did, and to this day I relish the delicious, juicy, melony, taste of peas. It's all in the presentation, I suppose.

Postmarks

During my childhood, the nearest store of any kind was thirteen miles away in Victoria, a town with a population in 1930 of 637 people, of whom 633 were German Catholics. The remaining four, Mr. and Mrs. Shook and their two children, were English and Protestant.

Regardless of whatever sense of alienation the Shooks may have felt because of their outsider, non-Catholic status, Mr. Shook's job as postmaster placed him at the very center of the daily hum and buzz of the community. Whether his assignment to Victoria was at his request or the luck of the draw, I do not know, but as postmaster Mr. Shook was probably the only one in Victoria who knew everybody's full name and address. This included the hundred or so living outside Victoria along RFD (Rural Federal Delivery) No. 1. Our mailbox, Box 54, stood alongside the road in front of our one-room schoolhouse, the Hope Valley School.

We children always hoped Mr. Shook would come by during recess so we could wave to him, and see him wave back through his car's open window as he stopped to push the mail, often just the *Hays Daily News*, into our box. One day he surprised us by coming into the school, interrupting Teacher's reading of *Tom Sawyer*. Our flag was not flying properly, he explained. We, the five students and Teacher, followed Mr. Shook outside, where the flag looked "more like a rag than a flag," Mr. Shook was saying.

Irene Behrens and my sister Armella, the oldest two students that year, ran to the pole and lowered the flag. The bottom eyelet had torn through the fabric on that windy day, leaving the flag attached only at the top eyelet and flapping all disheveled in the Kansas wind.

Mr. Shook was a veteran—I want to say of World War I before remembering that it was just called The War back then. His time in the trenches in France may have made him especially sensitive to improper displaying of the flag—that and the fact that flying the flag was a daily ritual, weather permitting, at his post office.

Visible testimony to Mr. Shook's service in the war was a glass eye, courtesy of a German hand grenade. I learned of the glass eye before I was old enough to go to school. It was during a visit to the post office with my father. Mr. Shook made a present for me, the paper band encircling a cigar he was about to light up. I truly treasured the "ring" he placed on my finger, where it was way too large, but after we left I told my father that Mr. Shook had a funny way of looking at me. Dad then explained about the glass eye, which made it appear that Mr. Shook was looking at someone else while looking at me too.

I have sometimes wondered about Mr. Shook's feelings about being the only non-Catholic in Victoria. My oldest sister, Georgine, boarded with the Shook family for her first year of high school in Victoria, and her impression was that Mr. Shook felt completely untroubled by the lack of any Protestant church in Victoria, let alone one of his persuasion. He and his family may have even thought of it as a godsend, Jean mischievously mused, leaving them at leisure on Sunday mornings to pursue interests other than going to church.

Crime and Punishment

When she heard that I was going out to Kansas to visit our brothers a few years ago, my sister Jan, who lives in California, sent me a bunch of questions to ask them about our dad. Jan is the youngest of us, and my only surviving sibling now. When she was born in 1936, I was already eight, Virgil ten, and Alvin eighteen. "Did he ever spank us?" she asked. Dad's treatment of her was always gentle, and she couldn't imagine his striking any of us in anger. But might he have been harder on the six older children, especially the boys?

Alvin told me that yes, he got whaled once, and Alvina too, when the two of them almost burned down a wheat stack. Their sin had been playing with matches, and had it not been for a sharp-sighted and quick-thinking neighbor, a stack of unthreshed wheat would have gone up in flames.

That was the only formal spanking Alvin could remember—but whether with razor strop or belt or hand I could not make out, being hard of hearing. Alvin was ninety-three at the time he told me this, and his advancing emphysema often left him without enough air to force his words through my increasing deafness. "In general," Alvin mused, "Dad's hitting was an open-handed slap to the head, never hard enough to hurt though, so that it was the humiliation that made you cry."

Virgil agreed. Dad didn't go for laying you across his knees, he said. A cuff to the head sufficed. He thought Mom employed corporal punishment more often than Dad, but that her cuffs were even lighter.

I myself remember only one swatting. I'm sure there were more, but this is the one I remembered: "I was about five or six," I told Alvin and Virgil. "I was standing outside the granary when Dad came running up, looking as angry as I'd ever seen him. He whacked me across the head, and I went bawling into the house. There was probably more to it than that—some talking or yelling or explaining—but that's all I remember."

Alvin asked me what had made Dad so mad, but it was Virgil who answered. "Alec Behrens had parked his tractor in our yard for Dad to repair," Virgil said. "I took a small rock and pounded a nail into the radiator to see what would happen. Water leaked out. It looked like the radiator was peeing. I made two more holes, but then no more water came out. I was leaving when Dad came along. When he saw what had happened—a little water was still dripping—he got really, really mad."

Virgil stopped. Silence. Then Alvin gathered enough breath to ask, "But why did Dad hit Loren?"

"Because I told him Loren did it," Virgil said.

Grandmother's Ghost

We always stopped in for a visit with Grandma and Uncle Frank on our way back from mass at St. Boniface Church on Sundays. On one of those visits, I can vaguely remember Grandmother scolding my father for not bringing her a stick to help her walk. She was upset because she needed support to walk to the outhouse. Was Daddy supposed to make her a cane? Or maybe he was supposed to buy a crutch in Victoria and forgot?

Another visit I remember much more vividly. Armella was telling Grandma all about our catechism lesson. Grandma couldn't speak English, so Armella was speaking in German. Then Georgine and Alvina jumped into the fray, talking about the lesson in English. Grandma silenced all those around her and immediately summoned Daddy and Momma. Grandma complained about our speaking in English around her, saying we would forget how to talk in German. She warned Daddy that the time would come when his children would not be able to visit with her, their own grandmother.

In the car on the way home, Georgine, the eldest, said we should all talk in English all the time. She was driving. We should try not to sound like stupid *Rooshuns*, she said, using the then-common slang for Volga Germans. Mother pointed out a hitch in the idea of speaking only English—the fact that Grandma might be too old to learn English. Daddy, on the other hand, told Georgine to keep her eye on the road. "*Bass uff*," he said. "*Bleib im vegh*" (Look out; stay on the road). By then Georgine was turning the car into our yard and when it came to a stop, Bert, our collie, began racing in circles around it, wild with joy at seeing us all back home.

Grandma's gloomy prediction about language decay eventually came true, sort of. When all of us got together in 2007 to celebrate Georgine's ninetieth birthday, the social status pendulum had, by then, swung the other way, sweeping the descendants of Volga Germans all the way up into the highest ranks in Ellis County, Kansas.

We seven siblings were seated around the main table in the banquet hall of Corpus Christi Church in Lawrence, where Georgine then lived, over 200 miles from the old farm. We said grace in unison, and Jean added thanks to her brothers and sisters for traveling long distances to come to the reunion. She added a tribute to our late parents, to which we responded with a hearty and heartfelt "Amen!" Then, as we started to eat, someone suggested that for old times' sake we should speak in German. Great idea! But after a few "*Vie gehts*," and "*Sehr guts*," the ghost of Grandma descended. We found that after a slow start we could not keep a conversation going in German. Then Alvin broke the silence: "Well, we sure don't sound like a bunch of dumb *Rooshuns*, do we now?" And we burst out laughing, which sounds just about the same in any language.

Sound Advice

I don't recall his exact words, but the gist of my father's advice was that if at first you don't succeed, try again, and if you don't succeed on the second try, it's perfectly fine to give up, right then and there.

At the time I was trying to play a song on a pocket comb. In case you're unfamiliar with this musical adaptation of a comb, here's how it works. You take some wax paper and fold it tight over the comb, teeth upward. Now you have made a *kumspieler* (comb-player, in English), an instrument that resembles a harmonica. But instead of blowing into it the way you would a harmonica, you hum against it, which makes the wax paper vibrate in tune with your humming.

The resulting sound is unlike that made by any other instrument I've ever heard, so it's tricky to describe. Perhaps the angry wail of a distant police siren sounds something like it. Anyway, I stopped playing my *kumspieler* at my father's gentle request long before I exhausted the full range of its musical possibilities.

Another piece of advice that I took to heart came from my maternal step-grandmother. My mother was not fond of her stepmother, and Die Pfeifer Grossmutter was not fond of my mother or her children, either. But I, ever ready to please, decided to entertain Die Pfeifer Grossmutter on one of her infrequent visits.

We were alone—everyone else having discreetly vacated the room, as usual, when she entered it. I knew better than to treat her to a *kumspieler* sonata, so I decided to tell her a funny story about school. I was just getting into the funny part when Die Pfeifer Grossmutter interrupted me, saying I should either laugh or talk, but I should not do them together. Then she imitated my laughter-laced storytelling, cutting loose a cacophonous cackle that startled me out of my shoes. Never again have I ever laughed while talking, or talked while laughing.

Don't misunderstand: I have continued talking, probably more than I should, and certainly more than I have laughed. Do you remember that dour, gloomy detective on the TV show *Barney Miller*, way back in the days when there were some really good sitcoms on TV? Fish was his name. I am sure that Fish laughed sometimes, at least when off camera. As for me, I have laughed too, from time to time—as often as I have deemed appropriate—as often, even, as twice on the same day, weather permitting. So, no, I am not a proponent of unremitting gloom, the way poor Fish appeared to be.

Now I'll conclude with some advice of my own. Smile. It will cheer you up, even if there is nothing to smile about, as will likely be the case. But the physical act of smiling will lift your spirits anyway. If you like to take fifteen-minute walks, as I do, schedule some smiling into one of them. Although it's not good to laugh and talk at the same time, as we all know, it's easy to walk and smile at the same time. So once a week or so, schedule a smile into your walk. Try it; you'll like it. And if at first you don't succeed, well, try again—but just once.

Grandfather's Business Ventures

"Grandpa was a man of many talents," Virgil said to me as we were driving back from Victoria to Lawrence, Kansas, in October 2009, not the least of which was a penchant for pranks—at one point, he painted the neighboring nuns' backyard fence bright red in the middle of the night, teasing them over their fears of a communist revolution. Virgil and I had been out in Victoria visiting Alvin, all three of us widowers at that point. Both of my brothers lost their wives in 2008. Virgil's Rita died in April and Alvin's Celeste followed her in November. My own wife, Mary, preceded them two years earlier in 2006.

The three of us brothers had visited for an afternoon together in Alvin's new living room, not lamenting and not exactly celebrating either, just reminiscing and feeling good about being together for the weekend. Alvin did most of the talking, though there were stretches of silence too, while he stopped to catch his breath. Unwilling to yield to the emphysema he'd been battling for upwards of twenty years, he tended to speed up his speech as he neared the completion of a thought, thus getting every last word in ahead of the pause for air.

Alvin was eight years older than Virgil and ten years older than I. He was sharing some anecdotes from times back further than his own memory reaches, telling us about a business venture of Grandpa's almost a hundred years ago.

At the time a stroke laid Grandpa low, he owned two houses. The first was the large, two-story limestone house he'd built in Herzog (also known as Victoria), Kansas, when he arrived there from Russia in 1892. The second was the large, two-story farmhouse on the 320 acres he owned thirteen miles south of town. He convalesced from his stroke out there. From his bed at first, and then his wheelchair, he instructed his two oldest sons—Mike, sixteen at the time, and Uncle Joe, fourteen—in running the farm. As time went by, Grandpa graduated from the wheelchair to moving about with the help of a cane. Meanwhile, Dad and Uncle Joe's farming ability matured, so that Grandpa's supervision, if continued, would have dwindled into busy-body meddling.

Virgil wondered aloud how an immigrant farmer like my grand-father had the means to build a house so soon after arriving in America. The short answer is that he must have brought money with him, this despite the fact that the Volga German immigrants were, by and large, quite poor.

Back in Russia, individual farmers in the Volga German colonies never owned, nor were they permitted to own, the land they farmed for over a century. Instead, land was allocated by the Russian state to each colony, who in turn allocated it to farmers for *use*, but not own-ership. Those who wanted to leave had no land to sell. Instead, the primary means of raising the money to immigrate was the auctioning off of personal possessions. Worse still, my grandfather's departure from Russia in 1892 came at the end of a three-year famine caused by crop failure that left the colonists so desperate they fed the thatch from their roofs to their livestock in an unsuccessful attempt to keep them alive.

After arriving in America, my grandfather and his family stayed with relatives in Kansas before building his house, relying, as so many did, on networks of extended family for support. They stayed with my grandmother's older sister, Magdalena Appelhans, who'd arrived earlier with her husband, Martin Riedel. (The Apfelhans family mentioned earlier and the Appelhans family mentioned here are two different families. The former are relatives on my mother's side, the latter relatives on my father's side.) The ship manifest from his journey to America lists him as a "farmer," which is exactly what he was, though that certainly does not preclude other economic activities. In fact, he'd operated a shoe-making business in Russia in addition to farming. He brought his shoe lasts with him to America; my father used them to resole shoes—ours and many neighbors'—and Virgil and I played with them as toys. I've also heard references to another business activity of my grandfather: money lending. Still,

Ship manifest from the *Italia*, 1892, which brought my father and his family to America (they are the first five passengers listed).

I cannot say if that was the origin of, or a subsequent consequence of, his wealth, relatively speaking. I do know that we—and he himself—regarded him as a man of means (again, relatively speaking).

The point, though, is that by the time of his stroke, Grandpa had two houses, one out on the farm and the other in town. Not wanting to feel useless or in the way, Grandpa left the running of his farm to Dad and Uncle Joe, and moved the rest of the family back to the house in Herzog. There, he spotted a need in Herzog's economy and seized the opportunity to supply it. Grandpa converted the downstairs of his house into a saloon. The business flourished from the first day on, especially on Saturday nights and Sundays. Yes, Alvin explained, Grandpa kept the saloon open on Sundays too, but with the church being in plain sight right across the street, he was careful to observe the Sabbath proprieties, if not the laws. He refused to serve drinks while high mass was going on.

Grandpa never bothered to get a license, saying that nobody would ever look into a small operation like his, way out west in a little town like Herzog, Kansas. Being neither naïve nor dimwitted, Grandpa's thinking was actually the product of spending his formative years in Herzog, Russia. The law did not reach very often into the German villages along the Volga River; the Russian government pretty much left those German enclaves alone. The way it used to be in Herzog, Russia, is how it must be now in Herzog, Kansas, Grandpa thought. In any event, Grandpa's business venture might have continued to go undetected by any government had it not been for the advent of Prohibition.

With Prohibition, attention would be paid, with a vengeance, across the land to ventures like Grandpa's, wherever they were tucked away. Emissaries of the law descended one fine Sunday morning on Grandpa's enterprise. Using a sharp axe, the sheriff, a stern Baptist, and his deputies, all of them Protestants too, ruptured, one after the other, all the booze-filled drums that Grandpa had stocked in anticipation of the shortage Prohibition would create. So Grandpa's entire inventory went gurgling into the sandy soil alongside his house, irrigating the sunflowers and cockleburs that were growing there.

That ended Grandpa's venture into the saloon business. Alvin paused in his story and then chuckled. For the rest of his days Grandpa made rosaries. After a while, he actually made quite a bit of money doing that, Alvin said.

Flowers I Remember

Kansas, officially speaking, is the Sunflower State, but to us farmers, sunflowers were weeds. When picked, they leave a sticky residue that's harder to wash off than pine sap, so we always wore gloves when we uprooted by hand the sunflowers and their cousins, the cockleburs, that our tractor-pulled cultivators missed. Here in Rockland County, New York, the equivalent of a bouquet of sunflowers would be a bouquet of dandelions.

Picking flowers out in the pasture is among my earliest memories. Not that there were many flowers to pick on the parched Kansas prairie during the early 1930s. Nonetheless, in the springtime there grew some drought-resistant flowers, not in abundance to be sure, but enough of them to enable me, about four years old, to gather a bouquet for my mother when she hung the washing out to dry. It was only on the days when she was at the clothesline and could keep an eye on me that she let me wander alone where the flowers grew on a slope in the south pasture, partially protected there from the wind.

There were several kinds of flowers, and later in life, I learned that what we called them was not what they actually were. The daisies I picked were individual plants, and not ever seeing them elsewhere, I never learned their real names. Similarly the blue flowers we called bluebells were not at all shaped like the bluebells that now grow outside my house. The pretty buttercup flowers grow nowhere else on earth that I know and were no good at all for bouquet making, having such short stems. After seeing newly picked buttercups turn limp and ugly in my hand, I learned to let them be where they were.

I would, however, pick a fistful of the longer-stemmed "daisies" and "bluebells" and then run to the washhouse, scoop some water into a cup at the water barrel, then stick my bunch of flowers into the cup and give the bouquet to my smiling, grateful, sun-bonneted mother. (A bouquet I call it still, though in truth it was more of a floating mishmash of stems and petals.) But my mother, clothespin in mouth and clutching laundry in one hand, would use her free hand to give me a squeeze and a pat on the head. Then, after taking the clothespin from her mouth, she would ask me to put the wilting bouquet on a shelf in the washhouse for safekeeping.

I remember thinking that I would show my bouquet to my five older brothers and sisters when they came home from school, but I don't recall ever actually doing so. I ask myself now if I resented their returning from school to the family orbit, thereby diffusing my mother's attention to me. Such evidence as I can recall suggests otherwise. I remember going out to the road with Bert to wait for them at four o'clock when they would come walking home. While I did not run in circles around them like Bert, I surely did share the dog's joy. I also recall yearning for the day when I could go to school too.

My longing may have been heightened by a song my mother used to sing. I have never heard it sung by anyone else, and I suppose she learned it during her two years in grade school before her stepmother took her out of school to help care for her half-siblings as they came along. Because Mother loved school, leaving it was the great disappointment of her life—a great big lemon this was, that life handed her so early, and the song she sang to us children in her beautiful soft voice may have been sips of lemonade she made of it. The song goes something like this:

> Oh we sit up from nine to twelve
> Then one p.m. to four
> Then we quickly gather on the green
> When study hours are o'er.
> And we always sing so jolly-o
> So jolly-o

and so on to the ending, which goes, "What jolly boys are we."

My mother is buried next to my father in the Hays Cemetery. It is well kept and beautiful, as is the entire countryside of Ellis County now. The dust storms are long, long past, remembered now by only a few. Farmyards now—the remaining ones—display a floral abundance. In green pastures, meadowlarks sing and in the surrounding tilled fields is seen only an occasional sunflower.

The entire student body of Hope Valley School, 1934. From left: me, my brother Virgil, Elmer Behrens, my sister Armella, Irene Behrens.

Part 2

Grade School Years

I should prefer to have some boy bend them
As he went out and in to fetch the cows—
Some boy too far from town to learn baseball

—Robert Frost

Bilingual Cows

I was only seven when I first started milking. That was a bit young, even for us Volga Germans, but nothing could stop me from trying to keep up with my brother Virgil. Two years older than I, Virgil had been milking for a year, and I, suffering from sibling rivalry, begged to be allowed to share in the joy of milking our cows.

My jealousy of Virgil blinded me to the downside of milking, as evidenced by my oldest brother's pronounced distaste for it. Alvin excluded himself from milking on the grounds that his responsibilities as tractor driver exempted him from so lowly a chore. In any event, after about a month of milking Old White Face, the gentlest cow that ever there was (which was why my mother assigned her to me), I got tired of milking. The novelty of keeping pace with Virgil in doing grown-up work wore off. Milking was hard work; it tired one's hands until they ached. I wanted to quit, but alas, having begged my way right into the lineup, I was unable to beg my way back out of it.

In my first year, there were seven cows and four of us children assigned to milking them. Georgine milked Die Schippers Kuh and Red Face; Alvina did Rinya and Die Gutern; Alvin, her twin brother, avoided this chore by commandeering tractor duty on our brand new 1935 McCormick Deering tractor, so his place was taken by Virgil, who milked Die Gaela and Rinya Mit Hanner. Armella was so slow a milker that she could milk only one cow. Mother needed help in the kitchen, so she yielded to my imploring and gave me Armella's assignment, gentle Old White Face, and moved Armella from the barn to the kitchen.

I have no idea why some of the cows had German names and others, English. Since we were bilingual—mostly speaking German, but sometimes English—I suppose we assumed that the cows too were at ease with names in either language. We were also at ease with our bilingual nomenclature for milking; that is, cows had *zitzen* in German, "tits" in English. *Hanner* in German, "horns" in English. No big deal. When still a heifer, one of our cows had suffered the loss of one of her *zitzen* to surgery after an injury. Once she healed, we called her, inevitably, Three Tits, a name as matter-of-fact to us as Rinya Mit Hanner (Rinya With Horns).

It was in the year that Three Tits dried up for good that our primary language began to shift away from German. I still recall a moment when Georgine advised Virgil and me to improve our English—to speak English all the time, in fact.

We were in the barn after the evening milking, getting ready to run the separator, the contrivance that separates cream from milk. At that point, I was still a year away from becoming a milker and was just tagging along with Virgil. He had finished milking Rinya Mit Hanner, and was handing his pail to Georgine for pouring into the separator. It was mid-September, and I would be going to school for the first time the next week, while Georgine would be leaving at the same time for her first teaching job at the one-room Pleasant Hill School, about ten miles away in Protestant, English-speaking Rush County. Georgine, age eighteen and newly graduated from high school, no doubt felt the butterflies that flutter inside any new teacher. But she was burdened by the additional anxiety that her *Rooshun* accent might undermine her effectiveness as a teacher—might even eventually cost her her job. There was considerable bias against foreigners, especially Catholic ones, in Protestant Kansas back then. Because our forebears had spent several generations in German settlements along the Volga River, we were called *Rooshuns* with an intonation that was not always kindly intended.

So in advising her little brothers, Georgine was really advising herself, but she was also genuinely solicitous for us. That year, Virgil and I would be the first in our family to have a teacher who was neither *Rooshun* nor Catholic. Jean didn't want Virgil and me to disgrace ourselves in front of our new teacher, who was, we had been told, Protestant and English.

Our fears, it turned out, were unfounded. Dorothy Wallace, eighteen and at her first teaching job, did not ridicule my accent. She just ignored it while teaching me, not just how to read, but to love to read. We were blessed with Dorothy for the next three years. She was the best teacher I ever had, grade one right through my PhD, and I am so grateful that I was able to tell her so at my mother's funeral many years ago.

Disgrace over my language did eventually befall me, though not in the way I feared, and in an environment radically different from the Hope Valley School. When I was ready for seventh grade, the local school board closed our one-room school because I would have been the only student in it. It had remained open the preceding year to accommodate my eighth-grade brother and me, the two of us making up the entire student body.

But after Virgil's graduation, keeping the school open for just me would have been more expensive for the Hope Valley School District than my father's solution, which actually killed three birds with one stone. He rented an apartment in Hays, the county seat, a city then of about 6,300 people, for Virgil, me, and Armella, who had just finished high school. For my parents' educational plans, Hays was a perfect fit, with Hays Junior-Senior High School and Fort Hays Kansas State College. Armella would start college at Fort Hays State, Virgil would be a high school freshman, and I would be a seventh grader. The Hope Valley School District would pay my portion of the rent for the apartment. So off to Hays it was for the three of us in September 1940.

This new world was about as different as one can imagine from the familiar world of cows and chores. And the two worlds collided one day in prim and proper Miss Courtney's English class at Hays Junior-Senior High School.

I wanted Miss Courtney to like me, and the way to have her do that, I supposed, was to show her that I was smart. Although I was a *Rooshun*, the only one in her class, I thought I was smart anyway. But three weeks had gone by and no opportunity had arisen yet for me to show that, really, I was smart. Then toward the end of a slow class in the fourth week, Miss Courtney had us play the weekly word game. A long word would be put on the board, and we were instructed to see how many little words could be made from its letters.

By prearrangement, Cora Mae Simpson, the smartest girl in class and the teacher's pet, had selected the word for the day from a dictionary: *recalcitrant*. R-E-C-A-L-C-I-T-R-A-N-T Cora Mae wrote on the blackboard, then carefully mispronounced it re-cal-KIT-rant. It wasn't long before the class had run through a bunch of words (real, ant, etc., I don't remember how many). Cora Mae herself came up with the last one, "rant." Then there was silence, which told us there were no more little words to be found. But there *was*, I saw, yet one more. There it was, a hidden little gem of a word—two *t*s and an *i*— and everyone else had missed it! I saw my chance to excel, and went for it. "Tit!" I shouted, waving my arms excitedly in triumph.

I shall never, ever forget the look in Miss Courtney's blue, glistering eyes as they met my own yearning gaze. It was a look of naked hatred.

Warm Beds and Oddly Chosen Names

I was already eight when my youngest sister, Janice, was born, so in my childhood home before 1936, I was the youngest of six: three boys and three girls. Our farmhouse was a rectangle divided into four equal-sized rooms—I am guessing about twelve feet by fourteen each, though they may have been smaller.

There was no bathroom—that was added on, along with two bedrooms and a large kitchen, in 1937, a year after Janice was born. So for my first eight years, one room served as kitchen, dining room, living room, and just-about-everything-else room except bedroom. In it were a table and eight chairs, a washstand, and a coal-oil cooking stove. There was also a wood- or coal-burning stove off to the side. In a corner, a door opened into a pantry. Between the pantry and the table was the slop pail. Into it went the remnants that nowadays would be scraped into garbage disposals or compost bins, but in those days went into the pail and from there into a trough in the pigpen. Yes, we called that chore "slopping the pigs."

To the right of this all-purpose room was Mom and Dad's bedroom. One of my earliest memories is being in a crib at night alongside their bed and asking, "*Was war des?*" (What was that?) after being startled by a noise that sounded like a gasp. My father explained, "*Des var der Hund*" (That was the dog), and I remember being puzzled, because Bert, our Scotch collie, was never inside our house. But I went back to sleep without pursuing the matter, which soon became irrelevant anyway because of a change in sleeping arrangements.

My new berth was on the opened davenport in the room behind the kitchen, where I was sandwiched between Alvin and Virgil, ten and two years older than I, respectively. I don't remember ever feeling crowded in bed though, or anywhere else in the house for that matter. But my older siblings and my parents surely yearned for more space.

It can get very cold in the Great Plains in winter. I remember having the bed warmed for me on some cold nights. For those unfamiliar with this kindness, it consists of a sibling's getting under the covers at your place in the bed. Then after it is nice and warm there, they vacate it for you to slide into. Remember now, the bedrooms got freezing cold because only the kitchen had a stove in it. That's where we scampered in the morning to put on our clothes over the union suits we slept in. And though I clearly remember having my place in bed warmed for me a few times, I am less clear about whom to be thankful to.

The girls had to go through our bedroom to get to their bedroom off to the right. These three older sisters—Georgine, Alvina, Armella—mothered me and Virgil; the youngest of them, Armella, was seven years older than me. Virgil and I talked about that during a visit in 2010 when I flew out to Kansas. Virgil believes it was Armie who most often warmed the bed for one or the other of us. Alvin agrees that Armie was the gentlest of our older sisters, but that his twin, Alvina, though noted for occasional flashes of temper, was consistently compassionate and helpful. She got him, Alvin reminisced, through the early grades of school, explaining to him how to do his homework and even finishing for him what he was too lazy to finish himself.

From Alvin's memories of Alvina's helping him through the early grades, his thoughts turned to the flooding of the one-room schoolhouse in a valley formed by the Smoky Hill River. He would have drowned then had not a neighbor, Jim Truan, pulled him to safety. They built the new school—the one I would eventually go to—a mile north on higher ground, but kept its old name. So that explained for me, finally, why my school, which wasn't in any valley at all, was nonetheless named the Hope Valley School.

The Complicated Nomenclature of Dining

When I opened my lunch pail at my one-room schoolhouse, I most often found myself unwrapping a sandwich. The bread would have been homemade as would have been the jelly and the peanut butter too, on those occasions when a peanut butter and jelly sandwich had been packed. More often than not though, the sandwich was a simple bread and butter sandwich. Much more common still were egg sandwiches, the yolk broken and flattened out, fried hard with thin streaks of mustard crisscrossing the top. I loved those sandwiches, but when I make one today, I add a leaf of romaine lettuce and a slice of tomato if one is ripe in my garden. The addition of a slice or two of bacon would transform my simple sandwich into ambrosia, the food of the gods, but I hate to make the mess or take the time for fixing bacon and anyway, dining alone, I don't feel quite worthy of the trouble.

I no longer make the bean sandwiches my mother sometimes put in my dinner pail, though a bowl of noodles and beans is still an entrée I make for myself from time to time. That fancy word, "entrée," distracts me into thinking about the vagaries of dining nomenclature. In France, this word refers to a small dish at the entry (the *entrée*) to a meal. So it's an appetizer, not the main dish there.

Now I notice that I have unconsciously changed "lunch" pail to "dinner" pail. It's the same pail, but back when I carried it the mile and a quarter to school, I called it my "dinner" pail. "Lunch" was for later in the day: a glass of whole milk (the skimmed milk was for the calves) and a thick slice of homemade bread slathered with butter and apple butter that mother served Virgil and me when we came home from school and got ready to go out and milk the cows. (We never took apple butter sandwiches to school; the apple butter would make the bread too soggy.)

It is the school year 1939 to 1940 that I am remembering. We milked seven cows that year. Alvin, already out of high school, was available to help (however reluctantly) with the milking. The three older girls were away. Armella was a senior at Girls Catholic High School in Hays, and Georgine and Alvina were in Antonino (population that I estimate at about 250) where they were teaching in a two-room school, meaning one hundred percent of the students there had *a* Schmidtberger as his or her teacher. Little Janice was only four and too young to help. So after we finished the chores and came in to supper, there were six of us around the table.

If it was my lucky night, the entrée (in the American sense) would be rivel (rhymes with swivel)—soup, my favorite meal. Rivel soup is heated milk with blobs of fried dough the size and texture of clams, seasoned with lots of pepper and butter. Sprinkled over it in my bowl would be chunks of bread toasted in the oven. Small wonder then that my favorite soup today is New England clam chowder, a very similar consistency.

The school year 1939 to 1940 was the time that Virgil and I were the only students at Hope Valley School. He was in eighth grade and I was in sixth. Our teacher, Victor Roth, was in his first year of teaching. Typically, he gave Virgil and me the same reading assignments. During reading period, Virgil and I alternated reading out loud from our Bobbs-Merrill textbooks, Victor giving the signal to change readers. Virgil would sense when Victor, following along in his book, was getting drowsy. So Virgil would skip a word, then a phrase, then a sentence, and then a whole paragraph, leaving poor Victor helplessly adrift, but unwilling to ask for help. Victor would eventually signal that it was my turn, hoping, I suppose, to be able to locate where we were in the story during the transition. If he appeared confused when I began reading, I would continue Virgil's method, so that we came to the end of the assignment a page or two ahead of Victor.

But my memories of Victor today are fixed on the contents of his dinner pail. He would pull out of it unheard of luxuries like, for example, a Baby Ruth candy bar. But even more enchanting to my wide-eyed wonderment were the tins; opening one revealed a row of sardines coated with yellow mustard—a relatively rare delicacy on the dry, hardscrabble plains. Every Friday Victor opened one of those tins, and every Friday I watched him spear the sardines and transfer them onto a slice of bread. One Friday, perhaps wearied of (or embarrassed by) the attention his eating attracted, he offered me a mustard-coated sardine on a saltine cracker. It was as tasty as it smelled, more delicious even than I had imagined.

Der Gayla Barrich
(The Yellow Hill)

I have been told that I am even-tempered—told often enough for me to almost believe it. In truth though, if I do appear to be keeping my cool in the face of grievous annoyances, you are witnessing a studied response, not my natural disposition. Left unchecked, my temperament disposes me toward ranting and raving in response to life's displeasures. From adolescence on, however, I have practiced the art of concealing my temper, so I suppose that I have gotten pretty good at it. Nowadays they call it anger management, but I began practicing it long before these buzz words became popular. I had to.

I was eleven, in fifth grade. Virgil was in seventh. After it happened, I was so shocked and ashamed that it troubles me still, over seventy years later.

Virgil and I were coming home from school along the dirt road, a section line that, like all section lines in western Kansas and elsewhere in the Great Plains, went straight as an arrow for exactly one mile—5,280 feet. Virgil and I used the road as a ready-made track. There was no danger from passing traffic—I do not remember ever meeting a car or truck on the way to and from school in this lonely part of the world.

We often ran some of the way. We both liked to run, and it was an obvious choice of sports, no other being offered at our one-room schoolhouse, which, of course, had no gym. The two-acre grass-covered schoolyard was large enough for team sports, but there were too few students to make up two teams, or even one, for that matter. The total regular enrollment never reached more than five, and once dropped to two—Virgil and me—in the seven years I went there.

Actually, the total enrollment may have exceeded five in the year that some of the Rohr boys showed up for school whenever their father had time to drive them. I have no idea where the Rohrs actually lived, but it was said to be too far for them to walk. Victor, Alvin, and Cyril (pronounced Cereal) Rohr attended sporadically for a year, mostly when I was in fourth grade, I think. Nicodemus, the oldest of the Rohr boys, rode up to school during lunch hour a few times to show off the horse and saddle the Pattersons—an elderly couple—provided him; he was working as a live-in hired hand on their farm nearby.

So under the circumstances, running was the only sport available. But Virgil's and my interest in running was amplified by our desire to emulate Glenn Cunningham, the Kansan who achieved fame for *almost* running a four-minute mile in 1938, a generation before Roger Bannister actually did it. Cunningham had already set a new world record for the 1,500 meter and the half mile.

It was the half mile we practiced, our choice predetermined by our road's topography. At just a little before the halfway point the road descended into a ravine. It went some twenty yards or so across the flat bottom before rising at a sharp upward angle. The road's surface at that point was a pale, yellow-colored clay, so we called this steep incline Der Gayla Barrich (The Yellow Hill), whether speaking German or English. Der Gayla Barrich presented way too formidable a climb for it to be included in any running. But once we arrived at the top of Der Gayla Barrich, the road stretched out for another half a mile or so.

In determining what constituted half a mile on our road, absolute accuracy was not an issue. Nor was keeping exact times of our runs all that important either, especially since we had no stopwatch or, in fact, any watch at all. For telling time we looked to see where the sun was. Though our accuracy with this method was remarkable it still wasn't accurate enough to measure improvement in running half a mile.

What I was competing against wasn't a matter of minutes or seconds or feet or yards. I was competing against Virgil, who was two and a half years older and far more physically developed. I wanted to run as fast as Virgil—to keep up with Virgil. Yes, I was delusional and yes, I was in the throes of a severe case of sibling rivalry.

Now Virgil's temperament ran toward accommodation. Although he must have yearned, as I did, for companionship closer in age and ability, he made do with what was handy and generally kept his mischievous bent in check. In fact, Virgil often let me keep up with him. After climbing Der Gayla Barrich, we would stop to rest a bit and then proceed—sometimes running, sometimes walking—home to the fragrance of apple butter on still-warm homemade bread, and then on to the tedious chore of milking the cows.

Sometimes though, Virgil ran at his natural pace, which of course was faster than I could keep up with for very long. But he would stop at the halfway point, where the ravine began, and wait for me to catch up. Then we would continue together across the ravine, sometimes lingering after we got to the other side of Der Gayla Barrich to sail flat rocks at jackrabbits. He actually nailed one right in the head one time. I remember it as having been around a hundred yards away, though that is surely an exaggeration of Virgil's prowess. (Our family didn't eat rabbits, plentiful as they were and hard as times were, though other families did eat them. We probably brought the rabbit home to feed to Bert.)

Then, on a bracing, perfect October day, Virgil's impulse to run faster and farther than he had ever run before coincided with his impulse to mischief. Instead of waiting for me to catch up with him at the ravine and going across together, he continued running down and across, heedless of my shouting, "Wait for me! Wait! Wait!" He may have actually jogged—not walked—up Der Gayla Barrich. My vision was too glazed over with tears of anger to see clearly. But I could make out Virgil still trotting on the other side of Der Gayla Barrich. He finally stopped and waved merrily to me, far behind now and just starting down into the ravine.

I should point out that there was another sport we loved, Virgil and I. We often boxed, using regular winter mittens for boxing gloves. We took turns being Joe Louis and Tommy Farr after we listened to their famous match on our family's new Philco radio. Before Tommy Farr came along, we were Max Baer or James Braddock, but one of us was always Joe Louis, and we rotated that honor. We followed the rule about not hitting below the belt and we did not allow any punching to the head either. I imagine Virgil made up this rule to avoid knocking my block off with a mittened right hook. I don't think he ever broke the rule—I would surely remember if he had—and I broke it only once.

I remember struggling up Der Gayla Barrich, to where Virgil now stood waiting for me. I was out of breath from yelling and climbing and in a white-hot rage while Virgil was doing what?—I don't remember. I swung at his head—rules all forgotten—oblivious to the fact that, as I launched my arm, my fist was not inside a mitten, but was clutching my dinner pail.

I cannot remember anything after that—whether Virgil picked the tooth up off the ground or if he spat it out, if there was much bleeding, or if I said I was sorry. I just don't remember anything at all of the aftermath—not our walk home or whether Bert ran around us in circles of joy as he usually did when we came into the yard.

Virgil did not tattle on me. He told our parents that it was all an accident, leaving out the fact that I was having a tantrum when we were "just playing." I don't remember being punished or even scolded, so I suppose my parents accepted Virgil's explanation, or more likely, were too preoccupied with more pressing matters—such as the cost of replacing Virgil's tooth—to pay much attention to my role in the need to replace it.

Homework and Short-Lived Rebellions

My talent ran toward obedience. By obeying, I would remain in the good graces of my parents and then my teachers, I thought. And that's how it pretty much worked out over the course of my education.

So I have difficulty trying to recall something I rebelled against in my formative years. Didn't I refuse to do my homework at least once, the way everyone does? No, I never rebelled against doing my homework because throughout grammar school, I wasn't given any homework. Farm kids all had chores to do—something every rural school district was perfectly well aware of—so the schools never burdened their students with homework.

When we came home from school, our job was to milk the cows. That done, we poured the milk into the separator, whirling the milk through and making sure we had a clean gallon can placed under the spigot for the resulting cream. The skimmed milk went into the pails we used for feeding the calves; the cream we poured into a five-gallon can for shipping to a creamery, the same creamery whose checks got my family through the poorest times during the Depression.

After milking was finished and other chores like gathering the eggs were done, we went in for supper. Then we played a game or two of pinochle, unless it was Tuesday and after 1935. That's when we got a Philco radio, which allowed us to listen to *Fibber McGee and Molly*. In 1935, rural electrification had not yet made its way out to our farm, so the Philco was powered by a car battery that we recharged with a wind-powered generator housed atop a windmill that my father put up. That wind charger is now long gone, but not too far from where it once stood there now revolve the long blades of the turbines on the Smoky Hill Windmill Farm. In any event, by 1937 times were getting better, helped along by the paychecks of $60 a month Jean was earning as a teacher and from which she had bought us the Philco. Things had actually begun to get better even before then, back in 1936, when Dad rented the fertile bottomland that we knew as Across the River.

Before I was old enough to milk, I hung around in the barn to watch, playing with our many barnyard cats. I remember everybody milking at one time or other, starting with Mom and Dad, but the cast of characters keeps changing in these chronologically sequenced scenes from childhood. We milked by hand. Georgine was the fastest. By 1936, the year I started milking, she was away at her teaching job in a school called Good Hope down in Rush County, so it must have been in the summer or on weekends that I saw her milking. The same with the twins: they were away weekdays in high school. Alvin was always finding emergencies that needed tending to during milking time, whereas Alvina was afraid of milking, fearful of getting kicked.

Cows, like other animals, can sense fear, so Dad assigned the most docile cow, Old White Face, to Alvina. But Old White Face, in an uncharacteristic onset of assertiveness, directed a half-hearted kick against Alvina's pail, overturning it. Cats scampered to lap up at least a taste of the spilt milk before it soaked into the straw-covered dirt floor. Meanwhile, Alvina stormed out of the barn and out of the milking rotation too. So I have landed on a rebellion, but it was Alvina's, not mine.

Armella's tenure at milking was brief. After Alvina's revolt, Dad decided to have Armie take Alvie's place. So sweet-tempered Armie tried her hands on White Face, who, after her one little bout of waywardness, had reverted entirely to her customary docility. All went well: swish, swish, swish, swish—the milk hissed into the bucket, now over half full, when White Face swung her tail toward Armie, sweeping her across the face. She jumped up, overturning both her milk stool and her pail. The cats again tried frantically to salvage a feast while Armie stood there, weeping inconsolably over the spilt milk, whether over the loss of income it represented in these desperate times, or over having let Daddy down, or just over the general sorrow of it all, she could not say. But she cried and cried, and Mom and Dad found different chores for Armella to do in the kitchen.

There was not an awful lot of time for homework after I started helping with the chores, so it was fortunate that I didn't have to bring any homework home. I can't imagine what it would have been like to run half a mile, more or less, keeping up with Virgil, while shouldering one of those posture-breaking backpacks children stagger under nowadays on their way home from the school bus. I'd never have made it up Der Gayla Barrich if I'd been weighed down like that.

When Virgil graduated and Hope Valley closed, I went to Hays Junior High for seventh grade. We had two study periods in the course of the day and were encouraged to do all our homework during them. I can't remember the name of my homeroom teacher, but I remember very clearly how she told us that a good student does not have to take home any schoolwork. What I took home instead was book after book from the public library on Main Street. I had all that free time, formerly devoted to chores, to fill now. Some titles I still remember are *Les Miserables* (which I pronounced Less Miser Ables), *The Count of Monte Cristo*, and *The Three Musketeers*.

I tried to rebel against going back to Hope Valley for eighth grade when it reopened the next year, but to no avail. So there I was, with aging teacher Lidwina Vonfeldt, who assumed, quite correctly, that I resented being there—an eighth grader sharing space with two little first-grade boys and a fifth-grade girl. Lidwina apparently handled my inclination toward rebellion well because I don't remember complaining once school started. Instead, I mostly remember reading various volumes of *The Book of Knowledge* (an encyclopedia for children) while little Bobby Dean and Danny recited their ABCs within earshot, but without particularly distracting me. Virgil says he read all twenty volumes of *The Book of Knowledge* in his eight years at Hope Valley, but I don't think I read quite all of them in my seven, which, in a pinch, could count as an act of rebellion, although it probably had more to do with my preference for a more leisurely pace when turning pages.

The Pecking Order

On our farm, there were many scary things that crept or crawled or slithered around the ground, but the creature that really, really terrified me was a rooster who fed on them all. His name was Ed.

Ed was a Rhode Island Red, a common breed of chicken distinguished by the dark rusty-red color of its feathers. Both hens and cocks are heavyset, and many of them are destined nowadays for the supermarket as one of those enormous oven stuffers, so heavy you need both hands to lift one out of the display case. I don't know what fate finally befell Ed, but it seems to me that he was awesomely larger than the twelve pounds that Rhode Island Red roosters can reach.

A question comes to mind: Why was our rooster named Ed? For a long time, I thought our rooster was named after our hot-tempered, redheaded Protestant neighbor, Ed Hollandsworth. I was very much afraid of Ed Hollandsworth and thought he and our rooster shared a name because they were so alike in appearance and temperament. But no, it wasn't quite like that.

Alvin eventually told me that rooster Ed was just a little cockerel when Ed Hollandsworth bought him at a farm sale and gave him to Dad. A kind man despite his rough edges, Ed Hollandsworth was always picking up little things for us at sales in the area. But the only thing that ever got named after him in appreciation was the bad-tempered rooster that Ed eventually grew into.

I remember leaving the outhouse—the *donniker*—once, closing the door behind me and just taking a first step around the corner when I gasped at the sight of Ed crouched there, waiting for me, ready to spring, his curved, cruel beak protruding underneath his large, flaming red comb. But what I most keenly recall is the anger in his fierce eyes, burning into mine.

In a split second I stepped back out of Ed's line of sight, then all the way back into the outhouse, all atremble, and slammed the door shut. I don't remember how long I had to wait in my safe haven before anyone responded to my calls for help. But odd as it may sound, I remember thinking that I needn't hook the door because it was impossible for a rooster to pull it open. But I hooked it anyway.

Roosters don't normally attack people. Their instinct is to guard their hens from harm, and they learn early on that human beings are not predators (though we are, in fact, their worst predators). So they like to sit on a perch, perhaps three to five feet high, from where they act as a lookout for their dozen or so ladies. The threat these sentinels most often see—and immediately attack—is a rooster from a different part of the flock.

But sometimes a rooster goes rogue, unattached to any flock. I suspect that Ed had been ousted from his harem by a younger rooster and now, useless in old age, he vented his frustration on anyone scared of him. In my large family, Alvina and I—I think *only* Alvina and I—exuded fear of Ed, and he sensed it.

I don't remember if Alvina's run-in with Ed happened before or after my outhouse adventure, but it was definitely around the same time, and I have two images of Alvie's misadventure fixed in my memory. One is of Alvie running for dear life in the pasture about a hundred yards away, with Ed chasing her and leaping against the back of her overcoat in a flurry of beating wings. He releases his hold, falls behind, then catches up and leaps again. The other image is of Georgine and Virgil and me at the farmhouse's window, watching Alvie fleeing from Ed. Georgine is laughing and calling Mom to come and watch too.

Penance on the Prairie

In 1939, I was in sixth grade and a fairly decent pinochle player. Winter evenings, Dad and I would team up against Mom and Virgil for an hour or so of pinochle before bedtime.

How we loved to play! But by 1939 we were no longer completely dependent on card-playing for recreation on the farm—we had a Philco radio. So at our home in 1939, two nights were for radio, not pinochle: Bob Hope on Sundays, and *Fibber McGee and Molly* on Tuesdays. I don't remember when *Amos 'n' Andy* was on, but it was a Wednesday evening when I put my parents through an awkward conflict over pinochle.

I know it was a Wednesday because it was the first day of Lent, and the first day of Lent is Ash Wednesday. Lent is the time for doing penance during the forty days before Easter, and I still hadn't thought of a worthy penance. I was not yet old enough to give up smoking. Giving up candy should have been an obvious choice, but there was none to give up—the Depression still lingered on in Kansas, where Dorothy would have to wait another year before soaring away to somewhere over the rainbow. Say more prayers? No. Prayer should not be a penance, though, if truth be told, the rosary was of numbing length to me. Do a daily kindness to Virgil? Never!

Then I thought of it—a mortification, not of the body, but of the spirit—that would eventually waft me upward into the higher reaches of heaven.

I would give up pinochle.

I was so very proud earlier that day, long before the hour for pinochle, when I told my mother what I was giving up for Lent. How delightful it was to see her beaming with joy at the spiritual heroism of her favorite son. It would be a few years before my memory finally retrieved the trace of doubt in Mom's lingering smile.

Evening came. The cows were milked, cream separator washed, pigs slopped, and chickens enclosed for the night—all chores done. At supper we talked of this and that, but I did not mention my Lenten resolve, biding my time. Finally the table was cleared and the dishes were done. Dad and Virgil seated themselves at their accustomed places at the card table, but I sat down in a corner and opened a book, though there wasn't enough light there to read by.

Looking puzzled, Dad motioned me to the card table, and then turned to Mom, who was retreating toward the kitchen.

"*Vas iss los?*" he asked her backside.

She said nothing, leaving me to pipe up with the explanation: "I'm giving up pinochle for Lent."

My memory says Virgil snickered, but he probably kept a straight face. My father looked thoughtful—neither happy nor unhappy— just thoughtful. Finally he said, in English now, in his heavy German brogue, "Maybe you can think of something else to give up?" Then he faced Mother's frown as she stood in the doorway, and in German asked her if she couldn't think of a different penance for me. "Tsk tsk" was her disapproving reply as she turned away into the kitchen.

With a head gesture that I had often seen Dad use to entice a wayward calf into its pen, Dad smiled and beckoned me to the table. Mom was nowhere to be seen. My sense of piety, of holiness, of smug self-satisfaction faded away, displaced now by sorrow—and guilt too—on seeing how very much my father wanted to play pinochle. Yet there was the thought of how much my mother would want me to keep my Lenten resolution. But Mom was out of sight, while Dad was right there, and suddenly, more than anything else, more than any place in high heaven, I wanted to be Daddy's partner again at pinochle.

I went over to the card table and sat down. Virgil shuffled the deck. Then he gave it to Dad, who cut it and handed it to me for deal- ing. Mom was still in the kitchen. Dad nodded, so I began dealing three-handed pinochle. We played that hand. Dad was about to deal another hand, when Mom came to the table and sat down at her place across from Virgil. Dad dealt her in, so now we were back to playing four-handed pinochle again, the way we always had.

Old White Face

I've been leafing through *Century Readings in the English Essay*, the awesomely ugly textbook that was handed to me for my first teaching assignment one fine day in 1955. I haven't used it since about 1963 when the English Department at Saint Peter's College switched to a more attractive book—which I don't remember at all.

Many of the essays I come across now in *Century Readings* seem as fresh and new as they were on my first readings. "A foolish consistency," Ralph Waldo Emerson wrote in 1841, "is the hobgoblin of little minds, adored by little statesmen and philosophers and divines." How apt that thought is today as we're so often treated to the spectacle of little statesmen combing through the records of nominees for high office, ferreting out any changes of opinion, as though changing one's opinion were a character flaw. I remember that I once was in favor of the death penalty before I was against it, to cite just one of my own many flip-flops over the years.

Emerson kept a journal and his entry on May 25, 1862, is still delightful. He admires practical people who know how to do things, describing how he and his neighbor "struggled in vain to drag our big calf into the barn. Then the Irish Girl put her finger into the calf's mouth and led her in directly."

That anecdote brings me back to my boyhood on the farm. After we finished milking the cows, we ran the milk through a separator. We sold the cream, and fed the skim milk to the calves. But each newly weaned calf had to be taught how to drink milk from a pail instead of nursing from its mother. The trick was to get the calf to suck on your finger, then lower your hand into the pail. The calves usually caught on right away, and the intermediate stage of providing a digital substitute seldom needed to be repeated.

One calf I especially remember was Little White Face. Even after fully grown, Little White Face remained smaller than her mother, so her name remained accurate even as the mother's name gradually shifted from White Face to Old White Face. Old White Face was the gentlest of cows and an easy milker too, so she served as the beginners' cow when my brothers and sisters and I began milking. Naturally, I favored her offspring, Little White Face, the year I started feeding the calves.

I allowed Little White Face a sip or two more of milk than the others, and I did not whack her across the head in anger when she butted her head against the pail, sometimes causing the milk to spill. Let me explain that calves butt their mother's udder to increase the milk flow, so butting the pail is merely an instinctive reaction, albeit badly misplaced and exasperating. Interestingly, I read recently that it's been proved that cows with names give more milk than unnamed ones. That makes sense. People who give their cows names are likely to accord them more humane treatment all around. So the cows respond in kind by giving extra milk.

Meandering memory puts me into Virgil's car in May 2010, when the two of us drove the 223 miles from Lawrence to Victoria to visit with Alvin at the family farm. It was a beautiful day and the countryside was storybook green. I'd forgotten my camera, so we didn't stop to take pictures of the herds of cows grazing contentedly in the pastures alongside the highway. "What a pretty view," Virgil said. We were driving through the Flint Hills, but my mind was elsewhere, thinking of the god-awful conditions that grain-fed cattle are kept in today.

But this was free-range country we were driving through. No crowding here—a mere dozen or two Black Angus or Jerseys or whatever breed grazing along a vast expanse of prairie. Then a few miles farther on, we passed a herd of Herefords on a long hillside, and the sight of their white faces abruptly brought up a memory of Old White Face. This memory has our neighbor Ed Hollandsworth in it too. He lived about a mile to the south of our farm, and hauled cattle in his truck.

Without warning, I see Old White Face again. Memory has rewound all the way back to when I am nine or ten. I am standing in the barn, where I am not supposed to be, watching aghast. Unbidden and unwelcome, this image of Old White Face the last time I saw her oppresses me now, some seventy-five years later. She has gone dry for the last time. There will not be another gestation. This is Kansas, not India, where old cows are afforded a sacred retirement, wandering about and treated kindly wherever they be. Here in Kansas dried-up old cows are put to yet one more use.

This is not a pleasant memory. It was all the more shocking because I was so unprepared for it.

Wide-eyed with fright, Old White Face is in a stall in our barn. She is turning helplessly this way and that, crashing against each side of the sturdy rails that confine her. She is refusing to step onto the lowered truck gate that serves as a gangplank between the barn door and the truck bed. Ed Hollandsworth is beating her mercilessly. He lashes her hindquarters when she is facing the truck; then her face when her back is turned to it, then her body as she turns. He keeps shouting at her, trying to curse her onto the truck. Then my mother appears alongside me. She pulls me out of the barn and back to the house, but I break away from her and run to the far side of our machine shed where, far away from the barn now, the only sound I hear is my own sobbing.

To return now to where we began, *Century Readings in the English Essay,* and Emerson's amusing account of how to gently lead a recalcitrant calf into a barn. There are, I know, more kindly, less troublesome ways of urging an old cow up a chute too narrow to permit her any attempt at turning away. But that's not how it went that day, and from that day on for all my days to come, my most fervent prayer was that God admit our farm animals into heaven.

Smoke Enders

I was ten when I had my first cigarette. It was a Pall Mall, stealthily removed from my oldest brother's pack on top of the dresser in the bedroom I shared with Alvin and Virgil. At ten years of age, I was experiencing a big event in my yearning for adulthood. It was late spring and time to change from winter's long johns to summer's underwear. When I was handed my clean laundry for the week at bedtime, I expected the BVDs that little children wore in the summer back then, a lightweight, one-piece, short-sleeved garment that buttoned down the front and had a flap that buttoned across the back. But lo and behold, I had been given a pair of briefs like the ones my brothers wore, which, to me, signaled my graduation into manhood.

Always an earlier riser than my two brothers, I'd long been assigned the task of bringing the milk cows to the barn from the "other pasture" about half a mile away. But that particular morning I got up even earlier, eager to don my grown-up apparel. That done, I slipped into my overalls and was on my noiseless, barefoot way when, spying Alvin's Pall Malls—the red pack barely visible in the morning darkness—I took one cigarette from it, and one of the books of matches too.

I didn't light my cigarette until I reached the other pasture. It was only just dawn, and jackrabbits were frolicking about at their morning play, leaping high into the air as the cows were unfolding themselves upright. Then, squinting warily as any man would, I cupped my hands around the flame (though there was no wind) and lit the cigarette. I drew the smoke into my mouth, then blew it out slowly. No coughing, no reaction of any kind. Smoking a cigarette was exactly as I had supposed it would be, and exactly as it would be portrayed decades later by the Marlboro Man.

I took another puff or two before stubbing the cigarette into the mud at the edge of a cow pond. My new, macho underwear remained the major feature of the day. The cigarette had been a mere celebratory flourish. I followed the cows as they led themselves single-file through the narrow lane to the barn. They entered, each in her turn, and went to their assigned stanchions, waiting there to be milked by me and Virgil, Georgine, and Alvina, who were already there at the barn. The sun was fully up now. Chickens were scratching about in the yard and our hogs were grunting for their morning's slop. Standing tall—taller even than John Wayne would stand years later—I surveyed the scene through narrowed eyes, took a long imaginary draw from an invisible cigarette, and reviewed my heavy responsibilities for the day.

Then Georgine snapped me out of my reverie.

"Hurry up, *Hertzya*" (little sweetheart), Georgine called. "Hurry up, *Hertzya*," she called, for all the world to hear.

When Communists Invaded Our Farm

I was afraid of rattlesnakes when I was a child, but the only snakes I ever came across while walking around the farm were bull snakes. They looked like rattlesnakes; both grow to about six feet long and have symmetrical brown and black markings on their yellowish skin. The big differences are that bull snakes do not have rattles and are not poisonous, which are very big differences indeed.

I met a bull snake once or twice a summer while getting the cows in from the far pasture for milking, but the only time I heard the warning rattle of a rattlesnake was when I watched Daddy clear the schoolyard at Hope Valley School before the beginning of school one September. Alvin was along too, with a hoe, which he used to kill three or four rattlesnakes. He cut off their tail ends and gave one of them to me. It had seven rattles.

At the school, the snakes had slithered under the wooden porch to stay out of the hot sun. The space under the wooden porch at our farmhouse was snake-free because our collie, Bert, usually resided there. I scurried under that porch one summer day, not to get out of the sun, but to hide from Communists. That's what I thought they were when I saw them drive into our yard—Communists—four or five of them standing in the bed of a red pickup truck, each one holding a gun pointed upward.

From my hideout underneath the porch, I saw Daddy surrender to the man who opened the truck's door on the passenger side. I was praying hard to keep them from shooting Daddy: "Savior of the world, save Daddy. Savior of the world, save Daddy," over and over. In church we prayed that the Savior of the world would save Russia from communism, but now it was Daddy who needed to be saved from the Communists. Then another one of them hopped down from the back of the truck. Instead of coming to the house to capture the rest of us, he walked ahead of the truck and opened the gate to the pasture. After the truck drove through, he closed the gate and hopped back on. Then the truck headed east toward the other pasture.

Daddy seemed remarkably calm as he walked back to the house, though seeing me instead of Bert emerge from underneath the porch may have surprised him a little. Our dog was away with Alvin and Virgil, working in the west field, which is why he hadn't torn out after the Communists, barking them out of our yard. Inside, I heard Daddy explain to my mother that these men were hunting for coyotes. They had asked permission to drive through our pastures to the river bottomland where coyotes were more likely to be found.

Why would a ten-year-old like me be so afraid of Communists? My reading in 1938 included a comic strip about the Spanish Civil War. It was in a magazine called *The Young Catholic Messenger* that was handed out after Sunday mass. In this strip, the good guys were Catholics led by General Francisco Franco. Among his followers were two boys, brothers, not quite old enough yet to be soldiers. One of them, the older one, was named Virgil, and this coincidence absolutely solidified my empathy with Franco's army. The bad guys were an assortment of Spanish and Russian Communists. Every week, comic strip Virgil and his younger brother put themselves in great danger to help Franco's soldiers. The two brave, crafty brothers outwitted and outmaneuvered the godless, cruel Communists at every turn.

Back on the farm, I did not tell Daddy how scared I had been. In fact, I don't remember telling anyone, not even Virgil.

Daddy died peacefully thirteen years later, in June 1951, of leukemia. I was twenty-one years old and away in the Army at the time, having been drafted after North Korean and Chinese Communists invaded South Korea. I was not assigned to Korea, though. Instead, I served in the 53rd Anti-Aircraft Artillery Brigade, whose task it was to safeguard Philadelphia from air attacks, it being feared at the time that the Russian Communists were planning to bomb American cities. So I was on the lookout, once again, for Communists, and once again I emerged unscathed.

828

Two Longs and a Short

In Kansas in the 1930s, farmhouses were generally about a mile apart, so communication between them was often by telephone. Our farm was the last one on a communal line that originated in the telephone company's office in Victoria, thirteen miles northwest of us. We were more or less the lonely southern fringe of a German farming settlement, the center of which, Victoria, being a town of about five hundred immigrants.

Our telephone number was 828—that's all; just three digits—no two-letter prefix. Eight-two-eight was a party line. I believe that as many as twenty-eight parties could share one line, but there were only twelve on ours. Each of them was assigned a distinctive pattern of long and short rings. A full turn of the crank produced a long ring, and a slight push on the crank, a short one.

Our pattern was two longs and a short; Uncle Frank's, where Grandmother lived, was three longs; the Wittmans' was two shorts, a long, and a short; and so on. When one phone in the loop rang, all of them rang. Anyone could pick up. So our party line kept our twelve far-flung neighbors connected—not just the ones talking on the phone to each other, but also the ones listening in.

Obsolete now, the party line was once way ahead of its time in facilitating what today we call conference calls. One family, the Wittmans, made a conference call every morning. Around 9:00 a.m., Anna Wittman's daughter Lillian, who lived a mile down the road from her mother, would—I started to say "give her a ring." But this phrasing seriously understates the ringing that Lillian actually did, which was to crank two short rings, then a long one, then a short one. Then Anna, a mile away, and her daughter-in-law Twila, three miles further west, would each pick up.

Thus began the three-way conversation about this and that and what they'd had for breakfast, and how many cows they'd milked that morning, and if Twila's newborn daughter, Twila Mae, was eating solids yet, and that pregnant Lillian threw up only once this morning, and that the community drunk, Tony Schuler, drove his Model T into a ditch again last night, and so on.

Eavesdroppers in the loop enjoyed these early versions of the *Today Show*, different mostly in that the Wittmans' conversations were bilingual—mother Anna using German while daughter Lillian and daughter-in-law Twila used English. Eavesdroppers never dared chime in. Eavesdropping on a party line, though commonly practiced, was widely frowned on. So the story about an elderly matron who butted in on some particularly juicy gossip to ask if they couldn't please talk in German—that story is probably apocryphal.

There was no time limit on telephone conversations within the loop, though the phone company advised keeping them down to five minutes in deference to others who might wish to use the phone. If you had an emergency, you could always ask the people who were tying up the line to get off it. Calling within the loop was free—the desperately poor people who talked about what they'd had for breakfast in great detail and at great length would not have done so if time on the line had been a cost factor.

Calls could also come from outside the 828 loop, and these had to go through Central, which is what we called the switchboard operator in Victoria. As my older sisters moved away from our area to their teaching jobs in faraway places, their calls home would produce a sequence like the following.

Central in Victoria would get a call through Central in Topeka from my sister Alvina. She wanted to reach the Schmidtberger residence at 828. Central would connect her to 828 without looking at her routing chart because she knew all the numbers and patterns by heart. She rang our number. My sister Georgine would hear the phone ringing: two longs and a short. It's for us. Georgine would answer. It was Alvina in Topeka. When she comes home tomorrow, she will get off the train at Victoria, not Hays. "Got it," Jean says, "we'll be there." Georgine would then depress the receiver, but only for a second, thereby staying on the line. She heard two clicks. "Only two," she'd tell us.

In the scenario just described, Alvie's voice came through fairly well because there were only two eavesdroppers. Five or six more than that would have caused line overload, the bane of party lines. Each eavesdropper decreases the line's audio-effectiveness. As the talk on our telephone came to be about jobs in distant cities and calls came in from boyfriends unknown around Victoria, the number of eavesdroppers increased until it became just about impossible to make out what was being said. Then Central (Ernestine) would cut in, and, in both German and English, order the people listening in to get off the line. The clicking sound of receivers being cradled would follow, yet my sisters could not be sure *all* the eavesdroppers had hung up.

To this day, I am wary of discussing confidential matters over the phone. I cannot rid myself of the apprehension that others are listening in. And I still feel, though I know better, that I must hurry to end my call. So I do that; I end it. There once were reasonable explanations for this uneasiness with talking on the phone. It was expensive, especially the interminable chitchat my six children engaged in as teenagers. But now I am the sole user of my landline, and the cost remains about the same no matter the amount of use. "My hearing is bad," I explain to my family and friends. And so indeed it is. It is natural, therefore, and normal that I should prefer e-mailing to telephoning. But there is more to it than that—I'm afraid. Below these sane and sound reasons for my aversion to talking on the phone there lurks yet a specter, unvanquished still, waiting impatiently to use the phone, waiting and listening in.

The Food Chain

Two Perspectives

Looking eastward from our farm, the prairie seemed to stretch out forever, even beyond the distant horizon where the sky finally touched earth. From underneath that point, at dawn, there exploded upward, in slow motion, great sheets of scarlet flames, turning multicolored, filling the eastern sky, rendering the sun's slow regal rising gorgeous and glorious.

My daily familiarity with this scene in no way dulled its reversal in the evening. Instead, it was as if nature had saved her best display for last, the sunset its grand finale. But there was still more to come. Stars, unimaginably bright, myriad, bespoke a cosmic grandeur wherein I was but a tiny, tiny speck. These memories still inform, though they no longer define, my view of nature—nature seen from a distance, awesome and incomprehensible.

For a close-up view of nature there comes to mind, unbidden, the most amazing thing I ever saw. But here I am using "amazing" in its older, original sense, now obsolete, of being in a maze, which is to say confounding, bewildering.

When I was about thirteen years old, I was out in the near pasture on a warm summer day, just passing the time until I would fetch the cows from the far pasture for evening milking. I had my .22 caliber single-shot rifle with me, just in case I saw a rabbit resting in the shade of a stone post along the fence line. Bert was with me, hoping to catch a rabbit for his supper. He had never actually caught one that I knew of, yet Bert remained under the illusion that he could outrace and catch a jackrabbit. These weren't the little cottontail hares they call rabbits here in the East. Jackrabbits—short for jackass rabbits because their ears look like miniature donkeys' ears—are much bigger than the fluffy, white rabbits people keep for pets, and ten times tougher. Like all rabbits, they are prolific breeders, notorious for multiplying into incredibly high numbers in short periods of time, so we thought of them as pests who could demolish a garden and do serious damage to a wheat field.

Anyway, Bert was forever scaring up a jackrabbit and giving it chase until it got so far ahead of him that he realized that catching it was hopeless. Sometimes, though, a jackrabbit would tease him, letting Bert stay within a hopeful distance. Then, when Bert's tongue was about to hang to the ground from exhaustion, the rabbit would quicken his pace. Hippity-hop, skip-and-a-jump and away he would go, leaving Bert to stop and reel in his tongue and rest a while.

So on the day in question, I thought this particular rabbit was teasing Bert, letting him get to within ten yards or so. A little closer than usual today, it appeared, but Bert wasn't actually gaining ground, so I thought the rabbit would sprint away soon, since Bert was clearly tiring. But instead of doing the hippity-hop, skip-and-a-jump thing, this rabbit was slowing down too.

The rabbit was running in a direction parallel to mine along a slope that declined into a small ravine we called Coyote Canyon. The distance between pursued and pursuer closed to within a few yards, and then remained the same. Both animals were exhausted and moving ever more slowly. I was short of breath myself, having run to catch up with them. I was about to command Bert to stay lest he fall over dead from a heart attack, when the rabbit, as if anticipating my command, stopped—sat down. Bert, about eight feet behind, stopped— sat down too, panting like I'd never heard before, or ever heard since. So there we were, hunted, hunter, and I, the three of us a tableau out on the open prairie.

I moved first—I pointed my rifle and squeezed the trigger, hitting the rabbit. I was edging closer to see if I needed to finish the job, when I saw the first tiny bunny coming out, and I knew now what had slowed this rabbit down. Bert did not have a collar, so I laid my rifle down, took off my belt, and put it around his neck to hold him away. By the time Bert's panting was down to only about twice the normal rate, there were four baby bunnies. Bert minded me throughout. I guess he was just too tired and too busy panting to heed his predatory instincts. Or maybe he was confused by the sounds I made in trying to keep from crying in my own confusion. But it was over with now. I picked up my rifle and we walked back to the barn. I stood the rifle in a corner, took the bridle down from its peg and put it on Pat, our pie-bald horse, who stood waiting for me in the corral. I rode bareback, as usual, into the far pasture to fetch the cows for evening milking.

While we were milking, I told Virgil what had happened, and after all the chores were done and supper was over, we walked toward Coyote Canyon and found the spot where the hunt had ended. It was getting dark, but it was still light enough to see some traces of blood, but that was all. The mother's body was gone, as were her four bunnies, which was to be expected in a place called Coyote Canyon. So in a way, my close-up view of nature ended with nothing much left to see.

Separation

While growing up, we seven siblings were forever bickering over this and that. My mother used to say, *"Der Gleesta gebt nah,"* when trying to calm a quarrel between any two of her seven children, hoping that this bit of wisdom—that in a dispute, the wiser one gives in—might inspire in each young combatant a yearning to act the part of the wiser one, thus ending the altercation on the spot. It never happened, of course.

Our spats erupted over small matters, like whose turn it was to carry water to the henhouse on a particularly hot day. Issues like this were of interest only to the parties immediately concerned—in this instance, Virgil and me—and, of course, the poor, thirsty chickens as well.

Most of our family arguments were prompted by the irksome need to do the chores. Cows had to be milked. Couldn't be put off to another day. The barnyard, unlike the government, can't be temporarily shut down.

Farm chores range from easy to hard, to really, really hard, with many gradations in between. Some cows are easy milkers, some are misbehavers. Who gets assigned to which cow can involve considerable negotiating over collateral issues like who has to wash the separator.

Running the separator sounds like fun. You pour milk into a container at the top of the separator, turn a crank, and then skimmed milk comes out of a big spigot while cream comes out of a little spigot underneath. As a child, I found this amazing to watch, but after my role changed from observer to participant, I discovered a downside to this marvelous contraption. After each use, the separator has to be *cleaned*, which means disassembling its separating mechanism into its thirty-four metal parts, then washing, rinsing, and drying each part. So anyone would probably choose to milk a mischievous, misbehaving cow over cleaning the separator.

But anyone would opt to wash the separator *and* milk the crankiest cow over cleaning the chicken house. That was a really, really awful chore. Only Alvin was willing to do it—that's how much he hated milking and its ancillary chores. Also, there was this one advantage: cleaning the chicken house was not a daily chore, it came due only every other Saturday.

When that time came, Alvin went to work scraping chicken poop, some dried, some solidifying, some freshly wet, from the roosting boards, letting the slimy mess fall into the straw below. Once the boards were clean, Alvin wiped them down with Germazone, a popular henhouse medication back then. It was usually added to the chickens' drinking water, but it was also touted as a good disinfectant for their roosts.

Alvin thought Germazone was a quack medicine. "About as useful as snake oil," he would say, but Dad made him apply it anyway. Then Alvin would rake the poop-filled straw out from under the roost and cart it by wheelbarrow to the manure spreader, returning with bales of fresh straw. Alvin thought that instead of raking out the poop-seasoned straw every other week, why not just keep covering it with fresh straw until there was half a year's accumulation? Dad thought otherwise, so this was a second running argument between them. Since our chickens remained healthy, year in and year out, Alvin remained on the losing side of both arguments.

As good fortune would have it, the grievances and grudges of childhood and adolescence did not follow us into adulthood. Our sibling rivalries were left behind as we went our separate ways to distant places, married, and with our spouses established our own spaces. But distance notwithstanding, we remained spiritually close through the years, closer perhaps than is the norm, or so it has been suggested to me by friends whose own family gatherings at Thanksgiving are an annual exercise in putting a smile on the face of discomfort.

It is pleasing to think that it was our moral superiority—our special virtues—that sustained this sense of solidarity my siblings and I enjoyed to the end of their days. But there may be additional, less self-satisfying explanations. Perhaps we lived too far apart to get on one another's nerves. I wound up in the New York area, while Armie went to Seattle, Alvie to Portland, Oregon, and Jan to Oakland, California.

Virgil, after graduating from the University of Kansas, stayed in Lawrence, far from the family farm in Victoria, and Jean, in Washington, Kansas, was about 175 miles away from Victoria.

Only Alvin remained on the family farm. He took over running it after Dad retired. When Virgil and I visited Alvin in the summer of 2011, I asked him about the Germazone argument. Alvin looked a little troubled and said he wondered how someone as smart and savvy as Dad could have been taken in by the Germazone ads. Having done a little research myself about Germazone, I mentioned that a great many chicken farmers swore by Germazone. "That's true," Alvin nodded thoughtfully. Virgil, taking another sip from his Budweiser, thought that Germazone probably contained a drop or two of alcohol, and so may have done a little good as a disinfectant when added to the drinking trough, a possibility that tickled Alvin.

After Dad retired, Alvin tore down the chicken house, which effectively concluded the poultry era of our family farm. As a result, Alvin's theory about Germazone's not having any beneficial effect on the health of chickens was never tested. Remaining untested, too, was his belief that removing poop from the chicken house should be done as infrequently as possible. On researching the matter, I was pleasantly surprised to read in a recent issue of a farmer's journal that "the recommended practice today is to just keep covering it with straw until half a year or so has gone by."

One may wonder how Alvin handled it when no one was left on the farm except him to do the milking he so disliked. He simply let the calves stay with their mothers, so the cows got milked by their own calves. "Exactly the way nature intended," Alvin used to say. He sold the separator at a farm auction.

Changing Styles

As a professor of English for upwards of fifty years, I have lived much of my adult life in a milieu that is, charitably speaking, inattentive to the norms of proper attire.

But as I reflect on my earlier years, I find myself touching a few little scabs of discomfort. For example, I remember having nothing to wear except my overalls when the time for my first school dance came at Hays Junior High, so I didn't go. No big deal, that. But as I reach further back to my childhood on the farm, I begin to recover embarrassments too god-awful to talk about.

"Leave it alone," I say about the time when I was six years old, and showed up in the afternoon for a post-communion service wearing my older brother's hand-me-down knickerbockers instead of the white trousers the three other boys were wearing, and that I too had worn that morning for our first communion, and then—Oh, the shame of it—had accidentally wet soon afterwards. (Never mind the circumstances—it happened and that's it.) My mother did not have time to wash and iron my white trousers before the afternoon Vesper Service, and sent me off in my hand-me-down knickers.

So how should I have answered the priest when he singled me out from the group of four little girls in white dresses and three boys in their white trousers—when he pointed at me and, looking puzzled, asked why I wasn't wearing my white trousers too? That was long ago, and now, in my mid-eighties and experienced with the infirmities of age, the vagaries of the bladder, I calmly turn and face my ancient memory of Father Callistus Rechtenwald. I look up at this gentle, old man and, shrugging my shoulders, tell him that, "It happens." But I was only six and didn't know, then, that *it happens*. So instead of answering Father Callistus's question, not unkindly meant, I am sure, I burst into tears.

There was a time when I escaped an embarrassment, one so awful that to the end of my days, I would have had to endure humiliation after humiliation at each laughter-choked retelling of it. At family gatherings, at Thanksgiving, at every wedding and wake—especially at wakes—the story of how I once "dressed for the occasion" would have left friends and family in stitches, and me red-faced and forcing a weak smile.

It was a hot summer day on the banks of the Smoky Hill River in Ellis County, Kansas. At age nine, I was the youngest of the fourteen or so members of our local 4-H club. We and our parents and relatives were having a Sunday afternoon picnic, around thirty people in all. For recreation, we were planning to do something different from the usual horseshoes, croquet, and softball games. We were going to go swimming.

The drought and dust storms seemed about over, and the river, which in my memory had never run at more than a trickle, was now a steady flow on a bed of sand. My enterprising five older siblings had built a dam using sand-filled bags, thus creating a swimming pool a few feet deep—deep enough to swim in but not deep enough to drown in—this latter an important consideration, since most of us did not know how to swim. In fact, we had never been in water deep enough for learning to swim.

The teenagers who built the dam also had the foresight to come equipped with swimsuits. But I hadn't helped with the building, which may explain why I, unlike my older siblings, had no swimsuit. A word about that. Back then, men's swimsuits were really no different from women's one-piece suits today. And women's two-piece suits were still a bit daring, but it's important to know that its bottom half looked pretty much like the modest variety of trunks men wear today. The scant bikini was still a long way in the future.

Anyway, after the fried chicken and mashed potatoes and corn on the cob—and the deviled eggs too, of course—teenagers were seen heading off in different directions, the girls to a nearby wash-house, and the boys to a thicket of cottonwood trees, whence they emerged, running through the sweltering heat and leaping into the cool of our homemade pool. How they laughed and splashed and played, the boys ducking under the girls and then lifting them high, the girls shrieking with joy as they tumbled back down off the boys' shoulders and into the water.

And all I could do was watch. I had no suit. I stood in the heat, yearning to jump into and rollick about in the sparkling, cool water—but I had no suit. "I wish I had a suit," I lamented to Armie. She was skinny as a fence rail, so it made sense for me to think it okay to borrow her suit when she offered. It was still in a bag on the backseat of our car, Armie explained, because she was just too tired to swim, though I now realize that perhaps she wasn't quite daring enough to be the only girl sporting a two-piece suit.

Light-headed with thoughts of pleasure to come, I headed for the car, but even as I ran, a little cloud of doubt began to float across my mind—an uncertainty quite like the real cloud that was drifting over-head. But there on the backseat lay the bag, and in it, sure enough, was the knit suit, and the bottom had an adjustable belt as I had hoped. I grabbed it and headed for the cottonwood grove. But my internal cloud was darkening into anxiety, and I may not have noticed that the sun was disappearing behind a thunderhead too. "What should I do with the top part of the suit?" I wondered, perplexed, unable to decide. I can't reconstruct any kind of logical progression of my thoughts, and the whole field of swimming and swimsuits was new and confusing to me. I had no precedent to guide my way, and so it was that, standing behind the huge trunk of an old cottonwood tree, and about to emerge for all to see, I had pretty well decided that when borrowing a suit, the proper thing to do is to wear the whole thing.

But praise be! Fate is sometimes kind, and good happens too. Yes, good happens. A bolt of lightning split the sky, then the crash of thunder, and I barely had time to slip back into my overalls and run to the car for shelter, ahead of the cascading rain.

St. Boniface Church in Vincent, Kansas

Every year, after wheat harvest was over, St. Boniface Parish had its picnic. Considered geographically, the parish was huge, covering some twenty-five square miles. But in terms of population, it was small, tiny actually, encompassing about seventeen families.

At the center of this vast expanse stood the church, the priest's house, a two-room school, and a sisters' house for the three nuns who formed the school's faculty and administration. That was it for the town of Vincent—no store, no post office, no baseball field, nothing else at all. My point here is the absence of anything that would grab your attention or offer any possibility of recreation, not even off the beaten path and certainly not on it, in St. Boniface Parish, save for the annual parish picnic.

I still remember the booths that were set up against the school-house, the new wood smell of the two-by-fours that formed the booths' perimeters. There was the stand for soda pop, Orange and Grape Crush being the favorites. A bottle was five cents. There was Coca-Cola and there was Pepsi Cola, and it was true: you got twice as much Pepsi for a nickel. There was the ice cream stand: vanilla and chocolate and strawberry, all homemade, a nickel a cone. In charge of the booth for beer stood broad-shouldered and lantern-jawed Uncle Nick, who had fought in the trenches in World War I and with whom nobody, drunk or sober, would ever think of messing.

There were booths for candies, cakes, and pies, and people came from other parishes, nearby and afar, so there was quite a crowd at our annual picnics.

Alas, the picnic was a once-a-year affair, and it stood in stark contrast to the regular, much more isolated, weekly assembly of the parishioners. After mass every Sunday, the married women would gather in a circle right outside the church door. As best I remember, *Rooshuns* and *Deutchlenra* intermingled. *Rooshuns* were the Germans who came to the prairie after their century-long stay along the Volga River. *Deutchlenra*, on the other hand, were Germans who immigrated directly from Germany to Kansas. The distinction may be subtle, but socially speaking, it mattered greatly.

The men gathered about ten yards farther away at the edge of the road that ran past the church. Unlike the women, the men always formed two circles and I used to think one of them was for *Roosa* and the other for *Deutchlenra*, but I now realize that the group on the right were parishioners who lived north of the church, and the one on the left were parishioners to the south, though this geographical division came close enough to coinciding with the ethnic division to mislead me.

My father, Mike, and his brothers, Nick and Frank, stood in the south circle. Uncle Frank, the youngest, stood nearly a foot taller than my father. Uncle Nick was also fairly tall and had a barroom bouncer's build. He lost much of his hearing during his service in France. His demeanor back home remained that of a first sergeant, and like many men who are partially deaf, he had a booming voice. This, coupled with his bulk, made Uncle Nick a presence to be reckoned with.

After mass, the teenagers gathered around the cars parked across the road, then disappeared into them. Preteens like me would tag along with their older siblings. How I loved listening to the banter between them and their friends. How witty and wise they were! Seated in the Plymouths, Chevys, and Fords, they appeared to me as unsurpassable models of sophistication and urbanity.

But sorry to say, some of the laughter of these youths was at the expense of their elders. Seated in their parents' cars, the younger generation observed the older as from the box seats of a theater. On stage were the physical incongruities that have been viewed as humorous from Mutt and Jeff to Laurel and Hardy. The elder Schmidtberger men—short Mike, tall Frank, huge Nick—were a paradigm of disproportion that was multiplied by the Vonfeldt brothers, Frank and John, both slightly shorter even than Dad, but more often than not standing next to George Wellbrock, who towered over them at close to seven feet. Additional sources of mirth were endless: a hat that was misshapen or seemed too large, a pipe stem too long, lighting a household match by striking it across the buttocks, an expectoration of chewing tobacco gone awry, and on and on.

But there comes to mind a scene from 1938 that is sober enough and somber too. I was ten years old at the time. In my memory, the two circles of men have, quite unusually, converged into one large group of about fourteen and the conversations are animated. In our car we can't make out what is being said. Uncle Nick, a *Roos*, is standing with Tom Baier, a *Deutchlener* whose gas mask spared his life from the Germans' mustard gas. He had been just a bit late in putting it on, though, so his lungs did not escape entirely unscathed. That was why, it had been explained to us, Tom Baier's characteristic facial expression was that of someone who feels perpetually troubled. In my memory of the scene, the two veterans, Uncle Nick and Tom Baier, are on the south edge of the group. Then Uncle Nick steps aside and faces north so that he can be heard by all the men, who are turning their heads toward him now. We too in our car across the road can hear Uncle Nick saying, "*Es gebt viedermal Krieg.*" Uncle Nick was sure there would be war again.

Part 3

Hays Junior-Senior High School

The Sailor cannot see the North—but knows the
Needle can—

—Emily Dickinson

Remembering Pearl Harbor

On December 8, 1941, in the early afternoon, I was alone in the cellar when I overheard my parents talking about the bombing of Pearl Harbor.

Virgil, a sophomore at Hays Junior-Senior High School, was away in Hays and Alvin was already away in the Army, drafted a few months earlier under the Selective Service Act of 1940. His one-year conscription would eventually stretch out into five years, three of them with the Army Air Corps in the South Pacific. Virgil would graduate from high school and then serve three years in the Navy. My three older sisters were away at their teaching jobs at country schools. So the only sibling at home was Janice, eight years younger than I and old enough for kindergarten, but not going to school yet because the grades in Ellis County schools back then were one through eight. There was no K.

So why was I at home in my basement bedroom instead of at school when I overheard talk about Pearl Harbor? The date that lives in infamy—December 7, 1941—was a Sunday, but it was on a Monday that my parents were listening to President Roosevelt's speech, which he made in the early afternoon on December 8, a day after the attack.

Now December 8 is the Feast of the Immaculate Conception, a holy day of obligation for Catholics—same as a Sunday—which means that Mom, Dad, little Janice, and I had gone to mass at St. Boniface Church five miles away, had dinner (the noon meal), and then gone our separate ways on this work-free holiday when we rested from all labor save for necessary chores, like milking the cows. Janice had gone off to play her favorite game of imitating adult conversations,

Mom and Dad had turned on the radio, and I had gone downstairs to sulk in solitude and silence.

I was in eighth grade, and back in the one-room Hope Valley School, which had been closed the preceding year for lack of enrollment, while I was sent to school in Hays. Hays was only twenty-three miles from home, but in cultural terms, I had been transported to a place as distant from our farm as Dorothy was to Oz in the movie. For me, Hays was connected to Oz in another way because that's where I first saw the movie *The Wizard of Oz*. The first movie I ever saw was *Rosalie*, with Nelson Eddie, Jeannette McDonald, Ray Bolger, and Edna Mae Oliver, which came out in 1938. A year or so later, in 1939 to be exact, Georgine again piled us into our Model A Ford, drove thirteen miles of dirt road to Victoria, and from there ten miles more on paved U.S. Highway 40 to Hays where *The Wizard of Oz* was playing at the Strand Theater.

How glorious it was, that next year when I was in seventh grade, to actually live in Hays. Hays was in Technicolor, but unlike Oz, it was real. The closing of my country school had opened up a whole new urban world, and it was a wonderful one. There were city streets and green, water-sprinkled lawns, and my school had classroom after classroom filled by young people. There was a gymnasium; there were sports that called for more than one lonely participant; there were friends other than my siblings; there were no outdoor privies— instead there were gleaming white toilets that flushed.

I could go on and on, but suffice it to say that I was not glad at year's end when I would be going back to Hope Valley in the fall of 1941 for eighth grade. A surge in enrollments reopened the school: there were two new students in first grade, Danny Schmidtberger (a cousin) and Bobby Dean Von Lintel. Also swelling the ranks was a new fifth grader, Loretta Orth, the teacher's adopted little sister. So there were five of us in all, including the teacher, Lidwina Vonfeldt, unmarried and a little on the bitter side.

Separation of church and state was what got Virgil and me started with going to school in faraway Hays, whose citizens were mostly English-speaking and Protestant, whereas my other siblings had gone to high school in Victoria, where all the families, save one, were German and Catholic.

When Georgine, my oldest sister and our ringleader, decided to go on to high school, she was the first in our neighborhood to do so. I like to think that we Schmidtbergers had loftier intellectual aspirations than our neighbors, but the fact is that Georgine, and then my other siblings, had an advantage over the neighbors. The nearest high school was thirteen miles away in Victoria. Since transportation consisted of horse and buggy, then Model T Fords and dirt roads, going to high school meant having to board somewhere close to the school in Victoria, and that cost money. But our grandfather's family still owned his two-story limestone house in Victoria, right across the street from the church and adjacent to the parochial schools, elementary and secondary, both taught by nuns.

For many years, the Quint family had rented Grandfather's house, and Georgine simply moved in with them, as planned, after her freshman year of boarding with the Shooks. In succeeding years, the upstairs became the Schmidtberger apartment as Jean was joined by Alvin, Alvina, and then Armella. So Grandfather's house in Victoria gave my brothers and sisters a decisive leg up in being able to attend high school. Beyond this practical advantage, I also think that our mother's heartbreak at being taken out of school made her very willing to consider any solution—however unconventional—that would allow her children to pursue their schooling.

Now we come to 1939, the year I finished sixth grade and Virgil graduated from eighth: the township closed the school, leaving me to do seventh grade elsewhere. So why didn't Virgil start high school in Victoria like everyone else had, and why didn't I simply join him in the Schmidtberger apartment and do my seventh grade in Victoria? The answer is easy, though I did not learn it until Alvin explained it to me at my last visit with him some six decades later. For the township to pay for my education, it had to be in a *public* school, which ruled out schooling in Victoria's Catholic schools.

What were we to do? At this juncture, Armella, newly graduated from high school and wanting to go to college, chose, of course, to attend Fort Hays State. That was the lynchpin that held it all together. Armella could provide adult supervision for Virgil and me at an apartment in Hays. So off we were to Hays Junior-Senior High School, grades seven through twelve for Virgil and me, and Fort Hays State for Armella, the three of us housed in a basement apartment at 105 Fifth Street, owned by Carl Engel of Engel's Hatchery, which supplied our farm each spring with two hundred or so baby chicks.

So that's where the three of us spent the 1940/41 school year: Monday to Friday in Hays, and weekends back on the farm, twenty-three miles away. My eighteen-year-old sister with two little brothers—aged fourteen and twelve—under her sole supervision. But all things have to come to an end. That wonderful year ended, and in eighth grade I was back in my one-room school—a sophisticated, urbane, man-about-town, sharing space with two weepy first graders, a dour teacher, and her silly little sister the year the Japanese bombed Pearl Harbor.

I still can't explain why I wasn't at school on Monday, December 8, 1941. Hope Valley was a public school, and I don't think it ever closed for Catholic holy days. So my best guess is that it was closed because of the attack on Pearl Harbor.

A Dictionary, a Pen, and Our First Christmas Tree

The Christmas gift, a fountain pen, was perfectly appropriate for a schoolboy like me. It's what happened afterwards that is terrible. The pen was definitely not a ballpoint because ballpoint pens wouldn't be around yet—not until 1945 when they were first sold at Gimbels. But I got my Sheaffer fountain pen for Christmas in 1940, the same year that Virgil got a *Merriam Webster's Dictionary*—the desk size—not that great big one called *The Unabridged*.

Books were made to last back then, and I saw Virgil's *Merriam Webster's* again on a visit to Lawrence in 2012. Virgil did crossword puzzles, and I spied that dictionary lying slightly out of his reach alongside some other dictionaries closer by on his breakfast table. The others were specialized glossaries that crossword fans use more often than standard dictionaries. Infrequent use may have accounted for the remarkable longevity of Virgil's *Merriam Webster's Dictionary*. In any event, it surely has outlasted my Sheaffer fountain pen, which survived little more than a week.

By that Christmas in 1940, the crippling droughts and the Great Depression were things of the past. But I do have memories from that bleak, earlier era. One is of Grandma giving me a dime, my only present that Christmas. I hadn't been old enough for school yet, but I did recognize what a dime was. This one had something to do with Kris Kindle. The words, *Kris Kindle*, "Christ Child" in English, did not evoke any image at the time, nor do they today. So, in my memory I only see Grandmother and feel her warm hand pressing the dime into my outstretched one, and I hear her saying, more to my father alongside us than to me, "*von Kris Kindle, net von Santa Claus*" (From the Christ Child, not from Santa Claus).

So I learned to disbelieve in Santa Claus before I got a chance to believe in him. But no matter. A few years later, times were much better, and I got a fancy fountain pen for Christmas. Rain had finally fallen on the drought-stricken prairie, and rain continued to fall in timely intervals, refreshing the pastures and the wheat fields. Our acquisition in 1936 of the half section Across the River represented the tipping point toward prosperity. The sandy-loam soil there was delta-rich in nutrients and produced wheat and milo in record-breaking quantities. So all was going well: our hens were laying eggs, our pigs were fattening up, our cows were giving milk, Franklin Delano Roosevelt was reelected, and by Christmas 1940, we were exchanging Christmas presents and happiness. In a surge of Christmas spirit, my older sisters put up some Christmas decorations and implored Alvin—then twenty years old and able to do just about anything worth doing—to go out and get us our first Christmas tree.

Evergreen cedars, many shaped like Christmas trees, now dot the pastures in Kansas, but in 1940, these pastures were still as empty of trees as the Sahara. So Alvin, to whom his sisters' wishes were his commands, sped off to town to buy one. But Alvin should have sped off earlier. In our sparsely populated part of the world, entrepreneurs were not likely to overstock Christmas trees, demand for them being low and their shelf life being so absolutely terminal. So Alvin was gone a long time—a very long time—long enough to have searched every town along Highway 40 between Ellis and Russell. He returned long after it had gotten dark and brought the tree into the house. Even little Janice, who was only four, could see that the tree he carried in one hand while opening the door with the other was a leftover, a reject.

Before describing the reception Alvin's tree received, I must first explain that profanity and potty words were not uttered in our household. Nobody said them—not in English, not in German. Never. We used euphemisms instead to help ease us through our trials and tribulations. "Oh, sugar!" we would grimace when hammer hit thumb, but never "Oh, *scheiss!*" And while "Gol-darnit" might be heard, "goddammit" was not. The family's expletive of choice was "Soccer!" and when the going got really tough, "Soccer Dis!" (which I learned years later was a mispronunciation of the French for "sacred divinity").

On that occasion, mild-mannered Alvin, a man for all seasons, had just walked in with that poor little waif of a Christmas tree. Georgine, the alpha member of our pack, screams, "Where did that come from?" Others join in. Alvina. Even Armella. Even Mother. A bedlam of criticisms and withering witticisms. Cacophonous chorus assails Alvin and his poor little tree. Father shakes his head and leaves the room. "Where did you get that?" over and over again. Alvin strives to be heard above the din, and finally shouts a defense: "Do you think I can just pull a Christmas tree out of my ass?" Silence. Alvin, embarrassed, reddens. Self-consciously shrugs. Mother's "tsk tsk" turns into half-suppressed chortle. Father reenters room, looking solemn. Can't hold onto solemn look. Guffaws. Cloudburst of laughter. Thigh-slapping, coffee-spurting-through-nose laughter. The end. For the rest of their lives, the phrase, "where Alvin gets his Christmas trees," remained in the family lexicon of euphemisms.

At some point during this merriest of Christmases, we received our presents. I only remember Virgil's and mine. I may have looked disappointed, though I don't remember feeling disappointed. But I don't remember feeling appreciative either, and I certainly did not catch on to the possible symbolism in our parents' gifts—a dictionary and a pen—to Virgil and me.

One day during the first week back in Hays, I got home from school earlier than Armie and Virgil, so I was alone in our apartment when I decided to fill my pen. I hadn't tried to use it before. For some reason, I had a problem removing the cap. I may have been trying to twist off a cap that was a pull-off or vice versa, I don't know. I thought that heating the cap would help me unscrew it. I took a match from the holder in our kitchen, struck it, and prepared to hold the pen above the flame. Then my eye caught the faucet at the sink and I decided that running warm water would be a better way to heat the cap. But in that instant of hesitation, my pen was suddenly all ablaze. I flung it into the sink, where it sizzled into a small black mess. Shocked, I just stood there, saying over and over, "I didn't mean to do that!" My memory leaves me standing there in the kitchen, atremble, waiting for Armella and Virgil to come home and find out what I've done.

Licenses—Poetic and Otherwise

The Motor Vehicle Bureau in New Jersey was an object of endless complaint, ridicule, renovation, and reorganization during my forty-four-year sojourn in the Garden State. And I knew it well, having shepherded each of my six children through the process that began with a learner's permit and ended, eventually, with the issuance of a driver's license. By contrast, the New York Department of Motor Vehicles in nearby West Haverstraw handled my last request expeditiously and politely when I went there a couple of years ago, leaving me with nothing to complain about.

But let me peel back through those blood pressure–raising ordeals in New Jersey, back through hours wasted—whole days wasted—in long lines, in wrong lines, in lines that eventually terminated at desks or at counters behind which sullen people in uniforms told you that you should have filled out the blue form, not the yellow form, and to go to the back of the room to get the blue one and fill it out. Can you reserve your place in line, you asked? Such a stupid question did not merit an answer. So off you went to the back of the room, where there were many forms lying on a table. No blue ones . . . But they will have some more before closing time, someone said. They think.

Stop me before I get to the time that Mary, my wife, that gentlest of creatures, spat an expletive at one of those pens on a chain that would not write because it was out of ink and then burst into tears at the end of an afternoon spent at the Motor Vehicle Bureau in Jersey City. Let me instead go back to an earlier, simpler era in a rural area when bureaucracies were still in their infancy. Let me take you back to when I got my first driver's license, though the event was, well, uneventful, absolutely lacking any harbingers of indignities to come at various motor vehicle bureaus.

I can't even remember exactly how old I was. My best guess is that I was around thirteen when Dad and I pulled up in front of the post office in Victoria, Kansas, in our 1939 Ford, with me driving. Whether the postmaster, Mr. Shook, received extra pay for his additional responsibility of issuing licenses, I do not know. The job was certainly not labor intensive. For a couple of minutes or so, he and Dad talked about crops and cattle and the weather—no doubt we needed rain. Then Mr. Shook took out a form and wrote my name on it. Dad gave him fifty cents, and Mr. Shook reached into his desk for a card and told me to sign it on the line right under where it said "Driver's License." So after I signed it, I had my first driver's license. That was it.

I don't remember whether Mr. Shook told me to drive carefully. Probably not. But ridiculously enough, there are certain details that I do remember. It was a 50-cent piece, not a combination of smaller coins that Dad handed Mr. Shook. Mr. Shook was smoking a cigar and a whiff of its fragrance lingers with me still. He had a glass eye, which made it hard to tell if he was looking at me or at Dad when he waved good-bye. And that's all I remember about the day I got my first driver's license.

Welcome Back

While walking up the steps of the one-room school I was returning to for eighth grade, I wondered how I should address my teacher. In grades one through six at Hope Valley, we had been taught by a succession of three young teachers, and the respectful form of address was "Teacher." So why was I troubling myself now over what to call Lidwina Vonfeldt, the teacher I was about to greet?

My year at Hays Junior-Senior High had been a wonderful, civilized time for me, but now I was back in the country again. At Hays High, we did not call our teachers "Teacher." We used the appropriate appellative of respect, followed by the surname, as in Miss Courtney or Mr. Massey.

I remember that it was unseasonably warm that September day, and I actually worked up a sweat in the mile and a quarter walk to school. No surprises would await me there. I already knew all the other students at Hope Valley: my cousin Danny and Bobby Dean Von Lintel in the first grade and Loretta Orth in fifth grade. And I, in eighth grade, would round out the student population at four. What was troubling to me was the question of whether to greet Lidwina Vonfeldt, our neighbor, with the traditional "Good morning, Teacher," or to impress her with the urbanity of "Good morning, Miss Vonfeldt," as I had learned in my year in the city.

Unhappy as I was at having to leave Hays, I nonetheless wanted to get off to a good start with my teacher back at Hope Valley. I sensed that Lidwina Vonfeldt would expect me to have a chip on my shoulder over being yanked out of a city school and made to share a schoolroom with two six-year-olds. My case had been publicly discussed. It was unfair to me, this dislocation, my father had argued with the powers that be, but to no avail. Mr. Joseph T. Pfeifer, the county superintendent of schools, could not justify making the taxpayers of Freedom Township pay for my schooling in Hays, he said, when there was a perfectly good schoolhouse that would be reopening its doors only a mile or so from my home. It was further pointed out by a local wag that the addition to the student body of the teacher's little sister would provide me the companionship essential to my social development.

I'm not sure that my father had pressed my case for continuing in Hays as vigorously as he might have. There were many, many chores to be done on our farm, and what with Alvin away in the Army, my three older sisters away at their teaching jobs, and Virgil now away in high school, I would be a very welcome hand indeed for those endless chores: slopping the pigs, feeding the chickens, milking the cows, and so on. My father had already hired one farmhand, and my being at home would make it less urgent for him to hire another.

It was right after Hays High let out for the summer at the end of my single year that I heard the unwelcome news that I would have to go back to Hope Valley the next fall. Apparently I did not accept that turn of events with equanimity because I remember Virgil and Armella both telling me that my sulking was making our parents feel bad. Naturally, their efforts at fraternal correction, however kindly intended, sent me into a rage. After all, I, not my parents, was the victim here.

But as the summer days passed by, I drifted, without admitting it to anyone, into an acceptance of my lot in the year that lay ahead, perhaps because the long hours of work left little time for dwelling on my misfortune. Wheat harvesting, that busiest time of the year, began shortly after school ended. Dad had promoted me to tractor driver, replacing Virgil, who took over Alvin's job of hauling the wheat to town. Dad remained in his supervisory station on the combine. The self-propelled version of the combine had not been invented yet, so it was pulled by a tractor back then.

Driving the tractor was an exacting task that demanded full attention. You had to make sure that the cutting table's length extended far enough into the uncut wheat to utilize all of its twelve feet. You didn't want to be cutting over the top of stubble left from the preceding round. But if you pulled the combine too far inward, you left behind a trail of uncut wheat. So you had to pay close attention to the cutting table, which required looking behind you every few seconds, while keeping an eye on what lay ahead too. I won't even try to explain the intricate maneuvers involved in turning a corner without (1) leaving a patch of uncut wheat, (2) turning the tractor into the cutting table, or (3) taking forever. If you have trouble with parallel parking on a busy street, then driving the tractor in harvest would not have been for you. It was hard, difficult work, this tractor driving, no doubt about it.

The harvesting machine is called a combine because it combines what used to be two separate tasks. The first task, cutting the wheat heads, could be done in either of two ways: (1) a machine called a header cut and transported the heads onto a wagon called a header-box, which hauled the heads away for safekeeping onto stacks that would grow to look like a huge loaf of bread; or (2) a machine aptly named a binder, cut and bound the heads into sheaves, which were gathered together into shocks that look like miniature tepees. Whether in shocks or in stacks, the cut wheat is safe from destruction by heavy rain or hail as it awaits the arrival of the threshing machine, which completes the harvesting. It was one of these stacks that Alvin and Alvina once nearly burnt down during their experiment with matches.

While pulling a combine, the relentless prairie wind blows the chaff over the tractor driver, who has to wear goggles to protect his eyes. Having chaff blown over your body all day long in sweltering heat that reaches 105 degrees is not a joyful experience. But that is not the whole experience either, not by a long shot. In fact, there can be an almost transcendental quality to the harvest. I can still picture Dad signaling, for example, that the combine's tank is almost full and me stopping the tractor to unload. We are no longer tormented by chaff, and Virgil pulls our Ford truck alongside the combine so that its box is right under the tank, then takes his shoes off and hops into the truck box.

Meanwhile, I have climbed up the combine to the platform alongside the tank. I unhook the chute, dropping the far end into the truck box, then push down on a handle, which opens the hatch at the bottom of the tank. The golden-brown grain gushes down the chute into the truck box where it threatens to spill over the side because this is the third filling and the truck is almost full. But Virgil, ankle deep in wheat, uses a scoop to push the flowing grain to where there is still

Harvest, 1914. Photo courtesy of my cousin Marylee Hamilton, showing her relatives harvesting with a header and a header box.

room along the sides and in the corners. When the tank is empty and the truck full, Virgil hops down and puts his shoes back on, then rolls a canvas over the load, tightens it, and drives off to the grain elevator in Victoria. Meanwhile, I close the hatch, raise the chute, hook it back in place, rev up the idling engine, and get back on my tractor. Dad signals and we proceed down the field again, both of us, Dad and I, combine and tractor, once again enveloped in a cloud of chaff.

But the sight of golden-brown wheat flowing down the glistening, wheat-scoured chute is one that gladdens. It gladdens me in a way nothing else does—nothing I can think of. That's what would bring me back to the farm year after year, whenever possible, from my home in faraway New Jersey to help out at harvest.

By the time summer ended, I had changed my sullen attitude. When I walked into the schoolhouse at summer's end, I said, as cheerfully as I could, "Good morning, Teacher." And I had been right. I could tell that Lidwina Vonfeldt had been expecting a surly, arrogant, disdainful city slicker, but that's not who showed up. There was also a silver lining to the situation. In Hays my athletic abilities had been unremarkable. But here at Hope Valley, with only a handful of much younger children to compete against, I rose to the likes of Babe Ruth in the admiring eyes of little Danny and Bobby Dean and, yes, golden-haired Loretta Orth too. Surely no one at Hays High rose to such unrivaled athletic stardom as I did that year at Hope Valley in eighth grade.

Happiness—A Tilting Point

In September 1942, I was a freshman in high school in Hays. There was a war on, as we told one another at every turn, though I needed no reminder, with Alvin risking his life in the Army Air Corps somewhere in the Pacific. One of the patriotic things President Franklin Delano Roosevelt urged us to do was to buy war bonds—he bought the first one himself.

The Series E War Savings Bond cost $18.75, and would be worth $25.00 in ten years. So buying a war bond was not only the patriotic thing to do, it was a sound financial investment too. But not everyone could pony up $18.75. No problem. You could do it a little at a time by buying 25-cent stamps and pasting them into an album until it was full at $18.75, when you turned it in for a bond. For really poor kids like me, there were 10-cent stamps and matching albums. I cannot explain how you reached an exact $18.75 with 10-cent stamps, but my dime album was only at $14.70 when I stopped pasting stamps into it.

Here's what happened. Once a week at the beginning of the afternoon study hour, I went to the assistant principal's office, where Mr. Massey handed me a pouch containing the materials relevant to the school's war bond drive. These I delivered to the city post office. Why I was entrusted with this responsibility, I do not know. But I did have an ulterior motive when I volunteered for it. I could surely borrow a bike, I reasoned, and ride it to the post office, which was a long walk from our school.

Ah, to ride a bike! Joe Bickel had taught me how to ride a bike during my year in Hays for seventh grade, and he sometimes let me take a spin around the block. What a joy that was! But then I had to go back to our bikeless farm for eighth grade. Even if we had owned a Schwinn, dirt roads like ours would have discouraged bike riding. The only bike of any kind that I remember seeing on a dirt road was the one that the wicked witch pedaled in the first part of *The Wizard of Oz*. Now I was back in Hays—in bike-riding land, but with no bike to ride since Joe had moved to Texas. But sometimes things have a way of working out. And they did!

From my first day on as a courier, I borrowed bikes from the row of about twenty of them parked, most of them unchained, in a row of stanchions along a side entrance. I borrowed a different one each time, yet in my memory of biking to the post office, the bike is always a deep, shining blue, and the day a gorgeous, crisp, absolutely perfect autumn afternoon and I am gliding fast down the smooth, sloping street—floating, flying with the greatest of ease.

I cannot remember how I got the 147 10-cent stamps in my Series E War Savings Bond album before I cashed it in for $14.70. What I do remember is that the only way for me to get my hands on some nickels without lying about what I wanted them for was to liquidate my only liquid asset, my partially filled war bond album. There was no other way. I could not imagine asking my mother, my father, or my older sisters, all three of them teachers in country schools at the time, and certainly not Alvin, now in the Army, or Virgil, in whose charge I was—I couldn't ask any of them to give me some nickels to feed into a pinball machine.

It was Junior Thompson who introduced me to the pinball machine in the Cozy Café on Tenth Street in Hays. An unpopular kid from a well-to-do family, Junior bought friendships. He bought mine midway through the spring semester. We took turns playing pinball, he supplying the nickels. It wasn't long before I discovered that I had a talent for playing the pinball machine. I found that by strategically pounding on its frame, you could nudge the machine into awarding free games. But if you banged too hard, the machine went dark save for the brightly lit-up sign, *TILT*, and you had to start all over again with another nickel. If you banged too lightly, too soon, too late, or in the wrong spot, the ball rolled past the circular posts that would have clanged triumphantly if the ball had hit one of them. The trick was to sense the tilting point at each juncture as you navigated the ball down the slope of the pinball machine, even shaking it just a little—carefully, ever so lightly, but still enough to roll the ball into one of the glass globes. Oh, the joy then of hearing the rhythmic clanging of points being added, of free games won!

I became an addict, but Junior Thompson was a sore loser. I pressed my superiority at pinball too hard, tilting his ego, so Junior quit playing pinball, perhaps preferring to play games he paid for to playing games I had won for him. Whatever the case, my loss of a patron left me in sore need of starter nickels for the duration of the semester.

I do not remember ever having felt so strong a sense of deprivation before. Not having a dime or even a nickel to my name had, until now, simply seemed an immutable condition, like not having wings. It was not something to fret about. I did not have a sweet tooth, so it never bothered me that I could not buy a Snickers or Mars Bar after class the way almost everyone else did at the War Effort Stand in the hallway. But doing without my semi-weekly pinball sessions was something new and different. Playing that machine somehow filled a deep need I had not known before, so I cashed in my partially filled album, ignoring the disapproving "tsk tsk" of the lady at the window as she slowly counted out my money.

I do not remember where I hid all that money. My plan was to repurchase 140 stamps and paste them in a new album, leaving me with seventy cents—fourteen nickels, more than enough, I underestimated, to keep me pinballing through the rest of the semester. Instead of repurchasing all 140 stamps at once, though, which might have raised eyebrows, I thought I'd replace them in smaller increments.

I proceeded along these lines until the last week of school. Then I would be returning to the farm for the summer, which would end my pinball playing and my need for nickels. At the post office, I bought a dozen or so stamps, restoring my album to $13.40, not $14.00, as originally envisioned, fourteen nickels having been too few to sustain my playing. It was the same tsk tsk lady who handed me my stamps, and I thought that this patriotic purchase would restore me to her good graces.

I *mistakenly* thought that. At the end of English class a day or two later, Miss Kraus told me that Mr. Massey wanted to see me. When

I got to his office, he took my arm and, while leading me back into his inner sanctum, he began to talk about the stamp album I was filling. Panic stricken at the thought that Mr. Massey knew about my self-embezzling, I flailed about wildly, trying to think of an expenditure more worthy than pinball to explain the $1.30 I had made off with and squandered. But I needn't have bothered. Still holding my arm, Mr. Massey explained to me that liquidating my album to get the money for buying more stamps did not really help the war effort and did not increase the amount of money raised by our class even if it appeared to do so. That was all he said.

I was, of course, immensely relieved, although I did resent being thought dumb enough to believe that cashing in and rebuying stamps would help the war effort. But I stifled the impulse to come clean, deciding it better to be thought a simpleton than a cheat. But I was not a cheat either, I kept telling myself as I walked down Ash Street back to our apartment, where I continued to roll the matter around.

Would the whole truth reveal me to be a cheat? I wasn't sure. I had put back the money I had taken—well, most of it, anyway. Besides, it was my own money. Then I saw the whole truth of the matter revealed something harder for me to accept. Buying a war bond, which would help my country win the war and save the lives of soldiers like Alvin, was evidently less important to me than beating a stupid pinball machine. Just a little less important, to be sure. If measured numerically, the difference between $13.40 and $14.70 was not so very much—just twenty-six nickels that I had refused to give to save a soldier's life. I had never looked at the matter in quite that way before, and the thought, when it hit me, gave me a jolt that stopped my pinball playing forever.

Language Bias

My parents' farm was on the southern fringe of our Volga German settlement, so that our neighbors on three sides, each about a mile away, were English-speaking and Protestant. They were real Kansans, as opposed to us foreigners, or *Rooshuns*, as some of them called us.

But these *Englishe*, as we called them, did not offer my earliest example of linguistic snootiness. No, that was provided by a second component of the Volga German communities: German Catholics who came directly from Germany. These *Deutchlenra* considered themselves culturally superior to us *Rooshuns* and worked hard at retaining the minor differences in speech that distinguished the *Deutchlenra* from us *Rooshuns*.

To the dismay of *Deutchlenra*, the English-speaking Protestants bundled *Deutchlenra* and *Rooshuns* indiscriminately together, calling them all *Rooshuns*. But in some instances, the *Deutchlenra* got their backs up enough to get themselves disentangled from the *Rooshuns*. For example, when I first enrolled in the public school in Hays, the *Deutchlenra* could register in a category of their own: German. Interestingly enough, there were only two other ethnic categories: German-Russian and English. When I returned after my year at Hope Valley, Georgine mischievously persuaded me to register as German instead of German-Russian. So I did, and to her great disappointment, nothing happened. A bit of a social climber myself, I'd have tried to make it further upward into that elite English column, but I had a very detectable German accent, which had been no impediment, obviously, for passing as German, but which would have left me vulnerable to exposure and humiliation had I tried to pass as English.

There were no blacks or Asians in Hays High back then. But there was one Mexican in 1942, the year I enrolled. He was in front of me in the registration line, and the lady at the desk placed him—after just the slightest twitch of a pause—down where she assumed he belonged, in the lowest tier, in with "them *Rooshuns*."

I have no idea what purpose these statistics served.

There is an additional complication: Depending on where it was used, the term *Rooshun* could refer to several different groups, all of whom were lumped together under this less-than-tender catch-all. There were the Volga Germans, of course, originally brought by Catherine the Great to farm along the Volga River. But there were also the Black Sea Germans, brought by Tsar Alexander I to farm in what is present-day Ukraine.

The Black Sea Germans came to Russia later than the Volgas (beginning in the early 1800s) and generally left for America later as well. But because they had actually owned their own land in Russia, the Black Sea Germans accumulated much more wealth and typically arrived in the United States with greater resources than the Volga Germans. But their later arrival also meant that much of the best farmland had already been taken, so they settled less desirable land reaching northward from Nebraska to the Dakotas and on into Canada (with no offense to those fine places). Many also settled in Kansas, but along the Atchison, Topeka & Santa Fe Railroad, buying the pricier land the Volga Germans had passed up in favor of the cheaper land along the Kansas Pacific.

A third group of ethnic German Russians, the Mennonites, were also called *Rooshuns*. Known for their religious objection to conscription, the Mennonites largely relied on church networks for immigration into America, whereas the Volga and Black Sea Germans typically relied on family networks. All these groups had different histories, cultures, and religions, and yet, to the sometimes-unwelcoming gaze of the English-speaking population, we were all simply *Rooshuns*.

Gastrocycles

On the farm, dinner was the biggest meal of the day, and we ate it at noon. After I went off to Hays Junior High for seventh grade, Virgil and I walked the seven blocks back to our apartment to eat. Only the farm kids brought their lunch to school. Virgil and I could have brought sandwiches to school in dinner pails too, the way that the farm kids did. But it was classier to be a city kid than a farm kid, I learned in my first days at Hays Junior-Senior High. And farm kids did not serve well as friends, anyway. They were driven home to their chores after school, so you couldn't hang out with them in the afternoon.

I don't remember a thing about what we ate other than eggs. We always went home to the farm over the weekend. Daddy would pick us up after school on Friday, and Alvin would drive us back to Hays on Sunday night after supper. We brought back with us the week's supplies that Mom packed—loaves of bread and smoked or salted meats and the like. The food I remember carrying out to the car most often was a two-gallon pail filled with eggs, so eggs were surely a staple. To this day, when a need arises to fix something quick and easy, my first thought is of eggs—and often enough there is no second thought.

I do have one clear and lasting memory of supper on a Friday night on the farm after coming home from the week away in Hays. In this memory, Bert recognizes our gray '39 Ford when we pull into the yard. He runs in wild circles around the car, frantic with joy. He does not jump up on us the way some stupid city dogs would as we make our way from the car through the cold, winter darkness into our warm kitchen's bright light, for we have electricity now. Mom, Alvin, and little Janice are waiting for us at the big oak table as we come in, Armella setting down a bag filled with the week's laundry, followed by Virgil and me, and then Daddy. Big sisters Jean and Alvina usually come later, after we have already started to eat. They too come back every weekend from their two-room schoolhouse in Antonino, some twenty-one miles away. But today they got here ahead of us, and we are all talking at the same time, laughing and happy and hungry as we sit down to eat.

I have never been so hungry or eaten anything as good as the noodles and pink beans we ate that night. It's one of the dishes Mother made on Fridays when we abstained from meat. But I remember noodles and beans as a favorite dish any day of the week, whether for dinner or for supper or for lunch in between.

A Vision Envisioned

What first comes to mind on hearing the words "a vision" is James Russell Lowell's poem "The Vision of Sir Launfal," followed immediately by the phrase "visions and *revisions*," from "The Love Song of J. Alfred Prufrock," by T. S. Eliot. It's odd that Sir Launfal's lofty vision and Prufrock's belittling *revision* should be paired in my memory—the sublime and the ridiculous lodged in there together.

For me, what the two poems have in common is that I once knew both by heart. That accomplishment is by no means unique. Memorizing poems was routinely required when I went to grade school in the 1930s and high school in the early 1940s. I was a freshman at Hays High when I memorized "The Vision of Sir Launfal." Actually, we only had to memorize the well-known section that begins with "And what is so rare as a day in June? / Then, if ever, come perfect days," and so on for twenty-four lines.

Perhaps as a joke, Miss Kraus, our teacher, said that anyone who memorized all 347 lines of the poem would get an A in the course, no matter what their other grades were. I thought this was a pretty good offer, it being still early in the semester. But I think it was the opportunity for showing off rather than the assured grade of an A that persuaded me to memorize the whole thing.

It's a pretty good poem. A haughty young knight, Sir Launfal, rides off in search of the Holy Grail—the cup Christ drank from at the Last Supper. As he leaves the castle, Launfal scornfully tosses a coin at a beggar. Then, after years of searching, he returns, empty-handed, but chastened by the hardships he has suffered. At the gate he meets a leper who again begs him for alms. Sir Launfal, now acting in the true spirit of charity, dismounts and shares his last crust of bread with the leper. Then Launfal fills his wooden cup with water from a nearby stream and brings it to the leper, whereupon the wooden cup becomes—you guessed it—the Holy Grail.

I had an additional reason for wanting to show off. I wanted to show up Miss Kraus even though I liked her very much. But she had put me in my place after I had questioned the accuracy of a comment she made about the poem. We were going over it in class when we came to the line, "The priest hath his fee, who comes and shrives us." Cora Mae Simpson, teacher's pet personified, raised her hand and explained that "shrive" refers to the Catholic practice of going to confession. "Yes," Miss Kraus beamed, and added, "That's all they want: money." I was already feeling chagrined for not having volunteered to explain the meaning of shrive myself, fearful of advertising my Catholicism in a classroom filled with young Protestants. So I had let Cora Mae get ahead of me. Now Miss Kraus's misstatement (actually, the poet's misrepresentation) about Catholic practice was too much to bear. I raised my hand, and blurted out, "You don't pay to go to confession!" Miss Kraus looked at me sympathetically, kindly, and smiled, "Just wait until you are old enough to have your own money. You'll see."

I had no response to that, and I did not look up to see how the class reacted. I suppose that in some misguided way, I felt that reciting all 347 lines of "The Vision of Sir Launfal" before an admiring class would show Miss Kraus that I was no benighted fool.

Recitations were done loosely in alphabetical order, beginning a week later. Toward the end of each class, a group of three students would take their turns. Then after some critiques, class would end. My plan was to catch Miss Kraus by surprise. I would not give her any notice of the extended performance she would be treated to when my turn came.

When recitation time came, squeaky-voiced Adams, a bit shaky, started us off. Then the next two students, and in a few days we got to Merkel, who started back from line one of the poem, as did the student who followed him, each getting a little applause for the extra effort. Then my day came: Rumsey, Simpson, Schmidtberger. I had it figured out that my recitation would take me all the way to the end of class—no time left for the usual critiques. At the very moment I finished, the bell would sound, as if on cue for the outburst of applause that I would accept with a gracious bow.

Billy Rumsey began reciting at line one and went right through to the end of the June stanza at line fifty-six without a hitch. Then Cora

Mae Simpson, predictably enough began at line one and made it to and through the June stanza without a peek at the card she was holding out of sight in her hand—and kept going. On and on Cora Mae went—on through line 174, "down swept the chill winds from the mountain peaks." Never once opening her closed left hand, Cora Mae declaimed the lesson that Launfal's vision imparted in lines 324–325:

> Not what we give, but what we share
> For the gift without the giver is bare

The bell rang just as Cora Mae delivered the final line, 347, and then bowed politely to more than just a smattering of applause. But it wasn't really a standing ovation, I consoled myself. We had to stand up anyway because class had just ended.

It's in the Basket

What a whole new, delightful world Hays Junior-Senior High was to me after all those years in a one-room schoolhouse. Now there were twenty-five students, some of them friendly, in my classroom, one of many such rooms off the long, wide, soap-scented corridor. There was also a huge gymnasium. At each end of the gymnasium, suspended out of reach, was a rectangular board from which extended a round iron with some white netting attached.

This was before television, so I did not know what I was looking at when we were marched into the gym for our first phys. ed. class. But in no time at all I learned that the twenty-five or so seventh graders and I, dressed in brand-new khaki shorts, were on a basketball court. What took longer to learn, though, was how to play this game.

Not only had I never seen a basketball game, but I had never even read about one. Fortunately, selection for playing that day was alphabetical, so I wasn't on the first team chosen to go out onto the floor. I had a chance to learn by watching the game being played, and what I saw was ten boys wildly flailing their arms around whoever had the ball. The whole, jumbled crowd of players would surge toward one of the baskets and then someone would try to throw it in. If it missed, someone would catch it and try again.

But whether it went in or not, eventually the mass of boys would run to the other end and try to put the ball through that hoop. From time to time, whistles blew, stopping the game, and then starting it again. After one such whistle, my name was called. I begged that I didn't know how to play, but Mr. Rothgeb pushed me out on the court anyway, where I proceeded to run around the fringes of the pack, waving my arms up and down and shrieking, "Here! Here!" just like everyone else.

Soon enough, Mr. Rothgeb motioned me back to the bench. "I guess you're new here," he said, showing not even a trace of disappointment. "If you watch carefully, you'll catch on, and Joe, here, he'll help you out," he cheerfully added, turning to Joe Ward, star athlete of the class, I later learned, who did, in fact, go on to tutor me in the basics of playing basketball.

So a few weeks went by and my basketball agility developed to the point where I was allowed to join our team on a visit to nearby Washington School—but surely not to actually play. As it turned out, though, Joe was having a really good day, and by dint of his jumpers, turnarounds, and layups, we were ahead by twenty points or so. Mr. Rothgeb took Joe out and put me in.

So there I was now, running up and down the court. Naturally, nobody passed the ball to me, even when I was wide open. Nobody had ever passed the ball to me in practice. But then little Timmy Wasinger, surrounded by all five Washington players, desperately bounced the ball between their flailing arms and into my surprised hands. In the panic of the moment all I could think of was to shoot. I was oblivious to the fact that I was out of range, that Washington's five players had left all my teammates except little Timmy wide open, or that instead of passing, I could even dribble in for an easy layup. Of all these options, shooting from way out here was the only really dumb one. Yet that's what I did. I flung the ball as far as I could toward the basket and—Oh, my God!—it arced upward, then downward, then swished through the net, just like that.

The cheering that exploded was probably not as deafening as I like to remember it, but I had never before experienced the exhilarating sound of being cheered. So what did I do? I pranced and preened like a showboating football player strutting in the end zone. Then Mr. Rothgeb called a time-out and benched me. Joe came over to me, sitting on the bench, and patiently explained how one should behave after scoring a basket.

I can't say if I learned my lesson or not. You see, I never scored another basket at school in Hays, even though Mr. Rothgeb did put me into a game again for a minute or two a couple of times.

Part 4

The Halls of Saint Fidelis

Trust thyself: every heart vibrates to that iron string.

—Ralph Waldo Emerson

Could Anything Be Finer?

I left Kansas quite early, though not for good. In 1943, at the ripe age of fourteen, I boarded a train for the first time in my life. That train took me 1,150 miles from home to a place more foreign to me than any of the foreign lands I would actually visit half a century later. I would spend the next five years, save for summer vacations, at St. Fidelis Minor Seminary in Herman, Pennsylvania, about forty miles north of Pittsburgh.

Getting there was an odyssey. The trip was in three stages. At Victoria, I boarded a train on the Union Pacific line (the same line my forebears took in the opposite direction while coming west to scout land for settlement, though at that time the line was called the Kansas Pacific). My train was called the Pony Express, and it took me to Kansas City, 286 miles away. There, I waited several hours in Kansas City's Union Station to board, if I remember correctly, the Missouri Waltz on the Wabash Line for the 252-mile trip to St. Louis, where I changed to the Pennsylvania Railroad's Spirit of St. Louis for the last leg of 610 miles to Pittsburgh.

The Pony Express and the Missouri Waltz were ultra-modern streamliners. These sleek, comfortable, quiet trains were pulled by powerful diesel engines that left no trail of soot and smoke. The dining cars were the last word in elegant dining, as celebrated in the lines, "Dinner on the diner, could anything be finer?" To this day, I cannot think of an image that so epitomizes gracious luxury as the dining car in the days before flying became the preferred mode of travel. When I try to visualize heaven, I do not see puffy, white clouds and harpists and choirs; instead, I see place settings—silverware and Wedgwood bone china and Waterford crystal on starched, white napery in a dining car on the Atchison, Topeka & Santa Fe.

But I never actually experienced the heavenly delight of the dining car in the ten times, going and coming, that I traveled by train between Victoria and Pittsburgh. My dining on these annual trips consisted of sandwiches my mother packed when I was going to Pittsburgh in early September. When returning from Pittsburgh in June, I bought sandwiches from vendors who walked the aisles of the coach cars at some of the longer stops. I did sometimes peek into the dining car, and I once asked a steward if I could eat my sandwiches at an empty table on the Missouri Waltz. His rebuff blew me right back to my seat in my coach car and pretty well defined for me my station in life, and I never asked again.

At St. Louis, I changed from the Missouri Waltz to the Pennsylvania Railroad's Spirit of St. Louis, named in honor of Charles Lindbergh's transatlantic flight. This long haul to Pittsburgh was behind a coal-fired locomotive that belched huge puffs of black smoke. The soot floated past the windows and some particles came to rest *inside* the windows of the rickety, old-fashioned cars. A letdown this was, for sure. By the time I arrived at Penn Station in Pittsburgh, my white shirt, so carefully ironed by my mother, was soot-smudged all over, as was the rest of me, but where it didn't show so much.

From Penn Station I lugged my enormous suitcase—no wheels back then—the few blocks to the Greyhound Terminal, and boarded a bus to Butler, about forty miles north. There a van from St. Fidelis loaded me and some other students who had gathered at the bus terminal from towns in western Pennsylvania. After a five-mile ride through a quiet, beautifully green countryside, we came to the tiny hamlet of Herman.

It was there, after about forty hours of travel, that I finally saw St. Fidelis, where I would spend the next five school years. What first caught my eye when I stepped out of the van was a soaring tower modeled on the stunning Basilica of St. Francis, in Assisi, Italy, though I knew nothing of that architectural history at the time. All I knew was that the place was beautiful.

One might ask why I went to school so far away.

So far away was, in fact, a primary motivation. Although the ending of *The Wizard of Oz* reminds us that there's no place like home, equally memorable is Dorothy's singing about her longing to be somewhere else. Anywhere other than Kansas, that is. So my desire to see distant lands was quite normal, and it dovetailed with the hope my devout mother held that one of her sons would become a priest and I, her youngest, was her last, best hope.

More specifically, St. Fidelis was chosen because that's where Elmer Vonfeldt, son of my parents' best friends, had gone. After six years there, Elmer graduated from the minor (or preparatory) seminary and went on to a major seminary where he was now just a year or two away from ordination. So my following in Elmer's footsteps nine years after he imprinted them was a way of keeping up with the Joneses, who, in my parents' milieu, were the proud Vonfeldts. In addition, our local parish priest, Father Callistus, had long ago attended St. Fidelis. In Volga German farm communities, the parish priest was the most highly educated parishioner, and I think my mother took Father Callistus's advice "as gospel" not simply because of his spiritual office, but because of his educated status. And I'm sure the priority she placed on the education of her own children was partly in compensation for her own, sadly truncated schooling.

St. Fidelis was operated by Franciscan Friars, followers of the thirteenth-century saint, Francis of Assisi. Mychal Judge, the New York City Fire Department chaplain who was killed at the Twin Towers on 9/11, was a Franciscan whom most people may have heard of. The Franciscans at St. Fidelis were a branch called Capuchin Franciscans, or just Capuchins for short. A group of them from Germany established themselves in Pittsburgh after the Civil War, and founded St. Fidelis not too far away in Herman, Pennsylvania.

When Volga Germans settled in Kansas toward the end of the nineteenth century, the German Capuchins ventured out to Kansas to serve as the Volga Germans' parish priests. If a youngster in Ellis County thought he might want to become a priest—"had a vocation" is how it was phrased—his Capuchin pastor would naturally recommend faraway St. Fidelis. Very few youngsters heeded this suggestion though, their parents preferring the preparatory seminaries that weren't so far away. So the students at St. Fidelis when I first went there were overwhelmingly from the Pittsburgh area. Only Roy Baier, a senior, and I were from Kansas. The next year Roy quit, leaving me the sole representative from the windswept plains of Kansas.

The words "preparatory seminary" may have mysterious overtones, so I had best say a word or two about this type of school that has all but disappeared. I don't know how many there were when I eventually left St. Fidelis in 1948, my own departure contributing a bit to the declining enrollments after World War II. There still were 122 preparatory seminaries in the United States in 1967, but by 2010 that number had dwindled precipitately to seven.

Preparatory seminaries, also known as minor seminaries, covered a total of six years, four of high school and two of junior college. Their graduates then entered a major seminary for another six years of study that would culminate in ordination to the priesthood.

The course of studies in the first four years at a preparatory seminary, the high school portion, was essentially the same as the college-prep track at any high school, public or Catholic. The Catholic high schools differed from the public in having the extra requirement of a course in religion, and prayer at strategic intervals like the beginning of class. What, then, made going to a preparatory seminary different from taking the college-track courses at a regular Catholic high school? Considered academically, there wasn't any real difference. What distinguished education at a preparatory seminary was that seminarians generally did not go to their school, they lived there, sequestered from the normal ties that teenagers have to their families.

At St. Fidelis, there was virtually no contact with the outside world: no telephones anywhere, no TV (which was still in its infancy anyway), no radio save for a Philco in the upperclassmen's recreation room. But its transmissions were limited to Texaco's broadcasts of the Metropolitan Opera on Saturday afternoons, and Fulton Sheen's sermons on Sunday evenings.

We did see a movie every other month or so in our auditorium—
National Velvet in my senior year. Having spent lots of time astride
horses in my childhood, the film was especially interesting to me, but
its equine attraction was nothing compared to the crush engendered
by beautiful, young Elizabeth Taylor.

There was no newspaper for us except the sports section of the
Pittsburgh Post-Gazette, one copy in the recreation room. The screen-
ing of what could come inside the seminary walls worked in reverse
as well. To send a letter out you left it unsealed on a stand outside the
rector's office.

St. Fidelis was even sequestered geographically, out in the middle
of nowhere. Although we could get permission to take hikes over the
countryside on Saturday afternoons, as a small group of us often did,
these excursions did not take us out into "the world," which is how we
referred to that large, beguiling environment outside of and vaguely
counter to the seminary's raison dêtre: "acquiring during the formative period of adolescence, the habits of piety and self-discipline." The
only contact with "the world" within hiking distance was a crossroads
store. We were not allowed to carry money (no difficulty for me, since
I never had any money), but two of the members of our group of four
sometimes broke that rule, so our treks yielded the worldly pleasure
of a Snickers or a Mars Bar. I suppose it was the delight of forbidden
fruit that enticed my comrades into buying these goodies, since their
parents regularly included treats like these in the laundry bags they
sent them every other week or so.

Come to think of it, I was even more sequestered than most.
Because Kansas was too far away for doing laundry by mail, mine
was done by the service that did the priests' laundry. So communi-
cating and smuggling via laundry bag was unavailable to me. Also,
I was the only one in my class of forty-three who came from more
than a day's round-trip drive away, so everyone but me enjoyed an
occasional family visit. On these Visitors Sundays, I would have the
rec room or library or wherever to myself for several pleasant hours of
the afternoon. My only memory of Visitors Sundays was the jarringly
out-of-place sound of high heels click-clacking on the tiled floors of

the hallways and how the fragrance of perfume lingered incongruously there long after the visitors left.

Everyone else went home for Christmas and Easter vacations,
whereas I went home only during the summer. But I do not recall ever
feeling sorry for myself or homesick either. I suppose I developed the
habit of appreciating my own company back on the farm, especially
during the long summer days I spent all alone on a tractor tilling our
vast fields, with Alvin and Virgil still away in the war. But I felt their
absence those summers. I missed them very much.

Along the Way to Adulthood

It was at faraway St. Fidelis that I experienced my first initiation, which is sometimes construed as a step toward manhood, which, in turn, is sometimes thought to be the same as adulthood.

One October day, we freshmen—we were called minims, as in "minimum," the least—we forty-three minims were assembled on the spacious lawn in front of the main hall. I have trouble remembering how we got there on a Saturday after lunch, the area being off limits to all but those in fifth or sixth form, the term we used for college freshmen and sophomore classes. Anyway, there we were, nervously waiting for our ordeal to begin. Then eight sixth-form students—the entire class, actually—strode up, scowling, enormously displeased with us minims, it seemed. I remember thinking that they would yell at us to get off their turf, but no, they stopped in front of us, still looking fierce but a little eager too, and began calling out our names, taking turns about it.

I was almost the only one left when Eugene Smith, the tallest of the upperclassmen, called my name, so I joined the other four minims already standing close to him. We knew the drill: we were to be turned from boys into men that day. For the next three hours we were in the upperclassmen's complete charge. Insubordination would be most severely dealt with and so on.

My head was filled with these dire warnings as I headed for Smith's circle, but when I got there all he did was ask us where we were from and how things were going at our new school. Everyone else was from Pittsburgh or Butler, and when I told Smith where I was from, he laughed and said he guessed I would like to see some hills for a change.

Smith didn't start moving us toward the initiation area until all the other groups were already heading there. After following the others a few yards, he veered off to one side. Then we followed him on a hike through the beautiful, autumn-colored Pennsylvania countryside, which was absolutely gorgeous, especially by comparison with the treeless prairie I had left behind just a month before. We all talked about this and that, and Smith let each of us pick an apple from a tree alongside the path. Mine had a delicious tart flavor I had never tasted before.

Eventually Smith circled us back to a hillside overlooking the football and baseball fields and the adjoining shallow man-made lake, wonderful for ice-skating in winter, but perfect now for getting minims mud-soaked in the course of their hazing, which had been going on all the while we were hiking and which I have to leave undescribed because I saw none of it. By the time Smith had finally led us to the hillside and sat us down in the leaves to watch, the little groups of five were leaving the field and heading for the dormitory, much the worse for wear. So we got up from the leaves we had just sat down on and headed back to the dormitory too.

The initiation at St. Fidelis was the last one held in my years there. Whether Eugene Smith's noncompliance was even noticed I do not know. If noticed, I do not know if it was a factor in the decision to discontinue Initiation Day. I do not know what became of him, but I do know for sure that what Eugene Smith did that day was an adult thing to do.

Nobody's Perfect

I'm sorry to say that I did not accept the evaporation of a perfect record I nearly set back in the 1940s with anything like Armando Galarraga's generosity when his perfectly pitched game was rendered imperfect by an umpire's botched call. I'm afraid that my reaction to the bad call I got was a sorehead's reaction, and I still feel a touch of discomfort when I think about it these many years later.

My competitive drive lay dormant in my early years for lack of any actual competition. The population of my one-room schoolhouse in Kansas, never higher than five, eventually dwindled down to just my brother Virgil and me, so there were no team sports to compete in. Virgil, two years older than I, made up games for us to play together, though these tended to involve throwing stones at jackrabbits, which has never been recognized as a sport.

After I moved into a more populated school for junior high, I thought this might be fertile ground for victorious, physical exploits. Instead of victories, though, memories of humiliations, one after another, come floating down. There is the easy layup that would have won the game; the softball that slipped through my outstretched fingers out in right field; being selected last in a pickup game. Evidence like that made it pretty clear that my skills did not place me anywhere near the top tier of athletes. So I decided to make the classroom my playing field. After all, I had once come in third in a countywide math contest in eighth grade, though my sense of achievement at the time was diluted by the fact that Alvin and Virgil had come in first and second in earlier years.

Then Dame Fortune bestowed on me the opportunity of a lifetime when I transferred to St. Fidelis in western Pennsylvania. I was assigned Algebra I, a course in which I had just gotten an A in the preceding spring semester back in Kansas. After a couple of classes, I saw that the course would repeat what I already knew. "An easy A," I thought, and did not let my new friends know of my advantage.

In point of fact, having me repeat algebra was largely intentional on the part of Father Callistus, our parish priest in Kansas who had been so instrumental in sending me to St. Fidelis in the first place. I had a pronounced German accent back then, and like so many well-intentioned though ill-informed people, he assumed that a foreign accent (other than British) reflects slowness of thought. That and the fact that I had not gone to a Catholic school left him apprehensive about holding my own against sophisticated eastern youths who had been taught by knuckle-rapping nuns from Pittsburgh. Having me repeat a class was his way of giving me a little boost, a leg up.

At St. Fidelis, my first test was returned with a 100 percent marked on it instead of the A it would have gotten back in Kansas. That's when it dawned on me that percentage grades opened up a new, exciting possibility. Getting an easy A in algebra my first semester would be a good thing, but getting a 100 percent—a *perfect* grade—would be a triumph. I would finally knock one out of the park, to borrow a phrase from Samble, my best buddy now, who loved baseball better than books and, unlike me, excelled at every sport he played.

Exercising the greatest care with every assignment and every test, I amassed a string of 100 percents right through the midterm marking period. But when we were handed our advisory report cards in study hall, my grade in algebra was 99 percent, not 100 percent. Dismayed, I waylaid my algebra teacher, Father Carol—Sleepy Carol we called him, Samble and I, behind his back.

Sleepy Carol told me to see him after class. The instant class ended, I was at his desk, all aquiver, report card and sheaf of tests and assignments clutched in hand. In answer to my heated question about how could it be that I didn't get 100 percent, Father Carol calmly, drowsily, explained, "Because nobody is perfect."

"I know I'm not perfect, but my record in algebra so far is perfect," I protested.

"Nobody is perfect," Father Carol slowly rejoined.

Clarification was urgently needed. Logical distinctions had to be made. I tried an analogy. Baseball had ended about a month ago, but Samble and a few other students still talked with Sleepy Carol after class about the Pittsburgh Pirates, and, listening in, I heard stories about a pitcher named Rip Sewell. I saw my way to getting on base.

"If Rip Sewell," I began, "were to get every one of the twenty-seven batters out without a one of them getting on base, we would say he pitched a perfect game, wouldn't we? Not a 99 percent perfect game, but a *perfect* game." I may have even assumed the stance of an indignant manager making his case to an error-prone umpire.

Father Carol nodded slowly in agreement. "You're right," he said, "that Sewell sure is some pitcher." Then he addressed the point at issue: "But that's baseball," he said. He took my report card and held it up. "This here is school," he clarified, returning my report card to me. Sleepy Carol then repeated, "Nobody is perfect," as he gathered up his books and slowly left the room.

A few of my classmates, wearied from an hour of trying to balance equations that stubbornly resisted all balancing, had gathered around us, hoping for some more talk about baseball. Sleepy Carol's words, "Nobody is perfect," fell like balm on their troubled souls. Now they were nodding their agreement that nobody is perfect. Even Samble was nodding, oblivious to the depth of his betrayal.

I swallowed hard, accepting—what else could I do?—my imperfection as we returned to our places to wait for English class to begin.

A Foolish Decision

I did not choose to have chronic obstructive pulmonary disorder. I acquired COPD as an unintended side effect of a decision that became foolish only in hindsight. To be sure, at the time when I decided to take up smoking I was aware that butt-filled ashtrays were not beautiful objects of art, and that smoking *might* slow one down a bit at a track meet in the same way as wearing heavy work shoes would.

Smoking might handicap you, but it didn't make you less healthy overall, it was widely thought. Besides, St. Fidelis did not compete with other schools, so our athletic activities were only intramural. There was no varsity level to get into shape for, there being no varsity teams. Nor would starring at basketball win you the admiration of girls, there being no girls at St. Fidelis. So the possibility that smoking might cause a slight diminution of athletic ability was offset by the radio commercials that attested to the beneficial effects of smoking. "Feeling low, feeling tense, these eight words are common sense," the jingle counseled, "Smoke a Luh-uh-key to feel your level best." Smoking didn't just give you a psychological boost, it actually improved your health, some brands more than others, which was why the advertisements counseled, "Nine out of ten doctors smoke Camels."

But these purported medicinal advantages were not what seduced me into smoking. It was the pleasing, alluring fragrance of pipe smoke. Some of the older students would sit together after supper, smoking, enjoying an hour of relaxation until it was time to go inside for study hour.

I was a sophomore in the spring of 1945 and sixteen years old, the age at which pipe smoking, with parental approval, was permitted. (Cigarette smoking never was allowed.) I had turned sixteen the previous October and could have begun smoking then. I had in hand my father's written permission, but both parents suggested I put it off a year to see if I really wanted to. The year was almost up now, and I really wanted to—very much wanted to join these young men in smoking during the hour after supper. I relished their easy banter, their humor. Nowhere else in the world were there such quick-witted youths as these eight or nine pipe-smoking juniors and seniors at St. Fidelis. I imagined myself sucking leisurely on my pipe, and then slowly, thoughtfully expelling the smoke the way they did, these seasoned seminarians, into the enveloping aromatic haze. Doing that, I thought, would complete my sense of camaraderie, and that's just what it did.

When summer vacation began a month or so after I began pipe smoking, I temporarily discontinued it. Life on our farm back in Kansas was so different in every way from my life at St. Fidelis that the idea of communal pipe smoking after supper seemed ludicrous.

But September came, and back at St. Fidelis, our circle reformed, with me very much in it. Then Christmas came, and for two weeks I was one of just three students who had the whole place to ourselves. I have no memory at all of how the other two boys spent their time, but I spent most of mine working with one or the other of two janitors at refurbishing the place—cleaning and waxing the floors, patching and repainting walls, and so on. I was a good worker, and the janitors, middle-aged and partially disabled from injuries suffered in the steel mills, treated me like a man, which is to say, when either one decided to have a cigarette, he shook one out of his pack for me too. By vacation's end, I had learned to inhale. My memory is a bit shaky here, but I don't think I choked or felt anything very unpleasant—or pleasant either—about inhaling the smoke from a Camel or an Old Gold. I inhaled whichever brand came my way, and for no better reason than that I was able to do it, this grown-up, manly thing.

When vacation ended and students returned, I got rid of my pack of Old Golds and returned to pipe smoking during the allotted post-supper hour. But now I was inhaling the smoke from my Sir Walter Raleigh Rum 'n' Maple–filled pipe, and deriving pleasure from a slight, very slight, effervescing sensation, a mild tingling in my chest and head, especially during the first few puffs.

Then Lent came. For Catholic smokers, Lent is giving-up-smoking time. Would you believe it, I just about couldn't get through that hour after supper without smoking—the only time that smoking was permitted. The odd thing here is that at no other time of day did I feel a need to smoke. During that hour or so, however, the urge was intense—right up to the time that we went to study hall. But once I got through the hour, the craving went away soon enough.

Yet I did not always get through that hour. Unwilling to admit even to myself that I was unable to quit smoking for Lent, I took great care to keep my lapses secret. But sneaking a smoke in a seminary is not an easy thing to do.

Smoking was also permitted—usually—during the half hour or so after lunch. But we had to get permission from the rector, Father Victor, each day. This meant that every day we had to come up with a reason to celebrate. Any Franciscan's feast day was a sure winner. Nine out of ten times, whatever the pretext, however slim—a faculty member's birthday, or slimmer still, a student's birthday—it worked.

The happy word would be cried out by a student returning from Father Victor's office—"smokes today!" But it was not automatic. Every once in a while, the bleak, depressing refusal sounded: "no smokes!" During my junior year, the occasional denial was a disappointment but not a difficulty—yet.

Then in my senior year, an inhaler now, I did indeed find the occasional prohibition to be a problem. It would be some years before the word "addict" would insinuate itself into the lexicon of tobacco use, so I became one before I knew the word for it. I could not get through that half hour after lunch without inhaling tobacco smoke. Would you believe it? I could not.

Bombs Bursting in Err

In 1944, it was not uncommon to see more than one B-17 in the sky at the same time, each one going its own solitary way. Flying Fortresses they were called, these four-engine bombers. When they flew in formation, the number might be in the dozens. World War II was raging, and soon after Pearl Harbor, the Army poured slabs of concrete over large stretches of farmland ten miles north of our farm, transforming the wheat fields there into the runways of the Hays-Walker Army Airfield. As such, it was a rare hour when there was not at least one plane in the sky above the endless expanse of the Kansas prairie.

The base was used for training the flight crews of four-engine, propeller-driven bombers: B-17s, then B-24s, and then B-29s. The training included target practice, and we saw the planes overhead daily, flying in V-shaped formations or sometimes solo, droning their way to the practice fields in the Rocky Mountains. Once the crews were up to snuff, they were deployed to distant bases and from there they flew their missions over targets in Europe and in the Pacific.

I was sixteen years old, working on our farm, home for the summer from St. Fidelis, far away in Pennsylvania. The wheat harvest was over and I was on our tractor, pulling a twelve-foot-wide plow that turned over the stubble in preparation for planting in the coming fall. At the time that I looked up at a solitary B-17, I had just stopped the tractor, or rather, it had stopped itself—spinning its wheels into the soft soil. It had rained two days before, and there were still some soft places. The tractor had gotten stuck in one of them, so I was about to unhook the plow, drive the tractor forward to make a track, then back up, reattach the plow, and continue plowing.

As I bent over the tractor hitch, I gave the airplane a second glance only because it was flying so low. Unusually low, I saw, and coming straight my way. Then—Hey! One of its four propellers was standing still—not turning at all. The plane was almost overhead when— Oh, my God!—the bomb bay opened. Then, exactly as I had seen in war movies, a cluster of bombs drifted out and down—about fifteen of them. It happened too suddenly for me to form any thoughts. Responding to the same instincts that cause startled cats to hide, I dove under the tractor. Then, a short distance to my right, some bombs hit—thud, thud—sending up huge balls of fire that lasted for just a few seconds. Then nothing.

That was all. It was over with. I was alive. I waited a minute longer, still curled up under the tractor, hearing the incongruously calm, quiet sound of its idling motor. I crawled out and stood up, all atremble. I don't know what I thought. Most likely, I had no thoughts at all—was simply in a state of incomprehension, of bewilderment. But I remember hearing the torrent of expletives I was hurling in the direction of the airplane that was slowly droning northward and out of sight. I continued hearing myself curse a blue streak as I drove my tractor to the end of the furrow, where I stopped, cut the engine, and got off. Then I ran the half mile back to the farmhouse faster than I'd ever run that distance before.

I will not try to reconstruct the confusing account I hysterically blurted out between breaths to my parents and sisters. Instead, I'll explain briefly what actually happened that summer, some seventy years ago.

The bombs—there were only two of them—were 500-pound target bombs, identical in shape and size to the ones that smashed to smithereens places like Dresden, Germany. On impact, instead of exploding into shrapnel, target bombs send up a flare (what I had seen as fireballs), which tells the crew how close they have come to hitting their target. Had these two bombs been the real thing, I'd have become a stateside casualty of World War II. But airplanes from the Hays-Walker Airfield did not carry explosive bombs, only the ones for target practice, and so I emerged from under my tractor, physically unscathed, if mentally shell-shocked.

Much later in the day, a military van drove up to our house. It was the B-17's crew, doing a follow-up investigation. "Did we know anything about—"

"Yes," I cried out. "Did I ever!"

I hopped in the van with the five of them and drove through a half mile of wheat field to the craters where the bombs had fallen.

One of the bombs was half buried, but still largely intact. The other lay partially buried, broken into three jagged pieces. I pointed out the deep ruts that the spinning of my tractor's wheels had dug out. Two crew members, the pilot and the navigator, paced the distance from the bomb casings to the tractor tracks. Nineteen paces (about thirty feet) the navigator noted on his clipboard.

They were both pretty upset, and I became upset again too, though I tried not to show it. They swore that they had not seen me. They said they had looked very, very carefully before dropping the bombs, and hadn't seen me. It's true that my International Harvester tractor had not been moving at the time, which would have made it more difficult for the eye to pick it up. On the other hand, my tractor, like all International Harvesters, was bright red.

Why had they released the bombs? When one of their engines failed, they looked for a place to dump this extra weight to conserve fuel, they said. Also, they were afraid of making an emergency landing with the bombs aboard, worried that their flares could detonate and ignite the plane's fuel tank. Added to that was a touch of good, old-fashioned panic. In fact, the pilot confided that the navigator had to release the bombs because the bombardier was too agitated to do it himself. They didn't see me and my tractor, I think, because in their panic, they didn't believe it very likely that any human being would actually occupy a spot in that vast expanse below.

Did my family show any hard feelings toward the crew when we got back to the house? Absolutely not! There was a war on. Alvin was in the Army Air Corps somewhere in the Pacific. Virgil was also in the Pacific, serving in the Navy on a destroyer. We were all on the same side here. These soldiers, these airmen, were training to bomb the enemy into surrender. Once that happened, they—and Alvin and Virgil—would come home again. Should we complain about a trifling accident here on the home front?

"Tank God nobody vos hurt," my father offered, thinking more of the crew, it seemed to me, than of his youngest son.

My father signed the accident report that had to be filed, and hands were shaken all around. Then, with business behind us, my mother and sisters served these airmen the best home-cooked meal they would ever have while stationed at Hays-Walker Army Airfield. So all's well that ends well, as we say.

This experience raises three points that seem to linger with me. The first point is the unreliability of eyewitness testimony. I was absolutely certain that I saw about fifteen bombs tumbling out of the bomb bay. But for the evidence to the contrary, I would have been willing to testify in a court of law that around a dozen bombs fell—drifting out of the plane, one after another. But there were only two. Two craters means there were only two bombs—no other possibility.

Conversely, the crew was sure that they saw no human activity in the empty field below them. They said so over and over as they apologized. They never saw the tractor, or the plow, or me trying to unhook the two. So I saw something that wasn't there, while the crew *didn't* see something—me—that surely *was* there. The lesson, I think, is that we tend to see our own preconceptions.

The second point was one I didn't immediately realize. The tractor was stuck in the mud when I first saw the crippled B-17. And yet, in my panic after the bombs fell, I *drove* the tractor, plow still attached, to the end of the furrow before running back to the farmhouse. What was stuck had come unstuck. I think the shockwaves from the bombs might have jolted the tractor loose from the field's muddy grip. I have no other way of explaining this.

A third point has to do with my incredible streak of cursing. I was on summer vacation from St. Fidelis. "Oh sugar!" was about as intense an expletive as was heard from me back then, and "dad gammit" touched the limits of my profanity. So you'd think I'd have gasped "Jesus, Mary, Joseph" when I saw the bomb bays open. "Jesus, Mary, Joseph," an ejaculatory prayer, we Catholics call it, should have been my wide-eyed exclamation. So how is it that, had the bombs burst into shrapnel at the very moment I flung myself under the tractor, I'd have gone to my maker with "God damn!" stuck in my throat?

There is also this further point. When I returned to my school in far-off Pennsylvania and told my unembellished story, nobody believed it.

Me with one of the bombs dropped on the family farm in 1944.

Thrown for a Loop

His saddle horse did stumble, and on him did fall,
The poor boy won't see his mother when the work's all
done this fall.

—D. J. O'Malley

I don't remember when I first rode alone. Before then, Alvin, ten years older than I, held me in front of him on Babe, our gentle sorrel. We galloped across the prairie, Alvin holding the reins in his right hand, and his left encircling me, holding me tight against the safety of his blue overalls and their clean, wash-line smell. We rode bareback. Lest this sound dangerous, I should explain that for the bareback rider, a galloping horse offers a smooth ride. Trotting is bouncy, but galloping is as smooth as silk. The faster the gallop, the smoother the ride.

I don't remember when Alvin let me ride alone. But to get to a gallop, Babe had to first go from her walk to a trot, and the trot was more than I could handle. Although I hung on to Babe's mane for dear life, I would eventually tumble off one side or the other. Instead of jumping right up, I would lie there on the prairie grass, and Babe would look me over, ears bent inquisitively forward, nuzzling me almost as if I were her colt, checking to see if I was okay. I would then get up and lead Babe over to a stone post, where I used the attached wire as a ladder to remount. But Babe, after a few more spills, would refuse to be spurred beyond a walk. (I use "spur" here as a figure of speech. There were no actual spurs in our barn.) She would gladly gallop for Alvin and Virgil, but not for me.

Just before St. Fidelis let out for the summer of 1945, the whole student body was treated to the movie *National Velvet*, starring Elizabeth Taylor and a horse named Pie. When I came home that summer, I was seventeen and my legs were plenty long for bareback riding now, but for some reason or other on the day in question, I decided against riding bareback. I lifted the saddle by the horn from where it usually hung unused and saddled up Pat, our piebald. I rode the half mile to what we called the "other pasture" to see if the windmill there was keeping the stock tank filled with water for our herd of steers.

On the way back home, Pat pulled on the bit, wanting to be let out. Like most horses, he was always more eager to run toward the barn than away from it. So as we approached the downhill stretch, I loosened the reins and leaned forward, letting him run as fast as he wanted to. Just when I remembered the ridges formed by cow trails, Pat, galloping full speed now, stumbled and went down. All I remember is being in the air and then being on the ground and pushing upward against the saddle as I felt Pat roll over me. Why the saddle horn didn't crush my chest, I cannot explain. You have seen gymnasts flip one another, and I suppose that I sort of flipped Pat. As impossible as it sounds, his momentum carried him over my extended palms without his weight bearing down on me. Then I just lay there, moving my limbs one after the other. Nothing broken, it seemed, so I got up.

I was okay. Pat was standing up too, looking sorry, but still ready to head home to the barn. I picked up the reins and started to walk him. Pat did not limp. Incredibly, neither of us was hurt, and so we simply walked back to the barn.

My Letter Home

A month or two before summer vacation at the end of my junior year at St. Fidelis, I learned that Virgil would be coming home on a furlough from the fighting in World War II. His leave would end on June eleventh, whereas our school vacation would only begin on June thirteenth. The solution that absolutely leapt at me was to leave for Kansas early—if not two weeks, then at least one. I was doing well in all my courses and could, I thought, take my exams early.

Instead of appealing directly to the rector, Father Victor, I made a serious error of judgment. I followed protocol, proper procedure, and asked my proctor, Father Arnold, to make my case with the rector. I should have known better, having had an unpleasant altercation with Father Arnold earlier in the term. But I was still naïve enough to believe it when he'd told me afterwards that my apology had been accepted, and he would harbor no ill will toward me.

What I had apologized for was some sarcasm that I hadn't intended as sarcasm at all, but that he'd misconstrued as such. Here's what happened. Each year, Father Arnold had the members of our group, which got smaller each year, do an evaluation of the strengths and weaknesses of each other. Then Father Arnold called us in for an individual conference to go over the evaluations.

My conference did not go well, nor did it last long. Father Arnold began with the category called "attitude towards others." I expected to hear words like *friendly* and *caring*, or in a worst-case scenario, something like *vain*. Instead, I heard *supercilious*, whereupon, in disbelief, I interrupted Father Arnold, blurting out what I thought was a rational observation.

"You must have made that up," I protested. "They wouldn't know a word like supercilious."

Father Arnold had a temper, and his face would turn a light shade of purple when he lost it. Well, his light purple complexion was turning plum purple as he told me, through clenched teeth, to get out of his office. I hurriedly complied, of course. The next day I apologized remorsefully, profusely, abjectly (and truth be told, hypocritically) and he accepted my apology. He never did tell me, though, what other traits had been ascribed to me, and I forgot to ask.

That had happened two months earlier, but letting bygones be bygones notwithstanding, I should have known better than to present my plea for an early vacation through Father Arnold instead of going directly to Father Victor, the rector. Father Victor had a degree from Oxford, and we called him Chaucer. He seemed to have a sense of fair play, and I'd always admired the editorials he wrote for *The Fidelian*, our school newspaper. But he was known to be a stickler for following the rules, and when his answer came back through Father Arnold it was no. I was stunned, flabbergasted—pole-axed.

That evening, I wrote a letter to my parents explaining that I would not be able to come home before Virgil left again for the fighting in the Pacific. Then, exercising my newfound talent for sarcasm, I added an analysis of Father Victor's character as it related to his decision. That done, I placed the letter—unsealed, as school rules required—on the stand outside his office. I have no memory of exactly what I wrote. Of course I should have known better than to include this unflattering characterization in a letter I would have to leave open outside his door. Then again, maybe I wanted him to read it. Yes, that's my best guess now, seventy years later. Yes—but shouldn't I have had the guts to march into his office and tell him to his face? That would probably have gotten me expelled, which would have gotten me home, sure enough, in time to see Virgil. Oh well, another road not taken.

The upshot was that the next night Father Victor pulled me out of the line as we marched out of chapel to the dormitory. He took me into his office and began by saying, "I was not edified by your . . ." He continued a long, long time but I remember nothing of what he said because it was so long ago and I wasn't paying close attention. I was hung up on that word he had used—"edified." I thought I knew what it meant, but wasn't absolutely sure. It might be one of those words like "enervate" that means the opposite of what it sounds like, and I idiotically wondered if I shouldn't interrupt to ask what "edified" means, but the time for asking went by, leaving my question unasked. Apparently my anxiety made me appear to be attentive to and respectful of Father Victor's words that followed his opening expression of non-edification. He finally stopped talking and I made my way to the dormitory upstairs.

Nothing further came of the matter. When I got home on June fourteenth, Virgil had already returned to his ship. But there is this postscript. My mother had shown the letter to Father Callistus. I imagine she went to him to protest Father Victor's callousness. But the only clear memory I have of the matter is Mother telling me that Father Callistus looked the letter over, slapped his thighs, and chortled that it was the funniest thing he'd ever read.

I really regret that my letter didn't get saved, but at the time both of my brothers were serving in the Pacific and in real danger of being killed, so my bruised feelings were not uppermost in anyone's mind at home, including my own.

Left at the Altar

Surrounded by rolling hills and fields that were green or gold or brown, St. Fidelis was a beautiful place, and from my first day there I loved it. But with each passing year, I found it harder and harder to suppress my feeling that I would never go on to a major seminary—that I had no true calling to the priesthood.

I vividly remember setting out for St. Fidelis for the first time. We were in the farmyard in the fall of 1943—Virgil, Dad, Mom, Janice, and Georgine. We were getting into our '39 Ford to drive to Victoria, where I would board the train and set out for St. Fidelis, 1,150 miles away. As we were getting into the car, Daddy, who had said he was staying home to take care of some chore or other, pulled me aside. Speaking softly so as not to be overheard, he confided, in German, "Don't be afraid to come home if you don't like it there." Then he added, "*Machs gut*" (Take care of yourself), and I got into the car with the others.

Nine and a half months later—it was too far to come home for any holidays—I got off the train at Victoria. The first question (I can't be sure it was the first, but that's how I remember it) Mom asked me was if I was going to go back in September. My yes drew a pleased look, not exactly of joy, maybe more of relief.

This homecoming-for-the-summer scene was repeated each succeeding year for four years, but at the end of the fifth, my answer changed from yes to no. I had no earthly notion of what I wanted to do in life, but I had woken up one fine October morning that year to the realization that I was absolutely sure that I did not want to go on to a major seminary to study for the priesthood. I did not talk about my decision with anyone at all, ever. I stayed the year, but not the course. Like Roy Baier before me, I dropped out at the end of that year, my fifth and last at St. Fidelis.

I should mention that the high point of the annual graduation exercise at St. Fidelis was the announcement by each graduate, as he received his diploma, of the seminary he would attend. The majority would go to the one in Maryland run by the same Capuchin Franciscans who ran our St. Fidelis. Others would go to the seminary run by the local Pittsburgh diocese. The top student in the class ahead of me chose the Jesuit seminary at Shrub Oak, New York. I left a year before graduation because I did not want to face the embarrassment, when my turn came on stage, of announcing that I was going nowhere at all other than back to our farm in Kansas.

For some months I had been bracing myself for the moment of telling my parents my decision, fortified somewhat by my father's still-remembered advice and the feeling that he was on my side. I don't know what I expected. I can't recall my mother's response when I told her I was not going back. Probably it was restrained. Otherwise I would surely remember it. I knew that my "quitting" would be a deep disappointment to her, but I don't remember feeling guilty about my decision to quit, much as I had dreaded announcing it.

My father actually seemed pleased by my decision. He and Mom thought I should continue with college at nearby Fort Hays State, so Dad found me a place to stay in Hays when college started.

That August, I sent a postcard to the rector at St. Fidelis stating that I would not return. I showed it to my mother because I thought she might still be harboring the hope that I would change my mind, though she had not made a fuss when I told her I was quitting. I think she may have actually felt relieved. Two years earlier, Elmer Vonfeldt, who had stayed the course at St. Fidelis and then stayed the course at a major seminary, refused ordination in the hour before the ceremony began. I understand that his mother did not take Elmer's change of mind well. So my quitting fairly early, before even making it to a major seminary, spared my mother years of apprehending heartbreak at the altar.

I remain grateful to my mother for my five years at St. Fidelis. Going off to a place as far away as Pennsylvania was an enlarging experience back in those days, much like taking a year abroad for today's students. St. Fidelis was a major, positive influence on my life in many ways. For some time, though, I did harbor a touch of resentment over what I saw as unfair pressure on me to fulfill my mother's dreams instead of my own. Not that she hadn't noticed my doubts, or harbored her own, about the authenticity of my vocation or even the wisdom of taking a lifetime vow of celibacy in one's mid-twenties. Then too, alongside her vision of having a priest in the family was the practical consideration that I was getting a good education, which I could put to whatever use I wished should I not go on to a major seminary.

As for my father, you already know that when I was leaving for my first year at St. Fidelis, he told me not to be afraid to come home if I did not like it there. Five years later, I finally heeded his advice. So if my sojourn at St. Fidelis was, in fact, one of the best things my parents ever did for me, I think that it was a joint effort after all—Mom doing the sending, and Dad easing me home.

Georgine and Janice (the oldest and the youngest).

Twins Alvin and Alvina.

Virgil on leave from the Navy during WWII.

Armella, with me trying to get into the picture.

Part 5

College and the Army

Truly it was a vast and awesome world!

—Sarah Orne Jewett

Bullets and Bumpers

All the way through January of 1950—including my college years—our family drove a stolen car, a '39 Ford. The car we had before that, a '36 Ford, still had the old-fashioned mechanical brakes that did not work as well as the newer hydraulic brakes on Chevys and Plymouths. Dad had bought our car at Twinter Ford, where he was a frequent customer, having often bought tractors and other farm implements there. Apparently Dad complained often enough to Ed Twinter about his Ford's no-good braking system compared to Chevys and Plymouths for Ed to be on the lookout for ways to get Dad off his back—but with the least possible cost to his Ford dealership. Then opportunity came Ed's way and he seized it.

Here's what happened: In 1939, Ford finally installed hydraulic brakes in all its models. Whether this updated value was an inducement or not to a pair of thieves, I do not know, but they stole a brand-new '39 Ford in California and drove it all the way to Ellis County, Kansas, where, with the state police in pursuit, a tire blowout—not the car's hydraulic brakes—brought it to a stop. I do not know what happened to the thieves or how the car came into the possession of Twinter Ford instead of being returned to its owner, who was 1,400 miles away in California. It is not difficult to imagine a plausible explanation, though, and I remember one detail that may have affected the reasoning of the owner and the insurance adjusters: a small bullet hole in the right rear fender. Aside from that, the car seemed good as new.

I know nothing of the financial proceedings whereby Dad became its owner, though in family lore, "The car was a steal." Dad, Alvin, and

Georgine drove the "good as new" '39 Ford home from Twinter Ford, and Nick Dreiling, our occasional Man Friday and a notoriously slow driver, drove our brake-challenged '36 Ford around Ellis County to the end of his days. We drove the '39 Ford until long after the war ended, years after it had become possible to buy new cars again. The little hole in the fender had not been much more trouble to fix than a dink is, though you could always see a slight discoloration where a state trooper had shot through our car.

A Very Short History of All the Rescuing I Did

Back when I was finishing my freshman year of high school in Hays, I wanted to rescue a girl, though from exactly what I never really determined, and the identity of the girl remained vague as well. I was too skinny and shy to ask a girl to go out with me, so I thought of getting a date as my reward for having rescued someone from great danger. Drowning was the danger I thought of—which was a preposterously unlikely danger, there being no bodies of water deep enough for drowning anywhere near our farm on the parched prairie. Dixie Dugan from the comic strips in the *Hays Daily News* was my template, and I imagined her flailing about helplessly in an imaginary lake. When it came to playing my part—that is, diving in and swimming to the rescue—I had to abandon the fantasy because of a physical failing common to farm boys in my part of the world. I didn't know how to swim, not even in my imagination.

I didn't try to imagine any other rescues for getting a date because I went off to a Catholic preparatory seminary in faraway Pennsylvania for the next five years, which eliminated the need for a dating strategy. But the desire for feminine companionship lingered. It lingered and grew stronger year by year until it played no small part in my decision to leave the seminary.

Back in Hays for college, I was still as skinny as five years earlier, but I looked even skinnier because I was now a foot taller. But physique did not matter as much as I had thought. Getting a date was not all that hard to do, I found, after I shed some of my shyness.

To tie up a loose end now to this short narrative: I had learned how to swim, the dog paddle being my default stroke, during my years in Pennsylvania. At Fort Hays State there was a pool in Picken Hall. It was square, about thirty feet per side. On its windowless doors were listed the hours for men and for women. The times did not overlap. I didn't go for a swim there, not even once.

Push-Ups

I was pretty good at calisthenics when I took basic training in the Army—except for the push-ups. I could only do three of them, maybe four on a good day. In all the other exercises—squat jumps, pull-ups, and so on—I could actually do way more than the minimum, so this weakness with push-ups did not cause any problem through three years of military service.

Nor had it inconvenienced me all that much in earlier years through high school and college. At Fort Hays State, four credits of physical education were required for graduation. That meant four courses, one credit each.

In 1948, I looked at the fall course listings. Under the physical education section, I found basketball, boxing, golf, and gym, among other choices. Gym. Not very specific. The word "gym" left wide open the exact nature of the physical exertions that this course would demand. All that the course listing specified was a laconic "Wed. 3–4:50."

I selected gym because Wed. 3–4:50 fit perfectly well into my schedule. In hindsight, if gym had been listed as Push-Ups 101, I'd have known better than to register for it.

In gym we did a few other exercises too, but push-ups are the ones I remember, probably because the class included a couple of awesomely athletic young men who had a special way of doing push-ups. Enhanced push-ups, let's call them. These two athletes would add a flourish at the high point of the push-up: in the moment when the body stopped ascending but before it began descending, they lifted their hands off the floor and clapped them together, lightning quick, all the while holding their bodies rigid in a straight line, shoulder to shoes.

These two show-offs—the Clappers, we called them—would continue doing these enhanced push-ups long after the count stopped at ten, when the rest of us ordinary students, doing the regular push-ups, stopped. Actually, I could do only the first three regular push-ups. For the remaining seven, I did what I would call the relaxed push-up, the opposite of the enhanced push-up. By letting my knees rest on the floor, thus pushing up only my upper torso, I was able to keep up with the class until the count reached ten.

I got an A in that course. Coach Alex Francis gave everyone an A, it was said. So I needn't have worried about being disqualified for using my humble form of push-up. Coach Francis was also the football coach, and word was that he resented having to deal with lowly, required gym classes. Giving everyone an A relieved him of the onerous task of precisely judging the cut-off points in the descending levels of inadequacy below the Clappers, who were obviously the only two bona-fide As. Coach Francis did not waste his time sorting out Bs from Cs in this large group, who did regular push-ups well. Nor did he mess with ferreting out the D level of inadequacy, represented by rule-benders like me. He ignored the two or three Fs who couldn't do ten push-ups any which way at all. They strained, grunted, then collapsed, stretched out full length on the floor. These failures at push-ups, who either had not heard of my easier, economical mode, or who eschewed it as unprincipled, preferred to fail with honor intact than to succeed with their principles compromised. Without giving them so much as a glance, Coach Francis awarded each one of them an A too.

Although our grades in physical education courses appeared on our transcripts, they were not included in the cumulative average, so they didn't really count, which was probably why the dean let Alex Francis get away with his inflated, one-size-fits-all grading system. But other physical education courses were graded traditionally. I know this because I got a C in golf, which I took in my senior year.

In my freshman year at Hays High, I could do only one push-up. I remember Coach Art Leas showing me how to position myself better, but with no better result. The next year I went off to St. Fidelis in Pennsylvania where I got really good at handball and Ping-Pong, but never so much as tried to do push-ups. So the three I improved to in the Army—four on a good day—represent my lifetime high.

You're Not in Kansas Anymore

I was already twenty-three years old when I first saw the ocean. It was on a chilly February day in 1951.

I grew up not too far from the geographical center of the forty-eight contiguous United States, according to a marker alongside U.S. Highway 281 at Lebanon, Kansas. So both the Atlantic and the Pacific Oceans were about 1,500 miles distant from our farm, which was a bit too far for an outing to the shore.

For that matter, outings from our farm to anywhere were difficult to plan because there was hardly anywhere to go to—"anywhere" being loosely defined as within a hundred miles. Vacations were unthinkable during those hard times, though permanently leaving for the distant fields of California was not all that unheard of.

But around the mid-thirties, as rain in summer and snow in winter replaced drought as the weather's default setting, times slowly got better. Among the neighbors who still remained there were a few who, having made arrangements with friends and relatives for milking the cows, feeding the chickens, gathering the eggs, etc., freed themselves off to vacations. Their destination was invariably Denver, a few hundred miles into Colorado where the Rocky Mountains abruptly rise up from the Great Plains.

But our family stayed put. Vacations were not for us. Our rest and recreation needs were vicariously satisfied by tales our neighbors told of drives up Pikes Peak, at that time thought to be the highest mountain in the United States. "Going down, you have to shift into second gear or even low gear. Otherwise you'll burn out the brakes," we were told, again and again and then again by successive marveling vacationers.

Still, it wasn't until I graduated from college that I finally saw the Rockies for the first time myself, just a few days before I finally saw the ocean too.

The two events were really part of one single experience, and it was neither momentous nor awe-inspiring—nothing at all like John Keats's famous poetic description of what the Spanish conquistador must've felt in 1513 when, dragging himself up over the crest of a mountain and expecting to see nothing but more mountains, he unexpectedly beheld a vast blue ocean, stretching out endlessly, beautifully, serenely, far, far below.

For me it was different. First, the mountains. I was on a troop train that was transporting us new U.S. Army inductees from Camp Chafee, Arkansas, to Camp Cooke, California, in 1951. The Korean War had broken out, and I'd been drafted upon graduating from college at Fort Hays. On the train, I was sick as a dog, but not as a dog that is sick enough to be taken to the vet. I was lying in a lower berth, where a medic had told me to spend the day. I woke up in time to catch a glimpse of a deep ravine, a stomach-churning distance below. I remember feverishly hoping the train wouldn't tip over and tumble, topsy-turvy all the way down into it.

Five days earlier, I had boarded a bus in Hays along with about twenty other draftees. From there we went to Kansas City, and then, by train, to Camp Chafee, where the induction process included medical shots, one of which I had a violent reaction to, which was why I had such a bad time on the five-day train ride to California. Of that trip I have only two memories: the one about being scared the train would tumble down off the mountainside, and the other of shakily getting off the train at Reno, Nevada, to be treated to the sight of rows of slot machines. I inserted a silver dollar into one of them and got nothing in return when I pulled the lever.

Our train proceeded to Camp Cooke at Point Conception, California. Camp Cooke had just been reopened for the newly reactivated National Guard's 40th Infantry Division. But it was wholly unprepared for this influx of additional recruits from the prairies. For example, not all our bunks had blankets. At least one of us—me—had no field jacket, and so on.

Perhaps to make amends for our sorry reception, the regular members of the 40th Infantry, some of them doubtlessly disgruntled at their reactivation for the Korean War, decided to treat us midwest-erners to a view of the ocean. So our first lesson in marching took us out to Point Conception. I could probably have begged to take the day off, not having fully recovered my health yet, and even feeling a new rawness in my throat and a touch of discomfort in my jaw. But I wanted to see the ocean, so I marched along.

The chill, damp wind blew ever more briskly as we neared the shore, but finally we halted. Hugging my arms to my chest to con-trol my shivering, I beheld the Pacific Ocean disappearing into a gray haze. I heard the rhythmic pounding of breakers against the rock-strewn shore, and it probably was only in my imagination that the cadence of the sea matched every fourth beat of the throbbing in my head.

That's how it was. But there is an epilogue.

The 40th Infantry did get itself organized in due time. I was issued a field jacket. I got well. Eventually I really, joyfully, experienced mountains and seas, and those experiences affected me profoundly. Suffice it to say that even in my imagination I did not click my boots together, like Dorothy, and murmur, "There's no place like home."

My Security Blanket, Parts One and Two

I think that some of my memories of long ago are works in progress that I unconsciously adjust to meet an emotional need. Such is the case with my memory of one time when I was sick.

In this memory, I am about four or five. I have been sick for some days, but now I am getting well again. I am lying on the opened davenport that I normally share with my two older brothers. The room is dark, but there is light in the adjoining kitchen/dining/family room. I can see the coal-oil lamp on the table. I can't see my parents, and there isn't a sound except for their voices, each pitched softly just above a murmur. They are talking in German. I am not trying to make out what they are saying, but I overhear one word anyway: "Katya," my mother's name, or, more accurately, the nickname of endearment my father sometimes uses for my mother. He says "Katya," and then continues, his voice low and calm. Then I hear my mother's voice, calm, unhurried. As they talk I feel an enfolding warmth, a contentment that is complete.

My memory ends there and it is beyond my ability to describe the satisfaction of the sound of their voices. But I think there has been some editing that makes the memory even more comforting than the real experience was. In the scene I have reconstructed, there are no siblings; but in the actual event it is highly improbable that my five older brothers and sisters wouldn't have been around somewhere—that I would be all alone in the house with my parents after nightfall and all the outdoor chores done. Perhaps my memory has deleted my siblings from the scene, relieving me of the uneasiness that sometimes comes with having to share.

It was this memory that I once seized upon, panic-stricken. I was a senior at St. Fidelis. About an hour after we finished a game of softball, I felt a severe pain in my chest. It was thought I was suffering a heart attack. A doctor was summoned, and after he did an examination, the details of which I cannot remember at all, he said my heart was just fine, and the pain was from a chest muscle that I must've strained when taking too vigorous a swing at a softball—probably a strike, he joked, then left.

But his laughter did not relieve my pain, and I continued to whimper, more or less silently, on my cot in the infirmary. I don't remember being offered any medications, though I must have been given at least a pill of some sort, placebo or otherwise. What brought me around after everyone left was the memory I described earlier of my mother and father talking quietly. No sooner did I hear their voices, when the pain in my chest stopped just like that. Though my parents were a thousand miles away, their calm voices soothed me to sleep.

It was about five years later that I should have summoned my "comfort memory," that is, the memory of Mom and Dad's unhurried voices, to help me through an ordeal. I was in the Army, drafted in 1951, and during my basic infantry training at Camp Cooke, I began to feel a pain in my chest. Every day it got a little worse, which I attributed to the increasing rigor of our training.

Then one night I woke up in a panic, almost unable to breathe. I managed to wake up the trainee on the cot beside mine, and the next thing I remember is being lifted onto a stretcher. I do not remember any of the faces hovering over me, but I can still see the silver maple-leaf insignia on the cap of the man leaning over my cot. I had been in the Army long enough to know that a silver maple leaf meant he was a lieutenant colonel. I overheard him ask, "Why does this man's bed have no sheets?" I vaguely remember being pushed into an ambulance and then lying on a bed in a hospital, breathing comfortably, with my head inside a tent made of plastic, which I learned is an oxygen tent.

All these years later, I wonder if the good, solicitous colonel wasn't even newer than I to the 40th Infantry Division. I suspect he had been assigned to the camp to report on the 40th's state of military readiness at newly reopened Camp Cooke. So I suppose that he eventually learned that the answer to his question about the missing sheets was that none of the cots in our barracks had any. And in due course he probably learned why some of us had not yet been issued field jackets either, because it was surely my lack of one that had left me vulnerable to pneumonia.

My unfortunate experience was part of a larger logistical problem. Camp Cooke had been closed and abandoned at the end of World War II. When it was reopened in August 1950, "it was not immediately ready for use by the Fortieth Infantry Division of the California National Guard, which was mobilized at the same time," as a history of the division explains. "An advance party of the 40th . . . started ordering the vast stocks of personal supplies and equipment that were needed to prepare for the troops due to arrive just a week later." Our trainload of Kansans didn't arrive until two months later, but some items like sheets and jackets were still in short supply.

Why the need for jackets in sunny Southern California? Camp Cooke was located at Point Conception. It's that little bump of coastline about a third of the way up from the Mexican border where the coast turns sharply eastward for a ways. Two different ocean currents collide there, producing the three-word impression I have of that tiny region's climate: fog, drizzle, shiver.

I don't remember how much longer I stayed at Camp Cooke, but it was quite a while and all of it was in the hospital there. My doctor was a colonel, but there was nothing military about Colonel Kurtzman's deportment. Also, he spoke with a trace of a German accent. Probably because of my surname, he used a phrase or two of German while examining me, and I responded in kind. I have no idea what then prompted him, on a subsequent visit, to conclude a pleasantry with a Latin phrase, the opening line of Ovid's *Metamorphosis*, a poem we'd studied over and over at St. Fidelis.

"*In nova fert animus,*" he said, so I capped it with "*Mutatas dicere formas corpora*" (I sing about bodies changed into various forms). Capping a line is what you call it when you recite the line that comes after the one that your opponent has just recited. The first one of you who can't recite the next line loses. In this contest that Colonel Kurtzman had just begun, I could see myself losing about two lines further down, but his attention was demanded elsewhere and he never tested my Latin again. To my surprise, he loved the Leatherstocking Tales by James Fenimore Cooper, and as good luck would have it, I, like so many people my age, had read *The Last of the Mohicans*, the best known one of that series. He finally discharged me with orders for a long convalescent leave, which I took at my home in Kansas.

I wish I had asked Colonel Kurtzman how he came to be in the Army.

When I returned to Camp Cooke, the 40th Infantry Division had left for Korea without me, taking all records of my service up to the point of my hospitalization with them. With no record of who I was and how I'd gotten there, the Army decided that the simplest solution was to just put me through an elaborate do-over. I was sent back to do basic training, starting from scratch, this time at a long-established, regular Army training center at Fort Ord, farther north on the California coast near Monterey. Meanwhile, the 40th Infantry Division saw heavy duty in Korea and suffered some 370 casualties there. I learned this only recently while reading the history of the 40th Infantry Division on the Internet.

A Salute to Colonel Curtis

When the Korean War broke out in 1950, I was one of the first to be drafted, though I probably would have volunteered anyway, as both my brothers had in World War II.

After going through basic training a second time, I went to leadership school for eight more weeks of really intensive training. I emerged tough as nails. Then, for reasons that needn't be dwelt upon, I underwent an additional twenty-six weeks of rigorous training at Fort Bliss, Texas, whence I emerged even tougher than whatever is tougher than nails. I may be exaggerating my wonderful level of physical fitness, but I just want to make sure it's clear that after I finished all this training, I commanded a really snappy salute, the kind that generals find a joy to behold.

My first assignment after graduating was as aide-de-camp to Brigadier General Robert J. Wood, commander of the 53rd Anti-Aircraft Artillery Brigade in Swarthmore, Pennsylvania. Yes, Swarthmore, Pennsylvania—a leafy, upper-middle-class town about twenty miles west of Philadelphia, and definitely not Seoul, Korea. There was no military base in Swarthmore, just a single headquarters building that had once belonged to and now adjoined elite, pacifist, Quaker-sponsored Swarthmore College. The 53rd AAA Brigade was charged with defending Philadelphia from air raids being planned, it was thought, by the Russian Communists.

If you lived in Philadelphia or one of the other major cities on either coast in the early fifties, you may remember seeing small military encampments, each with four anti-aircraft guns pointing at the sky. Philadelphia was encircled by eight of these installations, called batteries. (New York, being larger, had sixteen of them.) Homeowners in the vicinity of these batteries were generally unhappy at having them there, one reason being that they noticeably decreased the value of real estate in the neighborhood. My assignment was to put a favorable spin on the presence of these batteries, thereby reducing the likelihood of public protests and, ideally, helping General Wood earn an additional star.

The gods of good luck continued to smile on me. Sympathetic coverage of the 53rd Anti-Aircraft Artillery Brigade appeared in the *Philadelphia Enquirer*, *The Evening Bulletin* (now defunct), and on WFIL radio. Another station, KYW TV, did a half-hour show explaining what a good job General Wood's 53rd AAA Brigade was doing in defending Philadelphia from potential Russian air strikes, and how happy and grateful Philadelphians generally were. Media coverage like that eventually helped smooth the way to an additional star for General Wood.

So wearing two stars now, General Wood went off to a temporary assignment in Paris, leaving Colonel Kenneth I. Curtis in charge of the 53rd AAA Brigade. But I was still General Wood's aide-de-camp, even in his absence, and I was left with nothing much to do, other than to phone the media every now and then.

Like other aides-de-camp in the Army, I was exempted from routine duties required of all other officers. At our headquarters, the most onerous of these, by far, was officer of the day, the duty detested by Hawkeye Pierce (played by Alan Alda) on *M*A*S*H*. In a counterintuitive twist, being officer of the day in the 53rd AAA Brigade was most onerous at night. Being officer of the day meant being in charge of all military matters during the long night while others slept—not just staying awake, but awake enough to monitor the complicated and ever-changing codes and procedures governing air raid drills at our gun sites. Russian planes never did fly over them, but the threat of their doing so was taken to be real, and woe betide the officer of the day at the 53rd AAA Brigade who screwed up during a mock attack. He was in for the grisliest chewing-out of his sorry life.

There were only twelve officers at our headquarters, so they had to face this ordeal two or three times a month. I, though exempt, nonetheless became very familiar with how the O.D.'s night typically began. At 4:30 in the afternoon, the designated O.D. would appear at my office, a large foyer just outside the commanding officer's, now occupied by Colonel Curtis. The O.D. might or might not (usually not) exchange a pleasantry with me as I got up to slip into the inner office to announce his arrival. "Major Worley is here to report," I would tell Colonel Curtis, who would nod to let Major Worley in. I would go back to the door and signal Major Worley to enter, stepping aside for him and then watching him stand at attention, salute, and say, "Major Worley reporting for duty as officer of the day, sir." Colonel Curtis would return the salute, and after an exchange of a few words, Major Worley's reporting for duty would be over with, and he would leave, passing me on his way out.

A while after Colonel Curtis replaced General Wood, it occurred to some of the officers that General Wood's aide-de-camp, Lt. Schmidtberger, having no general around to aid, really ought to take his turn as officer of the day. The upshot was that my turn came. On the prescribed day, promptly at 4:30, I entered Colonel Curtis's office, came to attention squarely in front of his desk, saluted smartly, and—burst out laughing. Was it the comical incongruity of presenting a formal, stylized "reporting for duty, sir!" at day's end to someone you've been in contact with the whole day through? I don't know. Probably it was just one of those inexplicable, unpredictable bursts, almost impossible to stop once started. Anyway, I started over: "Lt. Schmidtberger repor—hee-hee-giggle—hah." Holding my salute, I tried again, but the harder I tried to stop laughing the harder I had to laugh.

Looking somber, Colonel Curtis finally returned my salute and commanded, "At ease." Then he said, without smiling, but without anger either, "In the future, just tell me you are the O.D. Skip the formality. That is all. Dismissed." "Thank you, sir." I said, and left, omitting the snappy salute and about-face I had planned.

My story should end here, but I have to add an epilogue. Two days later, Colonel Curtis invited me into his office for mid-morning coffee, as he'd often done before. He told me a story from his days at West Point. A class on battle strategy called for the class to stand around a sand table. For some inexplicable reason, he found himself having to laugh. When the instructor asked him to stop, he had to laugh all the harder. Then being made to stand in the corner seemed funnier still, but having to remain standing there after the class left finally calmed him down. That was the memory going through his mind as he watched me saluting him through my helpless laughter.

All these years later, I still remember the lesson in tolerance of human frailty that Colonel Kenneth I. Curtis taught me. So I salute you, Colonel Curtis. "Thank you, sir!"

My American Dream

There was no military base in Swarthmore, just the brigade headquarters on Dartmouth Avenue in a building that had once been owned by Swarthmore College. There were no officers' quarters either, so I moved into a rooming house. It was a Georgian mansion owned by Mrs. J. V. S. Bishop, an elderly widow down on her luck, now supporting herself with the income from her eight boarders and from the lectures she gave on Alan Paton's book, *Cry, the Beloved Country*. I was the only member of the military in Mrs. Bishop's rooming house, but I soon became friends with the other lodgers. From these friendships, others developed, including the one with Betsy—lanky, classy, laid-back Betsy.

When Brigadier General Wood was promoted to Major General Wood, he was also given a six-month assignment in Europe, leaving me behind in Swarthmore with nothing much to do. I checked in at headquarters each morning, and with the media from time to time, but the balance of the day was pretty much what I wished to make of it, and I began to visualize what civilian life might be like in Swarthmore, Pennsylvania, instead of Hays, Kansas.

Was it preordained, I began to wonder, that I return to the job I'd held while still in college in the advertising department of a midwestern town's only newspaper, there to scan the treeless, windswept, empty prairie to the end of my days? Surely not! To prosper in Swarthmore after the war ended, to own a home along one of its leisurely, shaded avenues, to fall in love and marry and raise a family here in Swarthmore—these idle musings gradually coalesced into my own American Dream.

To become real, my dream needed a wife, of course. "But that key component is here for the asking," I fondly thought—"dear Swarthmorean Betsy." She had majored in economics at Lycoming College and now worked at Lincoln Labs on Columbia Avenue, not far from brigade headquarters. She still lived with her parents on Princeton Avenue (most of the streets in Swarthmore bore the names of hallowed colleges) and she showed up at Mrs. Bishop's lecture on *Cry, the Beloved Country* the evening that a couple of friends and I attended.

Betsy and I had both actually read the book, and we really hit it off over coffee and cake afterwards. We began to date and soon enough were "going steady," as the saying went. Our interests were remarkably similar and our differences minor, we said to each other. To be sure, she disapproved of smoking, but I planned to kick the habit anyway.

But there was a bump in the road. As is so often the case, it was over religion. I was Catholic and Betsy, Protestant—Presbyterian—but it turned out that neither of us was all that into the dogmas and practices that separated our different forms of worship. We easily agreed that our values were nonsectarian, interdenominational, and I felt no need to disclose personal details like my having spent all those years in a Catholic seminary. I think Betsy saw my Catholicism as an amusing, unessential accessory, like carrying a vest-pocket watch or having an oddly shaped cowlick.

Betsy's mother posed more of a problem. Much more. It wasn't over smoking. She tolerated her husband's cigarettes, only complaining every now and then in the course of an hour. What she couldn't stand—just absolutely could not abide—was the Roman Catholic religion. All her conversations, sooner rather than later, led to Rome, so I decided that there was no real need for me to flaunt my affiliation. "Least said, soonest mended," I quietly thought. But habits are hard to break, and Betsy's mother found out that I was a Catholic when I inadvertently made the sign of the cross as she finally finished saying grace at dinner. You know how the audience starts clapping to get a speaker to stop when he is going on too long? Well, that's what tricked me into starting to bless myself. I hadn't even gotten past my left shoulder before the outrage in Mrs. Hunter's eyes told me how, for sure, I had blown my cover, and my American Dream was over.

Part 6

Graduate School, Teaching at Saint Peter's College, Married Life

And gladly would he learn and gladly teach.

—Geoffrey Chaucer

My First Day on the Job

It was 6:15 in the evening of Tuesday, February 1, 1955, when I walked into Room 205 of McDermott Hall and placed my new brief-case on the teacher's desk. I turned to the blackboard, wrote E1 21, The Essay, and under it my name. Then I opened my briefcase, removed the textbook and a folder containing the roster and some instructions, placed them on the lectern, and faced the class. Saint Peter's College had entrusted me with introducing three sections of freshmen to the mind-stretching experience of reading essays throughout the spring semester. I would meet the other two sections the next day, so this was my first time behind the lectern.

I had absolutely no business being there.

To say I was unprepared is a stunning understatement. A week earlier, I had never even heard of Saint Peter's College, and I'd never given so much as a thought to teaching.

In the fall of 1953, just months after the end of the Korean War, I was still in the Army, serving at Fort George G. Meade, Maryland. A few weeks before being discharged, I bought a used '49 Studebaker, and when I was separated from the Army, I headed home on U.S. 40, arriving back in Hays, Kansas, in time for Thanksgiving and for my brother Alvin's wedding. I celebrated with family and friends over the holidays and paid a visit to my old boss, Frank Motz, at the *Hays Daily News*, where I'd worked in the advertising department before being drafted. It appeared that a position heading the advertising department was in the offing, but I think Mr. Motz and I both real-ized that I did not really want to settle down for life in Hays. Nor was I particularly eager to make advertising and public relations my

170

profession, no matter where. Preparing advertisements and writing publicity releases sometimes verged uncomfortably close to flat-out lying, it seemed to me.

I was footloose and fancy free, and like so many midwesterners, I thought it would be a fine thing to live in New York for a while. Also, and a bit less typically, I wanted to catch up on some reading. To finance that, I would use the G.I. Bill.

I already had a bachelor's degree from Fort Hays State in journalism, so I decided to enroll in graduate school. From a listing of universities I found in the appendix of a dictionary we had in the house, I selected Fordham University in New York, and on January 4, 1954, I headed for the Bronx in my trusty Studebaker with my college transcript on the front seat next to me. My only experience with the procedures for gaining admission to college had been with Fort Hays, where all I had done was produce my high school transcript. So I assumed that when I showed my college transcript to Fordham, their graduate school would take me in. I had taken the precaution, though, of sending a letter to the registrar, letting Fordham know I was on the way.

I don't remember whether the registrar's office ever received my letter, but a kindly lady there suggested I go to the English Department to talk over the possibility of applying for admission. By good fortune, the chairman was in and even more fortunately, he had a sense of humor. Professor Cronin listened to my tale and looked at my college transcript. For some reason it also included my high school record, which showed lots of Latin and quite a bit of Greek from St. Fidelis, which he commented favorably on. I learned much later that Professor Cronin had gone to Boston Latin School, one of the most prestigious prep schools in the nation. He told me that it was way too late for me to complete the application procedures for acceptance into the spring semester, where classes would begin in a couple of weeks. (Back in those days, the first semester ended a few weeks after the Christmas break.) He paused, then said it would be a shame to shut the door on me after I had driven such a long way. He said he would provisionally register me as an auditor in the normal four courses. If I did well, I could then matriculate, and the courses would retroactively count for credit. Oh, he added, in the meantime I should get two letters of reference.

I had not majored in English, so almost everything was new to me. To compensate, I applied myself to my studies more diligently, I suppose, than is normal for graduate students. So I made it successfully through the spring semester and was accepted. I had progressed through courses in the fall and finished my last final exam—making it one full year of graduate school—when Professor Geissman appeared at the door to my room in Dealy Hall and asked, "What are your plans?" (No, professors did not normally communicate with students by walking to their rooms. But back then, the only alternative for immediate communication was a pay phone, usually way down the hall and on a different floor.)

I thought Dr. Geissman was there to tell me I had flunked Methods of Research and that I should forget about whatever plans I had for taking more courses at Fordham. The final exam was the only test in his course, so I had no idea how I'd been doing all along. The other basis for the grade in his class was a research paper, and Dr. Geissman had not yet returned mine. I stammered that my plan was to get a master's degree. "Yes," he said, "I know, but what do you want to do with it?" I honestly had no idea how to answer because I simply did not know. So like anyone else when pressed hard for an answer, I told the truth.

"I haven't really thought about it," I admitted. "I guess I'll look for a job, maybe in newspaper advertising." Instead of guffawing, Professor Geissman told me that Saint Peter's College was in urgent need of an instructor, so this would be an excellent chance to see if I wanted to go into college teaching. Time was absolutely of the essence, he explained. Classes would begin in a week—next Tuesday—at Saint Peter's.

He gave me the chairman's name and phone number, driving directions to the college in Jersey City, across the Hudson River, and wished me luck. He didn't tell me my grade in his course.

On Thursday afternoon, I met Dr. George Yanitelli, chairman of Saint Peter's English Department.

My interview with Dr. Yanitelli was not really an interview. His only comment when I produced my trusty college transcript (which he hadn't asked for) was a mumbling of joy at all the Latin and Greek there. He was only the temporary chairman of the English Department, he explained. The Classics Department was his real domain. He did not comment at all on my lack of English courses, and began describing what I would be doing as if I were an experienced college professor and had already been hired. I would be teaching El 21, The Essay, to three sections of freshmen. There would be about twenty students per section. He handed me a fairly detailed syllabus, some sample tests, a copy of the departmental final exam, and the textbook, explaining with pride that Saint Peter's was probably the only college in the country still using it. He stood up to begin our tour of the tiny campus, leaving me no time to examine the textbook and other materials, which I stuffed into my briefcase.

The focal point of our tour was McDermott 205, where I would meet my first class on the following Tuesday. It was then Thursday.

My tour ended at the dean's office, where Father Edward Clark talked specifics. My salary for the spring semester would be $1,500, one-half of a year's salary of $3,000. That was pretty much the national average for beginning college professors in 1955, whether at Princeton or at East Overshoe University. Father Clark did not explain health benefits because those would not kick in until the fall, and my appointment was for the spring semester only. There was the possibility of renewal after we saw how it went.

Once back at my room in Dealy Hall at Fordham, I took the textbook from my briefcase and opened it. Had there been a telephone nearby, I'd have phoned Saint Peter's and told them I was going back to Kansas today. But there was no phone nearby.

Century Readings in the English Essay by Louis Wann was the most formidable, forbidding textbook I had ever seen, or would ever see in the fifty-one years of teaching that would follow. I doubt that page one of the thirty-four-page introduction would inspire anyone into further sampling. I never made it even halfway through the introduction in the several years I used the book. But never judge a book by its cover, as the saying goes—or by its introduction, either. The introduction was a barrier easily skipped and beyond it lay essay after essay on all sorts of topics by true masters of the art. "Why not give it a try?" I thought, and began to read carefully an essay by Montaigne translated from the French. And so began, at last, my own education.

These essays were a joy to read, but they were not always easy to read, directed as many of them were to a sophisticated audience. My task was to persuade my students to exert the effort required to experience the pleasure of comprehension. That seems a stuffy way of saying that the idea was to read capably enough for it to be fun. I had never even read many of the authors I was now expected to teach, but my lack of preparedness was not an insurmountable obstacle. Instead, I learned along with my students (I didn't have my master's degree yet at that point) and enjoyed the experience. I think I also developed a certain degree of fraternal indulgence toward those I would later encounter—students or not—who were, in their own individual circumstances, wholly unprepared.

As the years have gone by, some of the essays I read so long ago have become more and more timely. So I'll conclude this essay with a quotation from Montaigne that increasingly resonates with me as the years pass: "I speak the truth, not so much as I would, but as much as I dare, and I dare a little more as I grow older."

Overnight in Ohio

A Conversation about Race

When enrolling at Fordham and teaching at Saint Peter's, my naïveté was sometimes an advantage. But it didn't always work out that way. At the end of the spring term in 1954, I was driving from Fordham University in New York City to Topeka, Kansas. I'm very sure about the date because just a month earlier, the Supreme Court had declared the doctrine of "separate but equal" education unconstitutional in the landmark case, *Brown* v. *Board of Education*. The Board of Education in question was, of course, that of Topeka, Kansas.

But that epochal ruling meant little to me the day I drove westward from New York. I might not even have known about *Brown* v. *Board of Education* had it not been briefly discussed in my last class of the year, where the most often-heard comment was that the Supreme Court's opinion was morally correct, but impractical because "it was too soon." The country wasn't ready for it yet, the students generally thought. When the term ended, this pair of friends—Matthew, from Montgomery, Alabama, and James, from a farm outside Columbus, Ohio—and I, more their acquaintance than friend, got into my '49 Studebaker to head home. I gave no thought at all to the possibility of racial tension, even though Matthew was white and James was black. The origin of my obliviousness may have been the fact that I recently served, without any issues or conflict, in an infantry regiment that was fully integrated following President Truman's 1948 Executive Order 9981. I simply assumed that such pleasantly unremarkable coexistence among the races was the norm, not the exception.

Our plan was to reach James's farm by the first evening, stay overnight there, and then Matthew and I would continue to St. Louis, where he would catch a bus down to Montgomery and I would continue on to Kansas. Initially all went well. Both Matthew and James were originally Protestants, recently converted to Catholicism, so it wasn't surprising that their discussion turned to theological issues. I wasn't much of a participant, having to keep my eye and mind on the road.

We passed the lovely Amish countryside of eastern Pennsylvania, drove through the tunnels on the turnpike, and were north of Pittsburgh, heading for Ohio, when I noticed that the conversation, which had become increasingly heated, had stopped altogether. I hadn't really given any thought to the increasing stridency. We graduate students often argued with passionate intensity about abstract issues like the validity of logical positivism, or the symbolic versus literal meaning of transubstantiation. So it wasn't until Matthew and James had sat in silence for some minutes that I noticed they were no longer speaking, that Matthew in the passenger seat beside me had stopped turning, voice raised, toward the backseat—and that it was, in fact, the doctrine of transubstantiation they had been shouting about when I last heard them.

Then Matthew, apologizing in his best courtly Southern manner for the inconvenience, asked to be dropped off in Pittsburgh. "No problem," I thought. It wasn't very much out of my way. I don't remember the excuse he offered for this change in plans, but it apparently satisfied me. On the way to the bus depot, James said nothing at all, not even when Matthew asked him to convey to his parents how sorry he was for not being able to come after all.

But once back on the highway, James said a great deal, and an eye-opener it all was. Matthew had changed his plans, James explained, because he couldn't bring himself to stay overnight in a black family's home. This wounded James deeply, and James had been through a lot. In fact, James had white half brothers who refused to acknowledge his very existence. James had hoped to show his Baptist family that Catholics—even a Catholic from the South—would accept blacks as fellow human beings. Quite an education it was for me.

It wasn't until years later that I comprehended the depth of the hospitality afforded me at James's family farm—the deference his father and mother and three brothers accorded me as their guest. I wince now at the memory of how I enjoyed myself, and especially how I enjoyed the satisfaction of knowing how clear-eyed and virtuous a fellow I was—only to realize so much later how unaware I was. How could I not have realized that the double bed I slept in, in the only large room in this small house, was surely the parents' bed? Even the slightest glimpse of the farmhouse from the outside should have told me that this was the largest, most comfortable room on the inside, and James's parents had given it up for me. I was absolutely unaware.

James's parents and his brothers came out into the yard after the noon meal to wave good-bye as I backed out of the driveway. I drove down the road past the Catholic church where James and I had gone to mass that morning. It only dawns on me now—finally—as I write this, that James had chosen the pew all the way in back of the church to be as inconspicuous as possible and thus short-circuit any potential backlash from the congregation. I belatedly realize that James, the only African-American face in the church as far as I could see, had not proceeded up to the communion rail with me for the same reason.

The Things People Say

In 1956, I was on summer vacation from teaching at Saint Peter's when I drove my trusty '49 Studebaker all the way back to Hays, Kansas, where my widowed mother now lived. I went there to join her and two of my sisters, Alvina and Janice, on a drive to Seattle to visit Armella, who had relocated there with her husband, Angelo, and the first five of the nine children they would eventually have together.

We took my mother's '51 Ford for the 1,700-mile drive to Seattle, I doing much of the driving, but spelled by Alvie and Jan, all three of us still single. Somewhere in Idaho, we had a blowout, which seemed exciting at the time, but having mentioned it now, it seems pretty tame stuff. While I was putting on the spare, a highway patrolman stopped by and asked if we needed help. Like most patrolmen in Idaho and Montana, he was about seven feet tall and very polite. While towering over me as I knelt at the left rear wheel, he told us where we could buy a replacement tire at a service station about eighteen miles ahead. Then taking note of our Kansas license plates, he remarked, "I've never been back East, myself." I'd never heard, or even imagined, the idea that Kansas could be considered "back East." The patrolman wished us a happy vacation, hunched himself down into his police car, and drove off, leaving me with my first quotation for my collection of three on this trip.

At that point, we were in the heart of logging country, so it took forever to get to the service station, slowed down as we were behind wide, overloaded logging trucks that crawled slowly up the steep slopes. It was impossible to pass them. We finally got to the filling station, made, naturally, out of logs. The attendant was removing the gas cap on the passenger side—there was no self-service back then—when Alvie stuck her head out the window, pointed to the log cabin, and asked, "Are those logs native?"

That's two memorable quotations now; one more to go. Because of all the logging trucks on the road, we couldn't make it all the way to Seattle that day, so we stopped at a motel in eastern Washington State.

Mother was disappointed; she was so eager to see Armie. She was up at six the next morning, perhaps even earlier. She managed to roust me out of bed, finally, and then returned to urge Jan and Alvie to get up and get going. Frustrated by our slowness, she fretted about and then finally scolded, "After we've paid all that money for this motel, do you think we're just going to sleep here all morning?" That woke us up for sure. We got to Armella's well before noon.

We had a wonderful visit. Our long drive to our home "back East" in Kansas was without incident, as was my long, lonely drive even farther east, back to Saint Peter's College in New Jersey.

Swimming with the Current

For about two weeks I once lived in a swimming pool in the Bronx, not far from Fordham University. The odd part is that it was in winter—from a few days before Christmas in 1954 to a few days after New Year's in 1955. What made me remember this long-forgotten segment of my life was an essay I recently read, "The Turning Point of My Life," by Mark Twain. In it, he argues that no single experience in his early life was more important than any other, but that each one, however inconsequential he deemed it at the time, nonetheless led him to becoming a writer. That set me to reflecting on my pathway to becoming a professor, and the swimming pool episode was among those that came floating into memory.

I stayed behind when Fordham closed my dormitory for the Christmas vacation because I couldn't afford a plane ticket back to Kansas, and besides, I needed to finish a term paper that I had put off, and put off, and would be due in January after vacation ended. So the swimming pool presented a practical accommodation. A fellow graduate student, Bill Steo, lived there—no, not *in* the pool, which was of course drained for winter, but in the bowels underneath it that housed all the machinery. To get there, you entered at street level and then groped your way along a downward slope through a labyrinth that reminds me now of a scary fun house I once took my children through and that frightened them—and me—out of our wits. But prowling about in this passageway was not all that scary, and after a false start or two into curtains of cobwebs, you came upon the living area, an enclosure framed into a square by rows of lockers set at right angles.

There in the middle sat Bill, brow furrowed, hunched over his Underwood, a big desk model, fingers flailing away at his PhD dissertation on the flawed epistemology of Emmanuel Kant. He had fastened onto his typewriter a contraption that held a roll of paper that fed into the typewriter, eliminating the need to stop and insert a new sheet when the old one was filled.

Bill's paying job was to act as a watchman, to alert the police to any suspicious activity like a break-in. Bill owed me a favor or two—I had lent him my '49 Studebaker from time to time—so he unfolded a second cot and set up a makeshift desk for me, even placing a few lockers between us for privacy. He had a hot plate and one of those small student refrigerators. The area was heated somehow, probably with an electric space heater. So we had all the comforts of home, as it were, save one. There was no water. Idiotically, in our swimming pool, we had no water. Pipes would have frozen, of course. So for water, we had to trudge across the street to a Texaco station, a three-gallon bucket in each hand. One bucket, incidentally, was for flushing the toilet, which was accomplished by pouring water into the tank that, for reasons I never fathomed, hung about eight feet above the bowl. To fill the tank we climbed a stepladder that was kept there for that purpose.

But I am getting distracted into details of housekeeping. More relevant to my topic is the fact that I actually finished my paper, typing page after page—no fancy attachments—on my trusty Gray Royal Portable. It was about Samuel Johnson, who is best known for his publication in 1755 of the first good dictionary of English and for being the subject of perhaps the most highly regarded biography in any language, *Boswell's Life of Johnson*, a copy of which I had with me at the pool. It contains Johnson's famous remark about how the prospect of being hanged focuses the mind.

My situation was ideal for writing a good term paper. Unbothered by the distractions that surrounded other graduate students during the holidays—or even a window to gaze out of—I was able to focus exclusively on my paper.

When Christmas recess ended, I moved back into my room in Dealy Hall at Fordham, classes resumed, and I turned in my term paper to Professor Erwin Geissman. A few days later, he appeared in my doorway to urge me to apply for that last-second opening at Saint Peter's College, Fordham's sister college in Jersey City. I had never given a thought to going into teaching for a career, but I needed to supplement my meager income from the G.I. Bill. So I drove through the Holland Tunnel to Saint Peter's that afternoon, where I was offered the job. I took it, stayed there for fifty-one years, and that was that. A big turning point in my life, it turned out to be, to say the least. Professor Geissman had been impressed, I like to think, with my paper on Samuel Johnson, which, as I have explained, outshone my normally dry, dreary output because I wrote it in the inspiring solitude of a swimming pool in the Bronx.

The Betrothal

It was a late winter afternoon in 1958, and already dark when I picked up the engagement ring at Black, Starr & Gorham, located at 48th Street and Fifth Avenue. I hurried across the street and up a couple of blocks into St. Patrick's Cathedral, then proceeded up a side aisle all the way past the main altar where Mary would be waiting for me in the beautiful little chapel there.

Formalizing our engagement in the Chapel of Our Lady was a nice touch, we thought, because that's where Mary's parents had married. And the ring I was bringing with me from Black, Starr & Gorham had been purchased there, not by me, but thirty years earlier by Mary's father, Eugene, who died just a few years later when Mary was only two years old (and her younger brother still a month away from being born). She had no memory of her father, but her mother, Theresa, spoke often about him. Theresa never remarried and gave the engagement ring to Mary when she graduated from college, not so much a present as a way of commemorating her father, who had earned a master's in chemistry and then a law degree before dying at such a young age.

Mary and I had met only a year earlier. It was love at first sight for each of us. Soon enough, without either of us voicing anything so dramatic as a proposal, we came to accept as established fact that we wanted to spend our lives together. "But when should this happy conjoining begin?" we wondered.

Mary's first thought was to wait four years. By then, she reasoned, we would surely have our academic degrees, other loose ends would be tied up, and there would be nothing to becloud our venture into matrimony. Putting it off that far in the future was also a way of avoiding a vexing problem. A few months before I met Mary, she and her mother, along with her mother's two unmarried sisters, moved into a new house in Bellerose Village, just beyond Queens, New York. The four of them had scraped together the means for making this dream come true, each contributing a third to the down payment (the sisters, Helen and Loretta, counting as one unit) and similarly sharing the monthly mortgage and household expenses. So by tying the knot with me anytime soon, Mary would be leaving her mother and aunts in a lurch financially, which is why Mary had entertained the idea of such a long wait.

It was in spring that we first decided on a marriage four years in the future. Then summer came, and on one balmy evening at Jones Beach, we decided that four years was too far off, so we reduced it to three. Then on a gorgeous October day, after a long drive northward on Route 9, we reduced it to two. Then on a brisk walk at Jones Beach on a clear, cold day in early January, we reduced it once more, selecting the coming August as the time to get married (we would continue Mary's monthly payments, we decided).

That issue settled, it seemed that a formal engagement was now in order. Mary, in a surge of practicality, suggested that I give her the ring she had never worn, thus letting me keep my tiny savings account intact for financing our small wedding in August. So instead of buying an engagement ring at Black, Starr & Gorham, I simply took her mother's ring back to them for resizing and resetting.

From St. Patrick's, we had planned to revisit Librairie's, the restaurant where we first met the year before in the early spring of 1957. Richard Brown, my colleague both in the English Department at Saint Peter's and as a doctoral candidate at Fordham, had suggested that we double-date for dinner one evening. He had selected Librairie's, intrigued, no doubt, by the aptness of its French name, which means "bookstore," though at the time I thought it meant library. Dick and his date, Mary Heslin, were already seated at the bar when Kathy, a fellow graduate student at Fordham, and I arrived.

After introductions, we continued chatting while waiting for our table. Mary was in her sixth year of teaching at Brooklyn Technical High School, and was taking courses toward a PhD in English at New York University. She was telling us about a great lecture on Walt Whitman by G. Wilson Allen that she'd just come from when the maître d' signaled us to follow him to our table. I do not remember if we ordered drinks; I do not remember what I ate or if service was good or bad or fast or slow, so preoccupied I was with the thought that this Mary Heslin was the most attractive girl I had ever seen. I don't think

I broke the first rule of double-dating, though, which is not to flirt with anyone except your own date. A week or so later, when Mary and I met for dinner again at Librairie's—each of us alone this time—Mary assured me that I had been a model of decorum, had not flirted with her (or my own date either), had spoken very little, in fact, to anyone. I had been much faster than Richard Brown though, she noticed, with a lighter for her cigarette.

Mary was already at the Chapel of Our Lady when I arrived just before five o'clock, so we should have had plenty of time to plight our troth and then celebrate at Librairie's in the West Village, where we had reservations at six o'clock. But earlier that afternoon, I had received a message from John Benson, my good friend and departmental colleague at Saint Peter's. It came via a secretary from the registrar's office, who was waiting for me outside the door as I was leaving my afternoon class. Professor Benson hoped I could cover his class in Greek drama scheduled for 6:15 that evening, the secretary said, explaining that he had broken his leg while getting off an airplane at the Newark airport.

I could simply have begged off. The practice at Saint Peter's in cases like this was for someone from the registrar's office to go to the classroom and announce that the professor could not meet his class, and that took care of it. But this was only the second meeting of the class that semester, and I surmised that John did not want his students to get off to a no-show start. In addition, I owed John for a couple of favors he had done me. Plus, I knew the textbook he had ordered and knew the first play in it. So my answer to John's plea for help was yes, I would cover for him. Mary would understand, I assumed.

When I arrived at the chapel and hurriedly explained the change in our plans for the evening, Mary did understand. During our year's courtship, she had come to know John well enough to consider him her friend too. The central point of our meeting was immediately accomplished when we found that the resized ring fit Mary's finger perfectly, and we left St. Patrick's without further ado, postponing our prayers and commemorative verses for later. Mary, recognizably engaged now, and I hurried off to my '49 Studebaker parked nearby on 51st Street. We hopped in and headed for the Lincoln Tunnel, not having to inch our way through traffic back then as you do now. We made good time through the newly opened third tunnel, then zipped down Hudson Boulevard—now called Kennedy Boulevard—to Saint Peter's. Parking was just beginning to become a problem there, but we found a space only a block away, and arrived at John Benson's classroom with a few minutes to spare.

Mary took a seat in the back row, where she remained indistinguishable from the students, many of whom were older than we. She had come to St. Patrick's straight from Brooklyn Tech, so she was prepared with a notebook, which she opened and sat poised for taking notes when I strode to the lectern and began.

My task was to give an introduction to the play the students were to read for the next class. It was *Agamemnon*, the first in a trilogy by Aeschylus, commonly known as the father of Greek tragedy. This play is about a family known as the house of Atreus, which experiences a singularly horrific sequence of wrongdoing: cannibalism, filicide, nepoticide, mariticide, matricide, and just plain murder, which sweep through five generations. *Agamemnon* does not offer light-hearted entertainment suitable for joyfully celebrating an engagement.

The house of Atreus's troubles began long before Agamemnon was born, I began, and printed the name "Tantalus," high on the blackboard. For motives that remain unclear, Tantalus wanted to trick the gods into committing the abominable sin of cannibalism. To this end, he had his son Pelops killed and cut into pieces. He boiled the pieces and added them to a stew, which he served to the gods for dinner. The gods were not tricked, however; they recognized the presence of human flesh and were horrified at Tantalus's monstrous crime. They executed him at once, then packed him off to Hades where he was chained in a pool of water. But whenever he bent down to slake his thirst, the water receded out of reach. Above him hung clusters of fruit, but when he reached to pick some, the branches withdrew. Several students started to whisper knowingly, so I said, "Yes, that's where we get the word *tantalize*." Mary's nod and smile were a thumbs up. This class was paying attention.

Reassured, I printed "Pelops" below Tantalus on the blackboard while explaining that the gods put him back together again—very well, in fact, for he subsequently fathered two sons, Atreus and Thyestes, whose names I printed side by side below Tantalus. Atreus married a very pretty woman named Aerope, I continued. Thyestes, his brother, had an eye for good-looking women too, and while a guest at Atreus's home, he seduced Aerope. The pair became secret lovers, but when Atreus finally noticed what his wife and his brother were up to, he did not let on that he knew. Instead, he plotted revenge. He invited his brother to dinner. Thyestes, always glad to visit Atreus's house, came right on over. Dinner ended, and Atreus revealed that he had used their grandfather's recipe. The main ingredients of the stew Thyestes had just consumed were his two older sons. Atreus then banished Thyestes to a distant land.

Atreus forgave his alluring wife her infidelity and she bore him two sons. Both boys inherited their father's eye for pretty women. Agamemnon, king of Argos, married Clytemnestra, beautiful and strong-willed; Menelaus, king of Sparta, married her half-sister, Helen, whose beauty was celebrated the whole world over. One day a young man named Paris, who had traveled all the way from Troy, stopped in at the home of Helen and Menelaus. Now Paris was the handsomest man in the world and Helen was the most beautiful woman in the world, and while the two were visiting, Menelaus, surely the dumbest man in the world, went off hunting, leaving them alone together. When he returned they were gone, heading for Troy.

To get his wife back, Menelaus turned to his brother, Agamemnon, who organized a coalition of Greek armies to secure the return of Helen. In no time at all, the Greek leaders named Agamemnon as commander-in-chief of their armies, which were gathered at Port Aulis and ready to sail for Troy, hoping to return soon with Helen and with their ships laden with plunder.

The war there dragged on for ten years, ending finally—here I interrupted myself to ask, "Does anyone remember how the Greeks won the war?" Several hands went up, and while the young man one row in front of Mary was explaining the cunning treachery involving the wooden gift-horse, I was thinking how well, thank God, this class was going. That prompts a further thought now, over half a century later, that we English professors have an advantage over those who teach in other fields. Students credit us when they enjoy a story or poem or play that we are presenting. We entertain with entertainment crafted by others, and then enjoy the acclaim earned by them.

When the class ended, I told the students to enjoy reading the rest of the play, and they said they would. It had been fun seeing Mary in the back row, ring sparkling on her finger, smiling, frowning, looking shocked, looking thoughtful—reacting along with the class—so engaged she was.

A couple of days later I got an amplified, more accurate account of Professor Benson's accident, straight from the horse's mouth. It was actually his girlfriend who was deplaning. She was returning from Italy. In her carry-on bag was a fragile ceramic that John had asked her to bring back with her. In those days it was normal to meet disembarking passengers at the foot of the airplane's stairway. One could even walk up into the cabin to lend a hand to a passenger burdened with parcels. John was descending the stairway, his girlfriend's carry-on securely in hand, when he tripped and fell, injuring, but not breaking, his leg. The ceramic of Aphrodite was unharmed.

Wedding photo of Mary and me, August 16, 1958.

Lions and Hearts

An Old English Memory

When I was getting the mail today, I passed by, both going and coming, a framed poem hanging in the living room near the front hallway. If you look closely, you can see the name Mary Heslin in the lower right corner. Mary wrote this poem in 1957, but in Old English, or Anglo-Saxon as it is usually called. It was the language spoken and written in England between 500 and 1100 AD. As you can see, our English language has changed a great deal since then!

The poem hangs at the entrance to the living room where Mary would have been sure to see it when she came home from the hospital. That is, if she'd come home from the hospital. Because I'm so used to seeing it there, I've gradually ceased actually noticing it. But today's mail brought a card that pictured one of the two lions at the entrance to the New York Public

Anglo-Saxon poem by my wife, Mary.

Library. I looked up from the picture of the lion in my hand to the poem on the wall and saw it anew.

I have not visited New York's Main Library in decades, yet I remembered at once the lions' names: Patience and Fortitude. I used to walk between these two haughty guardians of the library several times a week in the mid-fifties when I was in graduate school.

Mary was with me one Friday evening in March 1958, just a few months before we were married. I remember it as if it were today, though I don't feel my heart beating like I felt it back then as I headed toward the exit, complicit with Mary in the only illegal activity she ever undertook in her life. I nodded courteously to the guard stationed there, and he brightened at pretty Mary's smile. We strode past Patience, both of us maintaining a pretended nonchalance. Then, resisting with all our might the impulse to hurry, we slowly headed toward the stone stairway and walked down the steps that would lead us into the bustling anonymity of Fifth Avenue.

Arriving there at last, we yet postponed our exhalations of relief at not having been caught. Not until we had walked far enough south to be completely out of sight of the guard at the door (and of those disapproving lions too) did we finally embrace our success and each other.

We went into a bar—I wonder if it is still there?—to rest, recoup, and celebrate. I ordered white wine while Mary reached under her raincoat and, after some tugging, produced a fairly large book, the *Bosworth-Toller Anglo-Saxon Dictionary*.

What was all this about? Mary was teaching full-time at Brooklyn Tech while pursuing a PhD in English at NYU. I was teaching at Saint Peter's College while pursuing a PhD at Fordham. We were each taking a course in Anglo-Saxon language and literature. My course at Fordham let out on Fridays at 6:10. Hers at NYU let out on Fridays at 6:45. So after my class ended, I would hurry down to NYU in my '49 Studebaker, arriving there just as Mary was getting out of her class. Then we'd go to dinner at the Jumble Shop in the Village on West 8th Street. We had salad, swordfish steak, vegetables, dessert (always pecan pie), and coffee for $2.50 each. They let us sit there for hours while we discussed our classes in Old English.

But today after our classes we did not go to the Jumble Shop. We met instead in the Reading Room of the library where dictionaries and the like are shelved along the walls. These reference works cannot be checked out. They have guards at the exits to prevent that.

Now Mary had always liked to think outside the box. For her research paper, instead of using the topic Professor Dunn had assigned the class, she asked his permission to translate into both modern English and Old English a poem, "Reitet der Ritter," by the German writer Rainer Maria Rilke. Her purpose was to explain and illustrate some predictable patterns in the way language changes. But if there were any hope for Mary to complete this elaborate research project by next Friday's class when it was due, she would need to use the Anglo-Saxon dictionary at home. Mary's thinking outside the box now required using the dictionary outside the library.

We finished our wine. Then I walked Mary and the dictionary, which she carried in plain sight now, to her snazzy red Plymouth. She worked on her paper all weekend and into some weekday nights too, but finished with time to spare by Friday, when we stealthily returned the *Bosworth-Toller* to its rightful place in the Reading Room before going to dinner at the Jumble Shop. The perfect crime. Over pecan pie and coffee, she handed me an index card with the poem on it. Here it is with the promised translation:

Freondas lifdon freolice	**gefindan friðe.**
Friends live freely	they find freedom
Leof ond lufode	**hi lofiað ða clommas,**
Lover and beloved	they love the chains
Tha salas wyn-sume	**ða sellice sindon.**
The winsome bonds	that are wonderful

Hwaet is ðeos run?

What is this rune [riddle]?

Mary's poem illustrates the rune, which is a riddle, often a paradox, in poetic form. You may have guessed that the answer to this rune is love.

Runes were popular toward the end of the Old English period. Mary used the poem to show her students at Brooklyn Tech how Old English employed alliteration, the repetition of two or more initial consonants (e.g., "Friends freely find freedom") instead of rhyming as a poetic technique.

A line of Old English verse was in two parts. The space between was called the *caesura*. Old English alliteration required that the second half of the line contain at least one word that repeated the alliteration of the first half.

Mary printed the poem on the blackboard, and the students copied it. Modern photocopying was not yet available, though just around the corner. You can see that "th" is represented by ð, a letter called an *eth*, which looks a bit like the letter "t" leaning backwards on a unicycle.

One of the students, an artist, inscribed and decorated the poem, and then the class had it framed and gave it to Mary, their favorite teacher, as a present at the end of the year.

Dog-Eared Pages, and Other Important Points in the Narrative

It was around ten o'clock in the evening. Mary was reading *The Great Gatsby*. She had reached the point where Nick Carraway names many of the people who came to Jay Gatsby's parties, when she handed me the book and said it was time to go, the destination being Harkness Pavilion of Columbia Presbyterian Hospital. Our first baby was about to arrive.

The date was December 27, 1959, a Sunday. At that time, we were living at 210 Clinton Avenue in Brooklyn, so we drove across the Manhattan Bridge, then across Canal Street to the West Side Highway. I'm not absolutely sure that you could still access the West Side Highway at Canal Street in 1959, or if you had to go all the way up to 57th Street as you do now. I just don't remember when the southern section of the highway started to shed pieces of itself onto the pavement below and so was closed off as unsafe, then finally torn down.

What I still have a very clear memory of is my having to screech over to the side on Canal Street and stepping out of the car to get rid of a cramp in my left leg. It was either that or lose all control of the pedals. I may have been aware, even then, of the ridiculousness of suffering leg cramps while Mary was in labor, and this perception may have helped to relieve the tension that caused the cramping. Whatever the case, as if in answer to my prayer, or *actually*—who is to say?—in answer to my prayer and Mary's too, the cramp in my leg subsided as suddenly as it'd started. I got back in our car and sped up to the hospital without further mishap.

I should have said, "without any mishap that I remember," because I remember nothing at all that happened between Canal Street and a waiting room at Harkness Pavilion. I was sitting there holding *The Great Gatsby*. I noticed that Mary had dog-eared (a practice we both deplored and each did anyway)—the page where the people who came to Gatsby's parties are named.

The next thing I remember is Mary being examined by a nurse, a heavyset, stern-visaged lady. She was moving some kind of instrument over Mary's bulging abdomen, and as she did this, she gave me a momentary troubled look that said to me that she'd detected something alarming. She started to shake her head in dismay, but stopped instantly, steeling herself, I realize, against betraying her alarming discovery—"No, this is something to tell only the doctor," she must have thought. She must not upset the patient or the husband. She remained expressionless as she left, and I never saw her again. Then Mary, smiling and waving good-bye and all unaware, was wheeled away into the delivery room.

I had brought William Faulkner's *Light in August* with me, but I remember being unable to make heads or tails out of what I was trying to read. The next thing I remember, it is early morning on December 28th, and Dr. Charles M. Steer is congratulating me on being the father of a healthy, ten-fingered, ten-toed, baby boy whom we would name Michael. "It was an easy delivery," Dr. Steer is saying. "But it will be a few minutes before you can see Mary." Then, maybe because I still looked so distraught, he added that there was a florist shop in the lobby and that I would have time to get some flowers if I wished.

Heavens Above

I remember the exact date of Yuri Gagarin's flight in outer space. It was April 12, 1961, same as the birth date of my second son, John. While I was waiting for the stork to land at Columbia Presbyterian Hospital that day, I peered over the shoulder of an excited man who had just entered the waiting room and saw a headline announcing Russia's triumph in the race in space. Then Dr. Charles M. Steer was suddenly at my side with the more important local news that my second child had just been delivered. Ultrasound testing was not yet used at Columbia Presbyterian back then, so a newborn's sex and state of health were news, and I was greatly relieved to learn that I was the father of a healthy, eight-pound, four-ounce boy—"healthy" rather than "boy" being the point of relief.

Only sixteen months had passed since we brought our firstborn home, but a great deal had changed since then in our lives. When we left the hospital, we still took the West Side Highway down to Canal Street, as we had before, but this time we headed west under the Hudson River via the Holland Tunnel to our home in New Jersey. We had moved from Clinton Avenue in Brooklyn, which was within walking distance of Brooklyn Tech, where Mary had taught for seven years but was now on a leave of absence. Our new home was on Hudson Boulevard—subsequently renamed Kennedy Boulevard—in Jersey City, a block from Saint Peter's College where I had been teaching for six years.

But if I wished to continue teaching there, my dean advised, I had to complete my PhD. I had been working toward that goal anyway, and had finished all the coursework. Next were the doctoral comprehensive exams. To help me clear that hurdle, we moved to Jersey City because the hours I spent commuting from Brooklyn to teach could now be devoted to studying for that dreaded ordeal. Generally called the doctoral orals today, back then they were still written exams, at least at Fordham, and they lasted through three successive Saturdays, 9:00 to 12:00 and then 1:00 to 4:00.

I had a year to prepare and prepare I did—assiduously applying myself as I never had before. I drew up a chart showing what materials I needed to cover and made a schedule, which I stuck to—even if it took until two or even three in the morning to complete that day's segment.

Then, almost exactly a year after Yuri Gagarin's journey into space and the birth of our second child, the time for examinations finally came. On the night before the first exam, which would be on medieval literature, I meant to go to bed early, feeling that getting a good night's sleep would be more beneficial than reviewing the Scottish Chaucerians, the only topic left on my long list. That material was so inconsequential, I thought, that I needn't bother with it. Except to the Scottish, the Scottish Chaucerians occupy about as important a place in the vast field of medieval English literature as the outfield of a good minor league team in the history of major league baseball, or the role of vice presidents in Reconstruction politics.

Still, I had a vaguely troubling feeling about one of the examining professors—today they call that sensation a bad vibe—so I decided to review the four Scottish Chaucerians and their literary accomplishments anyway. It was a long slog, but I worked through it. That done, there remained just enough time for a couple of hours of sleep.

I felt pretty well rested and confident when I set out for Fordham in my '56 Mercury. No worries—I was as prepared as can be. I may have been thinking along these lines while waiting for the light to turn on Glenwood Avenue, a lightly traveled side street. The next thing I knew, a face appeared at my driver's side window. A young man was saying something, but too quietly for me to make out what it was, so I rolled down the window (to this day I reach for the crank first, before fumbling for the control button). Still speaking gently, but audibly now, the young man was asking me if I was okay. He thought I might be ill, he said, because I hadn't moved forward during the whole time the light had turned green. Twice. I apologized for daydreaming and thanked him for his concern. When the light turned green again, I drove on to Fordham. I got there in plenty of time for my exam. And sure enough, the very first question was this: "Explain what is genuinely Chaucerian and what is not in the works of the Scottish Chaucerians."

One might wonder why the young man—a guardian angel, as it were—hadn't honked? Well, maybe he did, but lightly and I didn't hear. Why didn't cars behind him raise a ruckus? It was early on a Saturday morning on a residential side street and there were probably no other cars.

But what really strains credulity is that my last-minute preparation provided me with an A-level response to an incredible question. Had my guardian angel prompted me to review the Scottish Chaucerians at two in the morning—and gently nudged me through a traffic light? Again, there's no need to make that stretch; I was at times a perfectionist and given to inopportune daydreaming. But what on earth, I wonder now, possessed Professor Liegey to devise such an unfair question?

This was actually my second run-in with Professor Liegey, so my "bad vibes" were probably the result of my previous experience. It began during the very first week of classes in the spring semester, 1955. At Saint Peter's, I had just begun teaching, meeting my classes throughout the week. This obligation, however, would throw a wrench into the schedule of classes I planned to take at Fordham. There was a solution, though: I could drive to Fordham on Saturdays and take a class in medieval literature, that is, if the instructor, Professor Liegey, gave me permission as a late registrant. I tracked Professor Liegey down at the cafeteria where he was alone at a table, having coffee. I introduced myself and made my request. In response to his questions, I explained that I had not previously registered for his class because at registration time I had not known about my new job at Saint Peter's. No, I had no background in medieval literature, I responded, though I had heard of Beowulf and Chaucer in high school.

Professor Liegey listened sympathetically, I thought, and as he got up to leave for his class, he made the practical suggestion that if I had to choose between doing the reading and coming to class, I should do the reading. (As I view this matter through my retired professor's eyes these many years later, I wonder if Professor Liegey took umbrage at my telling him that it was for the convenience of its time slot that I would be taking his course.)

Taking Professor Liegey at his word, when the semester started, I heeded his advice. I skipped more classes than I attended, but I did all the assigned reading. A fellow student mailed me the reading assignments on the days I missed class, so I felt fairly confident when it came time to take the final exam. But when I was handed the question sheet for the exam, one look at it told me I had been betrayed. The questions were certainly *not* about the reading I had done. Had it not been for the generosity of my friend, who'd had the foresight to pass along a summary of her notes along with the reading assignments, I'd have flunked the exam and the course. As it was, I eked out a miserable C.

A few years went by. Now it was 1962, and I was scheduled for the doctoral exams. I stayed up half the night to review the obscure Scottish Chaucerians because Professor Gabriel Liegey was on the board of examiners. And sure enough, my premonitions proved well founded. But this time I was better prepared.

I see now why Professor Liegey may not have liked me very much. Professors, like politicians and plumbers, like priests and poets, have their egos too. And who knows, Scottish Chaucerians like Robert Henryson, neglected for centuries now, may come into their own some day soon.

The Faculty Lounge

In the fall semester of 1963, my last class on Fridays ended just before three in the afternoon. As I hurried down the hallway to the faculty lounge on November 22, I noticed that students and faculty were standing around in clusters instead of heading for the stairwells as usual.

"The president has been shot," I overheard someone say. I continued, without pausing, toward the lounge, where there would be a telephone. Unsettling as the news was, it did not disrupt my Friday routine of calling my wife after my last class to let her know I was on my way home. By that point, our family—now grown to include daughter Ann along with sons Michael and John—had moved out to bucolic Schooley's Mountain, just outside of Hackettstown, New Jersey. Our house was about fifty-two miles due west from Jersey City and the drive could take well over an hour, especially on Fridays, when traffic jams were likely. I always stopped at a telephone as I hurried to the parking lot, even though phoning Mary would delay my getting ahead of the traffic by a couple of precious minutes.

John Benson, professor of classics, followed me into the lounge. As I headed to the phone, I saw Bill Ellis, my colleague in the English Department, sitting by himself, and I heard Benson behind me, trying to get my attention.

Although I do not remember using the phone, I know that I telephoned Mary, but did not mention the shooting, which she learned about only after I came home almost two hours later. Here is what I do remember as clearly as if it were happening in front of me now: Professor Ellis is sitting to my left, and Professor Benson, alongside me now, is exclaiming, "He's dead. They killed him!" Then, directing his gaze straight at Bill, John spits out, "Filthy Southern scum!" and I see the weary pain on Bill's face as John's words hit home.

Immediately after the shooting, some commentators were suggesting that the assassination was motivated by anger over Kennedy's support of integration and civil rights, and the fact that the shooting happened in the Southern city of Dallas lent credence to this explanation. Looking back, I can understand that John Benson, Irish to the core and a Kennedy supporter, may have, in the stress of the moment, embraced the idea that the assassination was the culmination of a Southern conspiracy. So he lashed out at Bill Ellis as a part of it.

Bill was a Southerner, a courtly Virginian who tended to flaunt his graciousness and conservatism along with his Phi Beta Kappa key and his Harvard PhD. He joined our English Department two years after John Benson and I came to Saint Peter's in 1955. John, my first friend there, taught in the Classics Department and it was his class on Greek drama that I covered the night Mary and I got engaged. John's doctorate was from the University of Turin, Italy, and he was completing a second doctorate at Princeton. I mention this because it might have had something to do with the unthawing chill between these two professors, which probably had its frosty beginning in Bill's belief that John's degree from Turin was not really the equivalent of an American doctorate.

Not as petty, though, were the real differences of opinion between these professors in areas of consequence. Proposals for radical changes in key areas like admissions policies and grading standards were hotly debated at Saint Peter's, as in other colleges across the land. In my own humanities division, among many issues was the replacement of traditional white, male authors like Plato and Sophocles with readings like *Up from Slavery* by Booker T. Washington and Mary Wollstonecraft's *Vindication on the Rights of Women*.

But it was still early in the '60s—the Kennedy era before Robert McNamara's war had taken full hold—and we professors still voiced opposing opinions without altogether abandoning the customary civilities. It wouldn't be until a few years later that the intrusion of the Vietnam War into the halls of academe would bring incivility there too, as in the campus riots, notably but not only at Columbia University in 1968, and then the fatal shooting of four students at Kent State in 1970. But the disorders that lay waiting for us down the road ahead do not explain the discharge of hatred I saw back on November 22, 1963, in the almost-empty faculty lounge at Saint Peter's College on the day President Kennedy was assassinated.

Even now, I do not know quite what to make of those scenes. I feel I should be able to draw some sort of conclusion or—say something relevant. But my imagination fails me, so I fall back on Robert Frost and the closing lines of his poem "Fire and Ice" to say something for me.

Fire and Ice

Some say the world will end in fire,
Some say in ice.
From what I've tasted of desire
I hold with those who favor fire.
But if it had to perish twice,
I think I know enough of hate
To say that for destruction ice
Is also great
And would suffice.

Swing Low, Sweet Chariot

Going out to dinner with a friend, or with friends, has become a favorite social activity in my golden years, but none of us went out to dinner when I was young. There was no money for that. Besides, we called it supper out on the farm; dinner was at noon. When I was in college at Fort Hays State, I went to a few dinner dances, but I recall nothing about them other than the shameful social awkwardness of not knowing how to dance.

I do recall, however, the night I went to a formal dinner sponsored by Saint Peter's College. Mary and I had been married only ten years, and we were young in heart on October 22, 1968, when we left our growing family—now five children: Mike, John, Ann, Paul, and James—with a neighbor, and set out for dinner at the Plaza Hotel in New York City.

I remember feeling rather good in my rented tuxedo, and telling Mary how pretty she looked in her blue formal dress—no matter that it cost way more than we could afford—as we got into our '65 Plymouth Valiant for the long drive from Hackettstown into the city. I can't remember parking or walking to the hotel. I don't remember even one thing I ate, and I probably did not notice what I was eating at the time. I am not certain whether we sat or stood when grace was said. Mary, however, had a fully developed sense of the comic, and she remembered it ever after as the night we were prayed over at the Plaza Hotel.

The dinner was to honor Roy Wilkins, executive director of the NAACP. It was sponsored by the Saint Peter's Board of Regents, who were bestowing the Excelsior Award on Mr. Wilkins. I do not know if the board selected Wilkins for the award before or after Dr. Martin Luther King Jr.'s assassination six months earlier. Either way, the choice was appropriate. The college had awarded Dr. King an honorary doctorate three years earlier, and I had been at the college's luncheon for Dr. King, my tiny claim to that distinction being my recent election to the newly created office of chairman of the Executive Committee of the newly created Faculty Senate.

Now, three years later, I was president of the Faculty Senate, but instead of realizing that it was my high office that got me invited to the Wilkins banquet, I idiotically thought it was for my scholarly work, especially a recent venture into African-American literature. The Board of Regents generally did not share space with faculty members, unless they were Jesuits, so they probably thought that my ability to name some African-American authors might help make Mr. Wilkins and his entourage feel at ease in a college that was so emphatically white.

Father Laurence McGinley met Mary and me at the entrance to the ballroom. He had been president of Fordham for years, and knew everybody important in New York City. Now he was retired, but helping out as an assistant to the president of Saint Peter's. He mentioned somebody named Rider to us, and then he said he hoped Mary and I would enjoy our table. When he pointed to it, I saw two friendly hands shoot into the air and wave to me: the president and vice president of the Student Senate. I was slightly surprised to see students here, but no matter. Both were good students, I knew, having had them in class. After greetings were exchanged, I turned to the third man, slightly older, but still young. Father McGinley had mentioned the name Rider. Now, I thought I knew of an up-and-coming young African-American author named Rider. So it all made sense now. Mary and I had been invited to generate an easy flow of literary conversation with an esteemed novelist. The students were here as our audience. So I introduced myself and Mary and then asked Rider if he was at work on a new novel. Looking just about as uncomfortable as a human being in a tuxedo can look, James Rider said no, he was an assistant football coach in the Athletic Department.

After Rider told me who he was, I told him I taught in the English Department and Mary, bless her, at once engaged him in conversation about how old our sons should be before they could or even should start playing football. The students joined in, and talk was flowing easily by the time Father McGinley stood up to say grace. We bowed our heads and listened to Father McGinley ask the Lord's blessing on the NAACP during these troubled times.

That done, Father McGinley turned his head our way, making it clear he was directing the Lord's attention to our table as he begged Him to grant us, students and faculty both, the wisdom to understand that running Saint Peter's College was absolutely none of our business. He did not put it that bluntly, of course, but stripped of its polite wrappings, the message was that students should stick to studying and professors should stick to preparing their classes. The running of the university would thus be left to regents and trustees, as it had always been in the past.

Heads at our table remained bowed in embarrassment through soup and salad. But then it came time for dessert and Mr. Wilkins's turn to speak, and we hid our heads again. Father McGinley had gotten to him. The only thing I remember is that Wilkins turned, not just his head, but his entire body to our table to lament how students wanted to get into the president's office, but didn't know the way to the library. I do not remember what advice he had for the faculty.

The shame of it is that we at our table did not disagree with Father McGinley's earlier advice, or with Roy Wilkins's either. The rebuke was so off-key because it was so uncalled for. The most influential and wholehearted supporter of the Faculty Senate was the president of the college, Father Victor Yanitelli himself, and in no way did this new faculty organization encroach on his authority. The same was true of the Student Senate.

But the fear of usurpation of administrative authority by faculty and students was there in Roy Wilkins's mind as informed by Father McGinley—and with considerable justification. Earlier that year, students at Columbia College had occupied President Grayson Kirk's office and two other buildings, and Roy Wilkins had spoken out against these tactics. The students' forceful removal by New York City police was reported across the land, and student protests, primarily against the Vietnam War, became widespread. But not at Saint Peter's—yet—though discordant voices, still mute, were gathering strength to decry the Vietnam War. Elsewhere two priests, Phil and Dan Berrigan (Dan was a Jesuit whom I occasionally saw at events at

Saint Peter's), were protesting the war by pouring blood on or setting fire to the government's draft card records.

Within a few more months, dissension within the theology department that had been simmering for a couple of years came to a boil. It spilled over into other departments. A very popular professor of theology whose lectures were mostly—indeed entirely, it was reported—about the Vietnam War, was fired. Students protested. Soon enough disorder engulfed Saint Peter's too.

The discord on our campus in 1969—it lasted less than a month— pales in comparison with the unrest on certain other campuses. Still, the first sign of troubles ahead came the night Mary and I were prayed over at the Plaza Hotel.

Remembrance of Things Obsolete

Memories of obsolete things that I definitely do *not* miss are blocking my memories of obsolete things that I *do* miss. I have on the shelves behind my desk a packet of Lord only knows how many sheets of carbon paper. I can't bring myself to throw them out, feeling that they might serve some purpose in a catastrophic emergency of some kind. Or perhaps they could be used in a creative way for entertaining my younger grandchildren, the older ones having escaped into adulthood in the years my carbon paper has lain unused.

On the other hand, I have long since thrown out my supply of purple ditto masters, once used for fastening onto the drum of what we in the English Department at Saint Peter's called the ditto machine, an alcohol spirit duplicator that was also known as the hectograph or rexograph. It generated a distinctive, intoxicating odor that floated around the dittoed pages for some time after they slid out from under the rotating drum.

After about a hundred copies, the purple lettering faded, and the master sheet had to be replaced. (But if you got the purple pigment on your shirt, it *never* faded away.) Replacing a master sheet meant having to retype one, so for a project that required a great many copies, the duplicating machine of choice was the mimeograph. The mimeograph printed in black ink, equally indelible, but a mimeograph was more complicated to run than a ditto machine. Because English professors were deemed technologically inadequate to the task of operating a mimeograph, the English Department did not have one in our office. Instead, for mimeographing, we placed an order, in triplicate, with the college printing office, only one long block away. But one block is a long way to go if it is raining or snowing, bitter cold or sweltering hot, so the ditto machine remained the favored duplicating method, especially after an improved model enabled us to crank out about three hundred copies from a single master sheet. The Xerox

Corporation rendered our rexograph obsolete some time in the early '80s, and I do not lament its passing.

But what is something obsolete that I do miss? Overalls? Overalls instead of denim jeans, also known as dungarees, are not really obsolete, just unfashionable. Why, I don't know. Slipping into overalls is certainly simpler for someone like me who supplements a belt with suspenders so that I don't have to tighten my belt no matter what the state of the economy. Also, overalls are a tad more comfortable than the combination of belt and suspenders. I can't do without the belt, fearing that a suspender may come detached, with embarrassing consequences. A solution would be to use button-style instead of clip-on suspenders. But that would add the complication of sewing eight accurately spaced buttons into the waistband of all my jeans. So why don't I just buy overalls and be done with it? Am I a slave to fashion?

The answer, alas, is yes. I was not quite ten yet when I tried to switch from denim overalls to dungarees. It was late June when I developed a case of hero worship for a migrant farm worker named Dennis, who was from Louisiana. My father hired Dennis for the wheat harvest, which back then could last as long as two weeks. Dennis's job was to haul the wagonloads of wheat from the combine back to the granary in our yard.

Scooping wheat into a granary is backbreaking work. But to my worshipful eye, Dennis made it look like it was something you would want to do better than anyone else could do it. He was probably around thirty, muscular, and treated me as a young friend. Anyway, one result of our friendship of little over a week was that I wanted to become able to scoop wheat the way Dennis did. But that could wait until I grew up. Another result was that I wanted to wear dungarees the way Dennis did—but starting now. So the day after Dennis left, I dropped the bib part of my overalls inside and strolled about, now appearing to be wearing dungarees, just like Dennis.

I don't remember how long I did that. But it wasn't until two years later that I finally graduated out of overalls. When I was sent to school in Hays, someone (probably my oldest sister, Georgine) had alerted my parents to the facts of sartorial life in the city, and when I got into the car on Sunday evening with Armella and Virgil for the drive to Hays, I was wearing new dungarees.

I was not yet old enough to shave, but I enjoyed reading the Burma Shave signs we drove past on U.S. 40 as we neared Hays. These amusing little poems used to dot the sides of highways in rural areas: always five signs spaced far enough apart to make it possible to read them as you drove by. Here's the one that was on the way to Hays:

> The hero was
> Strong and willin'
> She felt his face
> Then married the villain.
> Burma Shave

Another one I still remember was on a stretch between Topeka and Lawrence:

> Just this once
> and just for fun
> we'll let you finish
> what we've begun.
> Burma Shave

So for old times' sake and with gratitude, I'm putting my pen to paper to finish what Burma Shave has begun:

> For little smiles
> On lonely miles
> For unexpected joys you gave
> Thank you, bless you
> Burma Shave

My Unruly Moment

When I presided over the Faculty Senate at Saint Peter's in the 1960s, I was such a stickler for following the rules that the one time I did *not* follow them stands out, all the more so because I got away with it. My successful abridgment of *Robert's Rules* remains for me a moment to remember. Yet I have rarely discussed it with anyone.

They were upsetting times, the sixties. Unhappiness over the war in Vietnam, unhappiness with traditions that oppressed minorities and practices that demeaned women—these dissatisfactions along with other smoldering discontents led to widespread demands for change.

In our universities, traditional assumptions about what students ought to learn and who should teach it to them were being questioned. In particular, it was thought that faculty members should start playing a larger role in the governance of a college. In Catholic colleges, the move toward increasing faculty input in policy decisions gained additional traction from the liberating force of Vatican II in the mid-'60s. Faculty senates sprang up at Catholic (and other) colleges, replacing whatever system, if any, that administrators had relied on previously for gathering faculty opinion.

At Saint Peter's College, the idea of formally (that is, actually) giving the faculty a say in the college's policies engaged the attention of most of them, from the starry-eyed to the terminally disconsolate. The faculty council that was drafting the constitution for a faculty senate became the talk of the faculty dining hall through the fall of 1964. At semester's end, the council, the "founding fathers" as it were, completed their task. Dr. George Yanitelli, who had chaired the council, now convened the faculty to ratify the constitution and "get the ball rolling." (Yes, it was the same George Yanitelli, professor of classical languages, who had hired me ten years earlier, and yes, George was the brother of Victor Yanitelli, president of the college.)

After Dr. Yanitelli finished reading the constitution to the assembled faculty, an elderly Jesuit who would retire at year's end, rose to suggest that the amending process seemed way too restrictive. "So we'll amend it, along with other loose ends at future meetings, but for now, our task is to ratify this constitution," Dr. Yanitelli ruled, putting off until tomorrow what was vexing to do today, and the constitution was ratified by an impressive vote of seventy yea, one nay.

Yes, seventy-one professors had shown up to vote—an extraordinary turnout. This high turnout, professors said to one another, boded well for the success of the Faculty Senate. To be sure, the ratio of attendance was seventy-one out of a total faculty of 114, which does not look all that impressive until one considers that the total full-time faculty included a significant number away on research projects, or on restful sabbaticals, or infirm, or congenitally indisposed to attending meetings. So seventy-one truly was a high turnout. What went unnoticed, except by the old Jesuit who had voiced the single nay and then quietly shuffled out of the hall—what no one noticed was that this high turnout would not have been high enough to pass an amendment—not even one that *everyone* favored and *nobody* opposed. The constitution we had just ratified prescribed a two-thirds majority of the *entire* faculty to pass an amendment. Now two-thirds of 114 is seventy-six, so it would have taken seventy-six affirmative votes to pass an amendment—five more than the seventy-one present at that day's impressively well-attended meeting.

Lest you misjudge these professors at Saint Peter's as constituting a unique assembly of dunderheads, it must be pointed out that the mistake of setting too high a bar for passing amendments occurs often enough in various organizations to have prompted a cautionary note in *Robert's Rules of Order*. "A vote of two thirds of the members should never be used in ordinary societies," that masterful guide warns, "as it is seldom that two-thirds of the members—that is, two-thirds of the entire membership—is ever present at a meeting."

The workhorse of the newly constituted Faculty Senate was its uninspirationally named Faculty Senate Committee. It consisted of one member elected from each of the eighteen departments. My colleagues in the English Department, after making way too much of me as a slacker because I had never served on any committee inside or outside the English Department, elected me their representative to the Faculty Senate Committee. A week later, Dr. Yanitelli assigned me the task of convening the committee. I had the foresight to select a time when nobody had a class, and the room, when we got there, was actually available. It was this display of organizational talent, I suppose, that made me unanimously elected chairman.

I was good at it. My colleague and friend from Nebraska, Connor Hartnett, gave me a copy of *Robert's Rules* and advised me never to call a meeting without publishing an agenda and never to have a discussion without a motion on the floor. I followed Connor's advice to the letter, having no idea of how committee meetings were traditionally run. It was viewed quizzically at first, my insistence on following *Robert's*. But it caught on, really took hold. Meetings were brisk and the committee did a prodigious amount of work, establishing professional procedures in all sorts of areas: academic standards, grading methods, core requirements for graduation, procedures for hiring, for firing, for granting tenure, and on and on.

Alas, the winds of discord roiling other campuses roiled ours too. Divisive issues that would ordinarily have been resolved in departments or in committees were brought to the floor of the Faculty Senate, where I now presided. As the faculty became increasingly polarized, attendance soared—and that brings up my unruly moment.

Years before the saying "Never let a crisis go to waste" was popularized, I seized on this crisis as an opportunity to amend the amending process, especially since it was seriously impeding the workings of the Faculty Senate. So after following all the rules about prior notification, I placed the matter on the agenda of a meeting that was sure to be well attended because of controversial items to be considered. The Notification of Meeting featured my plea for a high turnout. It would take eighty-six affirmative votes, my note explained, two-thirds of our entire faculty of 129, to replace the present unworkable amending procedure.

We had begun the practice of having a head count taken at the door, so when I called the meeting to order there were ninety present—four more than needed to pass the amendment. After the approval of the minutes, I read the motion to amend and called for a vote. "All in favor raise your hand," I intoned. A sea of hands shot up. "No need to count," I thought. Then, just to follow proper procedure—proper procedure having long since become the expectation, "All opposed?" I asked. To my astonishment a row of six arms went up. "Good grief!" I thought. No, "goddamnit!" I thought, knowing that the motion would be two votes short of the eighty-six needed, and that one of the six raised hands belonged to Professor Ellis, who would be sure to ask for a vote count if I failed to do so. So I proceeded to the doomed count.

I called again for the ayes, and walking down the middle aisle, I pointed to each upraised arm and sounded off each number loud and clear: twenty-two, twenty-three, until I came to the last arm, to which I gave extra emphasis—eighty-four! Then I turned to the row of nays for a quick, dismissive one, two, three, four, five, six, and returned to my lectern. Then I proclaimed, "In light of the *overwhelming* vote, eighty-four yea, six nay, the motion to amend is passed." There was not even a murmur of protest as I quickly went on to item two on the agenda, a motion about the furor over the firing of a highly vocal opponent of the war in Vietnam.

Teaching at Saint Peter's College (extract from the President's Report, 1964–65).

Consulting Emily Post

I have been going through the clutter in my study, and I came across a picture of me published in 1965, my tenth year at Saint Peter's College. The photo appears in the middle of the president of the college's annual report. There is neither a caption indicating who I am nor any clue whatever as to what event the picture is supposed to illustrate—what purpose it is meant to serve. The photo of me in my early maturity is flattering enough, but the episode I associate it with—a battle over turf in the groves of academe—deflates the image of high seriousness we academicians so solemnly strive to cultivate.

It was in the Faculty Dining Room that I saw this picture for the first time when I sat down next to Dr. Lawrence Malnig, director of Counseling Services. "What did you do to rate this?" he greeted me, handing me the report, opened to my picture.

Larry Malnig came to Saint Peter's a few years before me as a teacher of Italian. He disliked teaching, he would tell me when we visited in the hallway during the ten-minute breaks between classes. So he earned a doctor of education degree at NYU, and started the Counseling Center at Saint Peter's, thereby remaining within the college, but outside its classrooms.

On the day my picture appeared I was a nonentity. In the ten preceding years I had done nothing at all outside my classroom to merit attention. I had not even served on a single committee. Still, I saved the picture, and when I look at it, it calls to mind a letter I wrote in anger to Larry in 1979, fourteen years later. Yes, I was in a white heat when I wrote it. But I did not then tear it up as we are so well advised to do. Instead, I put it in the mail.

The quarrel was not of my making, and I ought not to have been a participant. In 1979, after serving thirteen years in minor administrative posts, including four years of officiating in the Faculty Senate and nine as chairman of the English Department, I longed for the peace and quiet of just meeting my classes and doing some research. But

Father Patrick Lynch, who had succeeded me as chairman, begged me for just this one favor. Would I act for him in the matter of the classroom the English Department shared with Larry Malnig, please? Father Lynch couldn't stand dealing with Larry.

The space at issue was a small room adjacent to the Counseling Office in the basement of Loyola Hall. In the closing years of my chairmanship, the English Department had obtained squatter's rights there. A surge in last-minute enrollments left the college with no empty classroom anywhere, and we needed a room for meeting with special ESL (English as a second language) students who needed extra, unscheduled help if they were ever going to pass the basic composition course. I had noticed that the room was unused when walking past it, as I so frequently did on my way to the personnel office, also in the basement and equipped with the only photocopying machine in Loyola Hall, where the English office with its fifteen full-time and twenty-six part-time faculty occupied the third floor.

When I first saw the room it had some tables and chairs, dust-covered and cobwebbed. It obviously had not been used in the five years that Saint Peter's had owned the building. I telephoned Dick Riccio, director of College Services. After I explained the department's desperate need for a classroom by the beginning of the spring semester the next week, Dick advised just moving in, and he even had a crew sent there to clean the place up. The semester began, and on Tuesday, Wednesday, and Friday afternoons, ESL students were meeting there to get the extra help they needed for learning to say, "Going to *the* Bronx," but not, "Going to *the* Brooklyn." So all was going well, until I got a call from Riccio. It turned out that the Counseling Center had legal rights to the room we were using. Larry Malnig had a document from the former dean assigning the room to the Counseling Center. They just hadn't gotten around to using it, but now they needed it for testing their clientele.

I pointed out that the instruction of students was an income-producing component of the college, so providing a place for faculty and students to meet surely trumped any other use for the room in question. Surprisingly, my argument carried the day, so Larry acceded, if grudgingly, I thought, to my "usurpation," as he called it. On my part, in a gesture of goodwill, I assured him he could use the room any time he wanted when classes were not in session there.

It wasn't long after I went out of office as chairman that Father Lynch asked me to stand in for him in the matter of the shared room, which wasn't working out at all. I think it may have been that some students and faculty were having lunch in the room and, still chewing over some points of English too, were a bit slow to leave when Larry Malnig and his entourage came bustling in. In any event, I eventually found myself in a meeting with Larry in Riccio's office. Lest someone think I am making this stuff up, I'll just reproduce Riccio's report of the meeting.

To: Rev. Patrick Lynch, S.J.; Dr. Lawrence Malnig; Dr. Loren Schmidtberger

Date: October 2, 1978

Re: Utilization of 121 Glenwood Avenue Basement Conference Room

This is to confirm my recent meeting with Dr. Malnig and Dr. Schmidtberger and my subsequent conversation with Father Lynch regarding the use of the room captioned above.

I am extremely pleased that all parties have agreed to the recommendations listed in the summary of the meeting held on September 29, 1978.

These recommendations are herein restated so that they may be used as a point of future reference should the need to do so arise.

1. No wall will be constructed within the room in question.

2. The Director of Counseling and Chairman of the English Department will confer prior to the beginning of each term to review the schedules of both departments.

3. The English Department will be given priority for the use of this facility as office space in accord with the teaching and office schedules of the members of its department.

4. The facility will be used by the Counseling Center during non-scheduled English Department use.

There were a couple of additional stipulations along with Riccio's repeated expression of gratitude for the wonderful spirit of cooperation etc., etc.

Finding out when faculty would be using the room was a time-consuming process, which it became my responsibility to undertake at the beginning of each semester. That done, I would dutifully telephone Larry and tell him when students would be meeting in the time-share room. But at the beginning of the 1979 spring semester, Mr. Anthony Merlotta, Larry's young assistant, answered the phone. Larry was in a meeting, Merlotta informed me, and could not be interrupted. "No problem," I assured him. "Just take down the hours and pass the info on to Larry." But Merlotta was aghast at my asking him to write down this information. "Please send Dr. Malnig a memo," he instructed.

It was the end of what had been a long day. I had no secretary. Coordinating the jumble of student placements, student schedules, and faculty schedules was a draining task. But I had learned that the easiest way of dealing with people who take themselves too seriously is to take them seriously too sometimes, so I took the paper on which I had jotted down the teaching hours for the shared room, folded it into an envelope, addressed it to Dr. Lawrence Malnig, Director of Counseling, and dropped it off in campus mail.

A few days later, I received a copy of a letter that Malnig had sent to the dean:

January 26, 1979

Dr. James A. Pegolotti
Chief Academic Officer

Dear Jim,

Enclosed is the note I got from Dr. Schmidtberger, sent, I presume, at the request of the Chairman of the English Department.

I find this note to be sloppy, unprofessional, ungracious and, above all, undeserved. It violates the intent of the written agreement we made with Mr. Riccio about the use of the conference room in question, and it ignores the most basic amenities one would expect to be observed between two departments of the college.

I shall do nothing about this until such time as there is interference with the activities of my department. When this happens I shall simply ask the occupants of the conference room to move out for the necessary period of time.

Although I am puzzled by the behavior of the English Department, the purpose of this note is not to involve you in this childishness but only to keep you informed.

Cordially,
Lawrence R. Malnig, Director
Counseling Center

Copy to Dr. Loren Schmidtberger

I don't remember ever feeling so angry. Strange to say, the very intensity of my anger had a calming effect. I seated myself at my electric Royal Portable and typed the following:

30 January '79

Larry:

Thank you so much for sending along a copy of your letter of complaint about me to Jim Pegolotti. I don't know if you expect a response from me, considering that a civilized one might be difficult to phrase.

But after checking through my copy of *Emily Post*, and on recalling that we have been friends and colleagues for upwards of twenty years, I feel that your behavior may fall into the category that Miss Post calls "Lapses by Dear Friends and Close Relatives," and I remember how my father taught us children to deal with the infirmities of our dear spinster aunt with whom we shared our home. When the poor old woman accidentally farted during grace before dinner, we children all pretended that nothing had happened.

Larry, I can't pretend that your eruption didn't happen (since it is now lodged in the Dean's office). I'm sure it was just an "accident" though, and as a gentleman, I shall ignore it.

Peace!

/s// Loren Schmidtberger

Before I put the letter into campus mail, I trudged downstairs to the Personnel Office to make a copy for Pat Lynch and one for myself. Father Lynch gave his copy to his close friend Father Ed Glynn, S.J., president of the college, who pinned it to the door to his room in the Jesuit Residence, apparently to regale his fellow Jesuits. Every time he saw me during the three years he remained as president, he would guffaw and ask, "How's your aunt?" For a month or so Jesuit colleagues would give me a confiding smile, but when they broached this topic, I waved it off, saying, "Didn't happen."

My relationship with Larry remained courteous and distant. He did start to talk about my note over the phone once, but I changed the subject immediately—to what I don't remember—the weather, probably.

A Lie

If I recall correctly, liars of various types lie deep in the innermost circles of hell in Dante's *Inferno*. Included are leaders who deliberately misled their followers and advisors who offered false hope.

My wife's aunt Loretta was victimized by a lie that offered her false hope. Her doctor told the lie. He told Loretta that she would get well—this, after exploratory surgery revealed pancreatic cancer. She would get well, he said, at our house—"at Mary's house"—where Loretta would go upon leaving the hospital on Long Island. The distressing story of poor Loretta's three-month decline into death from, well, from starvation in our house, is quickly told. But appreciation of the full awfulness of the doctor's falsification needs some background information, so let me begin at the beginning.

Loretta and two of her sisters lived together almost all their lives. One of them was Theresa, my mother-in-law, the only one who married. The other was Helen (known as Honey), blind from midlife on. Theresa's husband died in the fourth year of their marriage, after which Theresa and her infant children, Mary and her posthumously born brother Eugene, moved back in with her sisters, Loretta and Helen.

Mary was raised by these three sisters. She was their pride and joy and hope, and they devoted their meager resources to her upbringing and especially her education. Mary occasionally recounted the heartbreaking Christmas one year when her mother and aunts filled the space underneath the Christmas tree with Mary's old dolls because earlier in the year they'd spent what little they had on a set of encyclopedias for her and her brother. Thus the hopes, expectations, and certainly the faith in education that one generation placed on the next.

After we married, Mary remained in very close contact with these three sisters—her mother and her aunts—even though our home in New Jersey was almost a two-hour drive from theirs in Bellerose, New York. Eventually, Honey died. Following the death of Honey, whom

Theresa had cared for tirelessly through her long illness, Theresa herself succumbed to deep depression. My wife, feeling that a regimen of good food and exercise out in the country might restore her mother to good health, took her into our home in rural Schooley's Mountain, New Jersey, where our closest neighbors were—I'm not making this up—a herd of Black Angus cows.

Slowly but steadily, Theresa improved. After about four months, she was fully recovered. Her doctor, Theresa told us, was lavish in his praise of my wife's restorative powers. Theresa returned to her home with Loretta in Bellerose.

But as inevitably happens, illness invaded their home again. Loretta felt a persistent stomachache. She went to the family doctor that she and Theresa had in common, where test after test proved inconclusive. Exploratory surgery, however, yielded the stark diagnosis of pancreatic cancer. Now Loretta's medical knowledge was quite limited. Indeed, her store of general knowledge had not advanced much beyond her eighth-grade education. She did not know that, though only sixty-seven years old, she had, at the most, a few months to live. When she arrived at our home, it was clear that no one had told her. Loretta—kind, cheerful, large-hearted, naïve, and trusting Loretta—had absolute faith in doctors and priests, and in her niece and her nephew-in-law at whose home she was going to get well, just like Theresa had.

Before too long, a visitor planted the thought that this illness might be terminal. I didn't overhear their conversation, but Loretta had apparently expressed disappointment at not being able to hold food down and at losing weight, and the visitor let slip the likely cause. Now it was left to Mary and me to explain why no doctors were coming to treat her.

I wonder now why we did not get help from a hospice. Was such help even available in 1975 in rural New Jersey? Perhaps we were not good at locating help. Nor would we have had the money to pay for it. In any event, the ordeal lasted from early June to Loretta's death at the end of August. Mary, a full-time homemaker for our six children, added Loretta to her responsibilities. I was on summer vacation from teaching at Saint Peter's College. Instead of doing research, I took on the night shift at Loretta's bedside and helped out during the day between naps. She finally accepted the fact that she was dying—an acceptance delayed by her anger at her doctor and then at the priest when he told her that the anointing he proposed—it used to be called Extreme Unction—might help her get well. She flung her rosary— tried to fling it in her weakened state—at the priest's retreating backside, but he had just turned the doorway out of the room, so he didn't notice.

Loretta's doctor probably went to his grave unaware of the great harm he did her.

Off to School They Went

We sent all six of our children away to boarding schools for high school. For freshman year, though, each of them went to our local high school, West Morris Central High School, in Morris County, New Jersey. Then each one in turn went to a school some distance away, as if leave-taking for sophomore year were part of a preordained pattern. But this pattern evolved entirely by chance.

It might be thought that the children were simply following in their father's footsteps, since I left my high school in Hays, Kansas, at the end of freshman year to attend St. Fidelis Seminary in Pennsylvania, over a thousand miles away. But such is not the case at all. In my case, I had a specific goal in mind—more my mother's than mine, to be sure—that required going to a special kind of school. My children, by contrast, were not directed toward any vocational goals I was aware of and the selection of their schools turned on different considerations altogether.

Nor had their mother set a precedent. Mary went from kindergarten through college without venturing more than a few blocks from her home in Brooklyn. But her decision to change pediatricians from our local one in Hackettstown to a more highly regarded one whose office was over thirty miles away in Morristown became a turning point in the education of our children.

When Michael, our oldest, was nearing high school age, our new pediatrician, Dr. Ella Cummings, advised Mary that it would be a good thing for him to go to the Phillips Exeter Academy all the way up in New Hampshire. Dr. Cummings's husband had gone to Brooklyn Tech, where Mary had taught for seven years. So there was a shared interest in the advantages of rigorous schooling. In any event, we heeded Dr. Cummings's advice. Then Mike's experience provided a template for the rest of the children.

Of course it didn't all happen that easily, that effortlessly. After Dr. Cummings offered her suggestion, Mary wondered if the idea of sending Mike off to Exeter might not be a pipe dream ridiculously out of our reach. Money—or the lack thereof—was an undeniable reality for us. Raising six children on a teacher's salary meant that, financially speaking, we were usually stretched beyond the limit. So Mary did some research before bringing me into the loop. The brochure she received from Exeter indicated that the cost for the 1974/75 school year was $3,400 (a piddling sum now as compared with $47,790 for the 2014/15 year).

Yet back then $3,400 represented a sizeable chunk of my measly professor's salary, which I had to supplement with overload teaching, late at night and all summer. But take heart, the brochure said, Exeter's financial aid program enables any qualified student to attend (and if memory serves, the amount we would actually pay was around $500).

Mary was uncharacteristically cautious about this assurance. She found a guide to prep schools. Between its bright red covers, this thick volume disclosed all sorts of information, the most valuable of which, for Mary's purposes, was the size of the schools' endowments. These statistics, she correctly reasoned, would be a sure gauge of the financial aid the schools could provide. Restricting her search to schools within a day's driving distance, she sorted out the ones with the most dollars. Voila! Number one was the Phillips Exeter Academy, founded by John Phillips in 1791, 330 miles away in Exeter, New Hampshire.

When I first heard Mary's thoughts about sending Mike to Exeter—more accurately, when I first paid attention—I was easily persuaded to come aboard. To go to high school away from home—even a long distance away—seemed a reasonable thing to do, especially if there were advantages, and in this instance there would be a big one. It would tone down the sibling rivalry between Mike and his younger brother, John, giving each his own space. The 330 miles between Exeter, New Hampshire, and Schooley's Mountain, New Jersey, were just the right distance to put between them, I thought. Yes! Go for it! I thought, and filled out the financial aid form.

The procedures for gaining admission were not all that difficult, but by the time Mike had taken the PSAT, filled out application forms, written a personal essay, gotten letters of recommendation, taken a physical examination (Dr. Cummings being very helpful here), it was past the deadline for admission for September 1974. Mary called the admissions office and was advised to come up for a visit anyway to get an idea of the place. We should think of the trip as an early start for seeking admission in September 1975, they said.

So in August, all eight of us piled into our rusted-out Country Squire station wagon and headed for Exeter. We made a family vacation of it, our first one ever, by spending two absolutely delightful days of sightseeing in Boston, staying overnight in one of those Howard Johnson motels with an all-you-can-eat buffet, and where children stayed for free. We also scheduled visits, but not interviews, for the way home at Andover and at the Deerfield Academy in western Massachusetts.

My only memory of our tour of Exeter was that Mike hobbled about in pain, having broken his toe at the Howard Johnson swimming pool the day before. My other memory is of the seven of us seated in the admissions office, waiting for Mike to return from his interview with Robert Brownell, director of admissions. After maybe fifteen minutes, Mr. Brownell strode in, just in time to overhear Paul loudly complain that James had "farteries" instead of arteries. Hiding a guffaw beneath some throat-clearing, Mr. Brownell announced that he'd had a very pleasant chat with Mike, and now was delighted to meet the rest of the family. He shook hands with John, then Ann, then Paul—he couldn't suppress a chortle when he winked at Paul, who was still red-faced with embarrassment. Straight-faced yet smiling, Mr. Brownell then shook hands with James, then little Mary Frances, and then finally Mary and me.

In October, Mr. Brownell wrote us that if Mike wished, he could begin in the second semester after Christmas, which Mike did. After he reported on how things were going, nothing would do for John but that he be given equal opportunity. But John's adventures call for an essay of their own, as do the adventures of each of the other children, so I'll conclude with the barest of sketches of their schooling and careers.

After Exeter, Mike went to Columbia College, followed by Columbia Law School. Today he is the managing partner of Sidley Austin's New York office.

John went to Exeter. He actually preferred Andover, but the two schools had different schedules for holidays, so I would have had to drive 330 miles each way, then a few days later or earlier, drive 301 miles all over again. So we just made sure they stayed in separate dormitories at Exeter, and it all worked out. After Exeter, John got a BA and an MFA from the University of Pennsylvania. Today he shows his and other artists' work at SFA (Schmidtberger Fine Arts), a gallery in Frenchtown, New Jersey.

Ann, a good swimmer, got an athletic scholarship to the Peddie School, only sixty-three miles away in Hightstown, New Jersey—a welcome respite, especially in light of the gasoline shortages back then. She went to Franklin & Marshall College, followed by a master's in education from Saint Peter's College and a law degree from Pace University. After a career switch from a law firm, she now teaches English in a public high school in New Jersey.

Both Paul and James went to the Lawrenceville School in Lawrenceville, New Jersey, a mere fifty-one miles from home. Paul went on to Yale, and then Stanford Law School. Like Ann, he made a career switch from a law firm, and today he writes in addition to teaching in the law school at the University of Paris–Descartes.

James went to Columbia University, where he majored in chemical engineering. After working for the Environmental Protection Agency for a few years, he also switched careers, going to medical school at NYU. Today he is the chief of infectious disease at Gouverneur Hospital in New York City.

Mary Frances went 142 miles away to Choate Rosemary Hall, in Wallingford, Connecticut. When President Kennedy went there, his parents lived in Bronxville, seventy-one miles from Choate, so the future president traveled exactly half as many miles to high school as our Mary Frances did. Mary went to Columbia College, and today lives in Los Angeles where she works as an actress, having appeared in numerous movies and television programs, as well as a Broadway play.

Town and Country

I have an unsettling memory of moving to Jersey City from our home of twenty-three years in the countryside overlooking Hackettstown, New Jersey. It's something I don't like to think about because I still feel a little uneasy about our move in 1986 to 22 Glenwood Avenue, Jersey City, New Jersey.

I was the initiating and driving force behind that move, so I was not unhappy about moving there. But I can't say I was exactly happy either, my family being dead set against it, with my vote the solitary yea against a solid seven nays—wife and children were unanimously opposed to our moving into Jersey City. *Near* Jersey City, or *close to*, or *around* Jersey City might have brought Mary and the children around. It was *into* Jersey City where they drew the line.

Technically, the children ought not to have had any voice in the matter: Mary and I were about to become empty nesters, with the children all away at boarding school or college or graduate school or their jobs so that only during summers and holidays would any of them be staying with us. But their opinions about where we should move to, these they made known to us. (Their concern for us, whether from near or afar, endured to the end of their mother's days, I thankfully add, as it will endure, I know, to the end of my own.)

In a last-ditch stand against moving into Jersey City, Mary visited real estate offices in towns like Rutherford that were an "easy" commute to Jersey City, the agents said (and the commute was always by car). Mary saw attractive homes that were smaller versions of our sprawling five-bedroom ranch. But this reduced space was all we would need now. Alas, even these modest-sized homes were as wildly beyond the reach of my professor's salary in 1986 as they had been twenty-three years earlier when a modest-sized home was all we thought we needed. So the economic forces that had propelled us out beyond the commuting area where houses were much cheaper, now pushed us right back into the center of Jersey City, where housing was much cheaper.

While Mary searched in surrounding areas, I was looking for something within walking distance of Saint Peter's College. The normal stress of driving there all the way from Schooley's Mountain had included the heart-racing possibility of not finding a place to park at journey's end. So I considered it my lucky day indeed when I learned that a co-op apartment was available within a block of the college. Perfect. It was the right size, we could afford it, and it had central air-conditioning.

A happy end, I reasoned, to the wearying fifty-two-mile drive to work, one way—not every day, to be sure—my teaching job generally called for my presence three days a week—two of which included evening classes. After twenty-three years of enduring this tough commute, I was entitled to any reasonable way of ending it, I reasoned, and what more reasonable way could there be of ending my triweekly ordeal than by moving into this available co-op next to where I worked?

And yet . . . before I continue, let me share an old truth I learned from driving 104 miles round-trip to work. People generally have a hard time understanding things they haven't experienced themselves. If you have never driven to JFK Airport or on the Cross Bronx Expressway during rush hour, or in Los Angeles at any time, or from Schooley's Mountain into Jersey City, you, like my wife and my children, cannot begin to comprehend why I wished to discontinue driving to work. All logic favored my decision to move to Jersey City, yet disapproval confronted me at every turn from the time I put our house up for sale. Neighbors snickered when I told them we were moving into Jersey City. Friends were more polite; they just rolled their eyes and changed the subject to less sensitive matters like politics or religion.

It went on like that until moving day finally came. A huge Allied van rolled to a stop in our cul-de-sac and then backed down our driveway. Muscular men stepped out of it. While yawning and stretching themselves they looked around at the green expanse of our yard, at the wild flowers and the green shrubs, at the vegetable garden that flourished under my Mary's green thumb. Their eyes, wide-opened now, took in the herd of Black Angus cattle grazing in the adjoining pasture. Then, as if they were the chorus in a Greek tragedy, now in its final scene, they looked at me in shocked disbelief. "I can't believe you're moving into Jersey City," they intoned.

We lived there for ten years. Mary was able to return to high school teaching at the Academy of St. Aloysius, just a short walk down the block. She had always loved teaching and her return to it distracted her from her distaste for Jersey City. Also, there was the wonderful three-mile walk in Liberty State Park across from the downtown Manhattan skyline, and the advantages of a mere ten-minute ride on the PATH to the Big Apple itself and all it has to offer. During summers, one or the other of the children sometimes stayed with us to enjoy that convenience. Paul was our guest when, on summer vacation from law school in California, he had a job as a summer associate with a white-shoe Manhattan law firm.

Paul had an experience there that jolted me, when he told me about it, into comprehending at last what moving into Jersey City had meant to Mary. One of that august firm's partners hosted a dinner party at his home, a glorious mansion in Brooklyn Heights with every detail restored to its original grandeur. The guests were a few other partners, some select associates, and a handful of summer associates. Since many of the summer associates were, like Paul, from schools far from New York, a conversational starting point was the place where they were staying for the summer. Just after Paul said he was staying in Jersey City, one of those lulls occurred when everybody around the table is quiet at the same time. So everyone heard the partner's wife say, with good-humored intent, "That's very adventurous of you, Paul, to be slumming in Jersey City." And everyone heard Paul answer that he wasn't adventurous at all. "I'm staying with my parents," he explained. "They live there."

Part 7

The Senior Years, and the End of an Era

Piecemeal the summer dies;
At field's edge a daisy lives alone.

—Richard Wilbur

Georgine

An Elegy

As my brothers and sisters and I grew into our own lives, some of us took paths that led us far away from our farm in Kansas. Three of my sisters settled along the West Coast, Janice in Oakland, Alvina in Portland, and Armella in Seattle. I meandered eastward, eventually settling in Schooley's Mountain, New Jersey. Only Alvin remained back on the family farm outside Victoria. Perhaps his four years on various Pacific Islands during World War II persuaded him that there is no place like home after all.

Virgil, on returning from the Navy after two years on a destroyer in the Pacific, also came back to Kansas, but to the eastern end of the state, in Lawrence, about as far from Victoria as Pittsburgh is from New York City. He used the G.I. Bill to attend the University of Kansas and then remained in Lawrence. Georgine and her husband, Schu, after a few years in Chicago, returned to Kansas, though to the far-away eastern part also, first to the small town of Washington and later to Lawrence, where they lived a few blocks from Virgil.

Although the rest of us lived very far apart, we remained spiritually close, getting together every few years, usually in Hays, where our widowed mother lived until her death in 1980. But we always wrote letters. From time to time we telephoned, not frequently, preferring letters.

At Christmas, we generally wrote up little summaries of the year's events and tucked them into the Christmas cards we sent one another.

By the year 2000, the summaries arrived by e-mail. In 2006, my wife passed away, so the Christmas e-mails that year featured celebrations of my Mary's life. During the next year, 2007, Georgine, the oldest of us siblings, became the first to die. At Christmas that year, Janice, the youngest, commemorated both deaths, Mary's and Jean's. "Last year my beautiful sister-in-law sailed away," Jan's e-mail began, then continued, "and this year we lost our flagship." Jan put it so perfectly: "We lost our flagship."

Georgine as our flagship defines her place in the family. Jean—ebullient, zestful, energetic Jean—often led us all, in pranks and in toil, from my earliest memories on. That she was the oldest is of course a factor in establishing her as our leader, but I don't think it was the determining factor. The only bona fide extrovert among us introverts, Jean was the most assertive, though never abrasively so. Gifted with a pleasing demeanor and a personable disposition, she dominated effortlessly, though without domineering. Everyone liked Jean, my fun-loving oldest sister: our dourest relatives smiled at her, our friends crowded around her. She was loved by her teachers and then by her own students in the country schools where she taught for twelve years.

After her marriage to Schu, Jean left teaching to care for her twin sons when they came along. She also helped Schu at the Barnes International Harvester dealership in Washington, Kansas. They worked tirelessly, and soon enough the dealership became Barnes/ Schumacher International Harvester and then just Schumacher International Harvester. Through good management, prudent practices, careful investments, and some good luck, Jean and Schu reached that financial plateau they called "comfortable," whereupon they retired and moved to Lawrence, where they were "people of means." Not bad for someone who—like many others during the Great Depression— once wore clothes stitched together from the material in flour sacks.

It has been said by moralists that a vice is merely an excess of a virtue. Of her many virtues, thrift was one that Jean may have practiced to excess. But Jean had good reason to be wary of frivolous spending. In her formative years, she saw too many farms—and the hopes they contained—disappear into foreclosure. Where it mattered, Jean was generous to a fault. Where it didn't matter, she could be seen as, well, maybe not exactly stingy but maybe a little bit tight, if that is what it would be called to telephone long distance only on evenings, back when rates were cheaper during those hours. And never to mind rousing her brother, two time zones away, from his deep sleep to answer the phone.

Jean frequently added a touch of her own to social gatherings, turning happy celebrations into memorable ones. It was in Lawrence in 2007 that we had our last reunion ever with all of us. It was Jean's ninetieth birthday. She brought a photograph of the seven of us at a reunion twenty years earlier at Armella's in Seattle. She had us line up in the same positions we had back then, with Jean holding a copy of the earlier picture. "How lucky," we said then, "to have had each other all these years. How good it has been."

As I look at the second picture now, I can hardly believe that Jean died of pancreatic cancer that September, just three months later. I flew out to see her in early August after her cancer was diagnosed. She was an amazingly good amateur painter, and her medication enabled her to be up and around, so we drove around the countryside, looking at some of the scenes she had painted. We called on a very old friend of over fifty years, Father Lorin Wirth, a Volga German priest who had given the eulogy at Schu's death in 1988.

Father Wirth was retired and living by himself in a tiny house he rented in Manhattan, Kansas. It was plain to see that there was deep affection between them, sitting across from each other in his living room. Yet he seemed to regard the news of Jean's cancer, when she told him, as no more remarkable than any other news. It was raining and I had no umbrella, which is why I hadn't left earlier to let them say their good-byes privately without me as their audience. So I left anyway, saying I wanted to go for a walk and lying that I had an umbrella in the car. I waited inside the car for Jean, and in just a few minutes they came out and hugged good-bye. As Jean got into the car, she said we should drive by Wamego, a small, beautiful town, because the planting at a windmill known as the Dutch Mill, Father

The seven Schmidtberger siblings in 1987 (top) and 2007 (bottom). Jean is holding the earlier photo in the later one. From left to right in both pictures: *front row*, Janice, Alvina, Georgine, Armello, Virgil; *back row*, Alvin, Loren.

Wirth said, was exceptionally pretty this year. We drove there and the flowers were indeed beautiful.

Jean's medication enabled her to enjoy eating, so we stopped for a late lunch at an unrestored, picturesque country restaurant, just for the experience of it. And an experience it was. The salad was a congregation of three of the saddest looking, limp leaves of lettuce I ever did see. "Home-made Chicken Noodle Soup" could more aptly have been called "Fortified Salt Soup." I can't describe what came next, it being indescribably bad, lying in a puddle of shimmering, cold gravy. Jean's sense of the comic had always been her great strength, and the incongruity between our high expectation of the "artsy" and this inedible reality was too much. Red-faced with suppressed guffawing, we got the bill, each of us simultaneously added an extra dollar to the tip, and then we headed into the car where we finally burst out laughing like idiots and drove on to her home.

I flew out again over the weekend ten days before she died. Jean was bedridden then in her home, where she remained to the end. Her beloved daughter-in-law Lizzie was with her now, and Armella had come from Seattle too. There was a steady stream of visitors to the bedroom, and when these were relatives, there would be a few minutes of solemn silence and then peals of laughter would erupt from the overcrowded bedroom. Armie, Lizzie, and I were standing in the kitchen, where we could overhear them. Armie finally said what Lizzie and I had been thinking but were afraid to say. "I didn't know dying could be such fun," Armie said softly under her breath.

We used to imitate the way Jean would say, "It's so gooood," when commenting on a delicacy being consumed, prolonging the vowel in "good." To say, "It's so gooood," in imitation of Jean, whenever something really was good became a family standard. "It's been good," I said to Jean as I bent down and hugged her good-bye. "Yes, Lutzya," she said, calling me by the nickname of endearment that she, my motherly big sister, had used when I was a child. "Yes, Lutzya, it's been gooood," Georgine whispered by way of good-bye.

Alvie

Sounds of old songs echoed through my head off and on in early 2009, providing background for thoughts about Alvina, who had been recovering from a stroke. Recovering is the word to highlight here. An e-mailed update from her daughter, Anne, indicated that Alvie was trying so very hard to recover. Anne wrote,

> When I arrived this morning she was sitting in her wheelchair. . . . We did a few range of motion exercises. I read to her for a while and we tried to sing a little bit. Dave [Anne's husband] made a CD yesterday with some of Mom's favorite Neil Diamond and Simon & Garfunkel songs, so I was trying to get her to sing along with me on a few of them. She clearly wanted to say something and seemed frustrated that she couldn't (I can't even begin to imagine how difficult that must be), but she did try to sing along a little bit.

Alvie loved to sing, as did my other two older sisters too. I, their little brother, just loved to hear Jean, Armie, and Alvie harmonize. Alvie generally sang alto—an unbelievably lovely alto she sang—while Jean sang lead in their duets. Whenever Armie made it a trio, she sang soprano. The songs they sang at home were the songs we all learned at school—at the one-room Hope Valley School, whose curriculum of reading, writing, and arithmetic also included singing from a songbook. I don't recall the title, but how well I remember the songs. There were the patriotic ones, of course: "My Country Tis of Thee," "America the Beautiful," "The Star Spangled Banner." Others that come to mind are "Love's Old Sweet Song," "In the Gloaming," "There's an Old Spinning Wheel in the Parlor," "There's a Church in the Valley by the Wildwood," "Seein' Nellie Home," and on and on. By the time it came my turn to learn them at school, I already knew them well, having listened so often to my sisters singing them while doing the dishes.

After we got a radio in 1935, my sisters' repertoire expanded to include songs like "South of the Border," but the old songs learned earlier at Hope Valley remained the most frequently sung. There was one exception though. The song, "Du, du liegst mir im Herzen," which we never sang in school—where speaking German was absolutely prohibited—remained a signal closing song at home. An old German folk song, it translates roughly as, "You, you are in my heart."

We went our separate ways when we reached adulthood, my sisters first, to faraway places like Kansas City, Denver, even Chicago, but every year or so we converged back at the family farm, and my three older sisters invariably broke into song. By now I made it a quartet, thus adding to the quantity while diminishing, I fear, the quality. My younger sister, Janice, and two brothers, Alvin and Virgil, sometimes joined in, but more often remained an appreciative (I tell myself) audience.

The last time that Alvie, Armie, and Jean harmonized was in June 2007, in Lawrence, Kansas, where all seven of us siblings had gathered to celebrate Jean's ninetieth birthday. Oh, how we sang our hearts and lungs out, with "Du, du liegst mir im Herzen" as the grand finale. She was in good health then, but Jean nonetheless passed away a few months later, at peace with herself and the world to the very end. Alvie and I drove together to the Kansas City airport after our good-bye visit, she to fly back home to Oregon and I back home to New York. I kept my hands on the wheel and eyes on the road during the hour's drive to the airport, and Alvie sang softly almost the whole time. Alvie always did that. During times of tension and of stress, she would quietly sing.

The next year, in August of 2008, Armie, Janice, and I joined Alvie and her husband, Ed, in Portland, Oregon, for a reunion. Alvin and Virgil, hoarding their breath against emphysema, could not risk flying from Kansas, but assured us by phone that they were with us in spirit to help celebrate Alvie and Ed's fiftieth wedding anniversary. Celebrate we did, and sing we did too. Oh yes, Alvie and Armie and Janice and I, we harmonized on a dozen or so golden oldies and then concluded with, of course, "Du, du liegst mir im Herzen."

Alvie would have turned ninety the next July, but in March she finally succumbed to her stroke. I flew out to Portland to celebrate Alvina's life with her family, and was joined by my sister Janice, up from Oakland, and Armella, down from Seattle. When we were back in Alvie's house after the funeral, Armie and I started to sing, for old times' sake, I suppose. Jan doesn't always join in anyway, and after harmonizing on a song or two, Armie and I quit too. Without Alvie's beautiful alto holding it together, our singing sounded empty—lonely.

What's In a Name?

I was blessed with four sisters, all of them admirable, so I should be able to shed light upon a shared trait that makes me look good too. I think I'll begin with the word or phrase that pops into my head as I type their names and dates.

Georgina Johanna (1917–2007): Sometimes called Georgine, never Georgina, usually Jean. She married Clarence "Schu" Schumacher. Owned International Harvester dealership in Washington, Kansas. Alpha leader of our pack. Fun-loving. Caring. Dominating personality, verging on domineering. Frugal.

Alvina Marie (1919–2009): Twin sister of Alvin. Detested the pronunciation Alveena. Insisted on Alvina, and then Alvie. She married Edward Clapperton. Settled in Portland, Oregon. Beautiful. Artistic. Wonderful sense of style in personal attire, in home décor, inside and out. Lovely alto singer. Had a temper and a kind heart.

Armella Marie (1922–2012): Preferred, and then insisted on, Armie, unaware of the military overtones, as was I. She married Michaelangelo Ricci. They started two restaurants in Seattle in the 1950s, both thriving today and run by their children. Sweet, gentle Armie was always eager to please. Good soprano. Expert bridge player—as were her sisters.

Janice Luanne Marie (1936–): Alive and well in Oakland, California. She married William Elliott, music teacher (now retired). Jan has a hilarious sense of the absurd, especially in the political arena. A tremendously gifted writer with a great artistic eye.

The naming of JaNEESe (which is how we initially pronounced it until she had a say in the matter, whereupon it became Janice and then Jan) Luanne Marie says something about the level of religious sensibilities and tensions in the culture where we grew up. Our parish priest, Father Callistus, wasn't sure that Janice was a saint's name and Luanne sounded vaguely Lutheran (though only to Father Callistus), so he added Marie, just to be sure.

But sure of what? Sure of being allowed, later on, to partake of joys like going to confession? More likely, to make sure of averting dire consequences in the hereafter, like having entrance to heaven barred at the pearly gates for lack of an appropriately Catholic name. "What nonsense!" I'm thinking.

But I am getting drowsy here at my keyboard, and as I try to keep from dozing off I remember a nightmare in which I am still at my computer, trying frantically to access my record book in heaven. My account there should be filled with gold stars. You remember those rows of gold stars you got in grade school for perfect attendance and the like. Mother used to say to me, "you will get a gold star in heaven," if I did something especially virtuous, like pulling my little sister around in her shiny, red wagon. Around and around we bumped along, from washhouse to granary to barn to garage, this way and that, and then all over again, all for a gold star in heaven.

But I am old now, drowsing into dotage, getting sleepier by the minute here at my computer, which keeps telling me that the password I entered to access my heavenly account is invalid. Either my user name or my password is incorrect. "Please enter a valid user name," my computer tells me. "This name does not match our records," my computer insists. "Check your spelling," it advises. "Passwords are case sensitive," it suggests. Then, finally, impatiently, "Your time is up!" it scolds, and I sob myself awake, knowing I will never, ever, get into heaven to see my treasure of gold stars awaiting me there, all because I don't have a valid user name and have forgotten my password.

I think Jan and I have distanced ourselves somewhat further than our siblings from the religious assumptions we all grew up with. She once described herself as a cultural Judeo-Christian, and I suppose the label would serve me as well, but with a touch of Zen added to the mix. But I don't like to take chances. I say grace before dinner, and my favorite quotation is Hamlet's reply to his disbelieving friend, Horatio: "There are more things in heaven and earth than are dreamed of in your philosophy."

I recently e-mailed Jan to ask her about traits we share, and she replied that "we are both competitive, and love language and literature." She made no mention of shared theological leanings, focusing instead on the psychological. "Our whole family," she explained, "would assign reasons for people's behavior. After finding reasons, we could then forgive or live and let live as it were. We were not people to hold grudges."

True to her word, Janice has held no grudge against Father Callistus. She once explained to me the reason why so well educated a man could hold so ridiculous a belief about the name Luanne—that it had Lutheran overtones that might render it invalid as a Catholic name. I have forgotten the explanation, but in the end, it really doesn't matter. What matters more, I think, is the homage my mother paid in giving three of her own daughters the middle name Marie—an Americanized version of the name of her own mother who'd died so young and to whom no reference was permitted in the household for the remainder of her childhood.

Two Good-byes

I wrote the first words of this essay in one of the old test bluebooks I still had from the college while waiting at the Kansas City airport for my flight to Newark. It had been an unusual weekend—different in crucial ways—from all my earlier semi-annual weekend visits to Kansas the previous five years. To help understand how this visit leaves me feeling vaguely disoriented, I'll begin by describing the normal routine for visiting my brothers.

Alvin, at ninety-three, was blind from macular degeneration and in an advanced stage of COPD. Virgil, at eighty-six, was also struggling with COPD and a heart condition. The three of us had became widowers in a span of two years, I first, in 2006, and Virgil and Alvin in 2008. Since then, I'd taken to visiting them in Kansas twice or so each year. Two weeks before this particular visit, Virgil called 911 just before losing consciousness. At the hospital, he was not expected to live and was removed from life support, but after four days he regained consciousness and went into hospice care.

Virgil lived in Lawrence, in the eastern end of Kansas, and Alvin lived on the family farm outside Victoria, 231 miles west on Interstate 70. When I'd made my airline reservation a couple of months earlier, neither brother's health had deteriorated since the last visit, so I planned to follow the usual itinerary: that is, arrive at Kansas City on Friday afternoon, rent a car, and drive to Lawrence, where I would spend the night at Virgil's. Saturday morning we would head for Victoria, stopping midway at Salina for brunch at an IHOP, and telephoning Alvin to let him know we'd be coming soon. Once there, we'd spend the afternoon visiting and driving around the farm and local area, looking at cattle and crops and new machinery. But with each succeeding year, we did less and less of anything that required physical exertion.

We always had dinner at Gella's, a restaurant in Hays, about ten miles west of Victoria, at first just the three of us, but in recent years, Alvin's son and daughter-in-law, Tim and Pam, came too. We invited them along to treat them to dinner out, we said, but we really needed their help with the logistics of getting Alvin into the restaurant, first with his walker then with his wheelchair.

Sunday morning the three of us would go to church, and then to a lavish dinner that Pam prepared for us and their three children and their three grandchildren. Dessert invariably included homemade coconut cream pie, Virgil's favorite, as well as a banana cream pie. Then, after the pie had settled down, Virgil and I would drive the 231 miles back to Lawrence and eat a very light supper with Virgil's son Gary and his family.

Monday morning, Virgil would always take me out to breakfast. From there he'd go off to work at Lawrence Decorating Service, the paint contractors' firm he founded in the 1950s, and I would be off to the airport. That's where I was when I wrote those first words in the old-fashioned test booklet, reflecting on how this visit had been so different.

A few days before I was to leave for that weekend in Kansas, I found two unusual messages in my voicemail. The first message, from Alvin's son Tim, was that his father was in the hospital in Hays. Alvin was too weak to use the phone, but a visit from me would do him a world of good, Tim said. The second message, from Virgil's son Gary, was that his father was in the hospital in Lawrence. Subsequent conversations and e-mails assured me that both brothers wanted me to go through with the scheduled visit, so I decided to do just that. The last word I had before boarding the flight on Friday was that Virgil was in hospice care in Lawrence. The message came by phone from Virgil himself. He gave me the address of Pioneer Ridge Assisted Living, and said I'd be able to walk in and visit with him any time I wanted. He sounded remarkably calm and matter-of-fact about his impending death. Virgil's chief concern seemed to be that I remember the code for getting into his home where I would be staying.

My flight from Newark to Kansas City was uneventful, as usual, but I was nervous when I picked up my rental car and began the fifty-one-mile drive to Lawrence. I found the Pioneer Ridge Assisted Living's hospice section easily enough, and walked in on Virgil seated in a wheelchair, doing a crossword puzzle. He was his usual, good-humored self. Some of his grandchildren and a great-grandchild were there visiting. When the pizza eating and socializing were over, I drove to Virgil's house, where I remembered the code. I spent the night alone in my brother's house, where I'd slept so often before that I called it my time-share.

In the morning, I stopped by the hospice again before starting out for Victoria. Traffic on I-70 was light. I stopped in Salina for brunch and called Tim, who gave me Alvin's room number at Hays Hospital. It was around 1:30 when I arrived at the hospital and walked into room 310. I can't really describe how I felt seeing Alvin propped up in his bed and his greeting me, so I'll just summarize by saying I am very glad I came to see him.

I stayed with Alvin for the afternoon and we talked from time to time, Alvin resting between phrases and still finding space for laughing. That evening, Tim and Pam and I had dinner at the restaurant we always went to with its easy wheelchair access, for which there was no longer any need. Dinner done, we went back to the hospital. After they left, I stayed on until it got to be pretty late and then I went to the Hampton Inn a mile or two away. Apparently, the days of defined visiting hours are over.

Sunday morning, October 30, I went back to the hospital and said good-bye to Alvin. Tim and Pam insisted on having me to Sunday dinner, but now it was just the three of us at one end of the long table. Pam had baked a coconut cream pie and packed it carefully for me to take to Virgil, which is what I did at the end of my long, lonely drive back to Lawrence. Gary was there with Virgil, so we each had a piece, and then Gary put the remaining half into the little refrigerator in the room.

I spent the night alone in Virgil's house. In the morning, I stopped for coffee at a Starbucks on my way to the hospice. Gary and I arrived there at the same time. Would you believe it—Gary almost couldn't—Virgil with his walker was walking back from the bathroom! Gary went off to work, and I went off to breakfast where Virgil had always taken me. When I came back, a therapist was scheduling him for an exercise session that coming Saturday. Then it came time to leave for the airport and we said our good-byes. At the door I turned to remind him that there was still half a pie in his refrigerator.

That was on Monday, October 22. A day earlier, Sunday, October 21, I had said good-bye to Alvin. He died on October 30. Virgil died on November 11, twelve days after Alvin.

My Brother's Dictionary

Gifts were not easily come by during the droughts, dust storms, and Depression that coincided with my first eight years on earth. As a result, one gift per household member was pretty much the rule in my earliest memories of Christmas. By 1940 though, by which time I was twelve, rain and Roosevelt, respectively, had ended the drought and the Depression. But in our home, frugality continued to characterize our gift-giving, long after the need for such constraint had lifted, so a plastic Sheaffer pen was all I got.

But I didn't think of it that way. I was habituated to wanting little, so if a Sheaffer pen was all I got, a Sheaffer pen was all I expected. My setting it on fire was accidental, the product of slow thinking and ineptitude, not disappointment. Besides, I did not even know how really cheap these mass-produced Sheaffer pens were. I didn't know how flammable they were either. It caught fire as I tried to free the stuck cap with heat, and wound up a sizzling, dissolving, black mess in the kitchen sink.

So my Christmas present didn't last long enough for me to write even one word with it. Virgil's experience was just the opposite. He was fourteen that year, two years older than I, and he got a *Merriam Webster's Collegiate Dictionary*. He took very good care of his dictionary, as everyone could see, and it lasted him a lifetime.

A fountain pen and a dictionary suggest that our parents had an eye for combining the utilitarian with the recreational when it came to gift-giving, and I do remember that on one of the preceding Christmases I got a shiny red wagon and Virgil a wooden wheelbarrow painted green that Dad made. One good use we made of these presents was gathering dried *kühe knutla* (cow pies, in English) in the pastures. These *knutla*, when dried out, were an excellent fuel for heating the contents of the huge cast iron kettle that sat on cement blocks outside our washhouse. In doing this chore we honed another skill, which was gauging when *knutla* were *completely* dried out and *really* ready, therefore, for picking up and hauling to the wash kettle.

But our mom and dad didn't focus on all work and no play. They tried to maintain a balance. In evidence was a bat for Virgil and a baseball for me one year. It wasn't too long though before we ran out of exciting variations of the game of baseball-for-two. I don't remember what finally became of the baseball, but the bat splintered in Virgil's hand when he used it to break up a bullfight—a fight between two bulls, that is. Our white-faced Hereford, King Arthur, we called him, was pushing and shoving our careless neighbor's scrub bull (a scrub is the equivalent of a mongrel). Virgil, already fearless at fourteen, joined the fray. He whacked the intruding scrub over the head, sending him wobbling and groaning back through the broken strands of barbed wire and into his own pasture and pen.

Other purely recreational gifts were a pistol that fired red paper blanks and a bow and arrow. The arrow's head was a rubber suction cup that was supposed to stick to a target, which it never did, and we decided that the suction cup's real purpose was simply to keep the arrow from inflicting serious damage on anyone. The pistol was a disappointment too. The roll of blanks got dampened when left outdoors overnight and wouldn't fire anymore. I don't remember if the two of us even once tried playing cowboys—no, cow*boy* and Indian.

Then I went off to high school in Pennsylvania, and that ended my meager gift-giving-and-getting at Christmas, since I stayed at St. Fidelis over the holidays and mailing presents just wasn't a practice. The war came and then when it ended we were all together again, but only briefly, as marriages and job opportunities scattered us up and down the West Coast and to metropolitan New York. But Alvin, our older brother, stayed on the farm, and Virgil stayed in Kansas too, albeit some 230 miles east in Lawrence, where he stayed after finishing college there.

Virgil died (he always corrected me if I used a euphemism for dying) in November 2012, a week after I last visited him. He refused invasive treatment of his defective heart and spent his last few weeks in the hospice section of an assisted living facility close to his home. During the three days of my visit, I stayed in his empty house.

Virgil did a daily crossword puzzle. A specialized crossword dictionary was a fixture on his breakfast table as was his old *Merriam Webster's* alongside it. I was used to seeing it there on earlier visits, its blue cover much faded but the binding intact. Its pages were worn, but in good condition. Since I knew he did the local paper's crossword puzzle in the hospice, I asked him if I should bring him his dictionary. He said no, he could make do without it, and he was in fact doing a puzzle when I stopped by on my way to the airport.

As I think it over now, I should correct my earlier comment that Virgil's dictionary lasted a lifetime. Actually, his dictionary *out*lasted a lifetime and so much else too, for which I can't quite find the right words just now.

At Half Mast

I never licked the flagpole in freezing weather the way Ralphie's classmate does in *A Christmas Story*. But I had plenty of opportunities.

At Hope Valley, helping with raising the flag in the morning and lowering it when school ended in the afternoon were honors bestowed on me with increasing frequency as the enrollment decreased year by year until Virgil and I were the only students there. That year, we did the raising and lowering together every day. It did not become a chore, a burden, like having to carry water to the henhouse to keep the trough filled. We always treated the flag with respect, never letting it touch the ground. But we did not fold it in the proper thirteen-step sequence because we did not know that's how it is supposed to be done.

So licking a flagpole in freezing weather is a stupid thing I did *not* do. A really stupid thing I *did* do was to stick my tongue into a can of lye when I was about Ralphie's age. We made our own soap on the farm, and one day I found the can of lye in the washhouse. My mother and Georgine were preparing to make soap, which is why they had the lye out with the lid off. When I came upon the can, it looked like sugar. Now the easiest way of telling if something is sugar or not is to taste it—right? So that's what I did. No sooner did the tip of my tongue touch the lye, when I went howling to Georgine, who was just on her way into the washhouse. Would you believe it, there was a bottle of vinegar on a shelf. In a split second, Jean reached for it, twisted off the cap, and rinsed out my mouth. Never in my life have I tasted so cooling, so sweet a nectar as that vinegar. I was pretty lucky that day.

There are a few implausibilities here. First of all, why was there vinegar so close by? Well, our washhouse was also used for heavy cooking, and vinegar is one of the staples kept on hand in any kitchen.

Why did Jean know that vinegar is a good anodyne for lye? The answer is that Jean, twelve years older than I and a schoolteacher already, knew *everything* and that's that. Also, she may have read the instructions on the can's label at some earlier time.

How is it that Georgine showed up just when needed? Jean probably realized that she shouldn't have left an open can of lye sitting around, what with me wandering around in the area, and so she came running back to close it. As I said, I was pretty lucky. If she hadn't been there to neutralize the lye, there would've been no tongue left, and without one, I could hardly have spent fifty-one years wagging mine at the front of a classroom.

Jean's death in December 2007 signaled the ending of an era. Alvina went a little over a year later and then Armella in January 2012. Next, Alvin left on October 30 of that same year, and just a few days later, Virgil on November 11, each brother dying peacefully in his sleep. I think November 11, Veterans Day, was an appropriate time for Virgil's leave-taking. He and Alvin were veterans of World War II. They were examples of the Greatest Generation in so many ways beyond their military service, as were my three older sisters too.

Janice, my younger and sole surviving sister, lives on the West Coast. She and I were talking on the phone a few days after Virgil died. We agreed that we have been very lucky in our family.

"But it's the end of an era now," I added.

"Well, not quite yet," Jan gently corrected me.

Staying Connected

When I have trouble getting started on an essay, I do not feel frustrated, or anxious either. I just feel untethered—at loose ends—disconnected.

Maybe I just miss my wife. Mary has been gone now for, well, it's getting on to nine years. So why do I sense her absence just now, as I sit here, beginning to write? I used to call Mary "my helpmeet," using the word for wife that we learned when we were studying Old English together in graduate school. In the various administrative positions I held at Saint Peter's College, I sometimes had to issue a memo in a hurry. If I didn't have time to set it aside for a day or two, I would run it past Mary, my helpmeet, whose unerring eye would highlight whatever needed editing.

But Mary is gone, and with her passing in 2006 there began the exodus of almost all my women kinfolk. Both of my sisters-in-law died in 2008, both unexpectedly, Virgil's wife, Rita, in May and Alvin's wife, Celeste, in November. So in a span of a little over two years, the three of us brothers became widowers. Then Virgil's son, Gary, became a widower too when his wife Evelyn died of cancer just a little over a year ago. Evelyn was not quite sixty yet, and her early passing evokes memories of two other lives that ended way too soon. Armie and Angelo's son Michael had just reached early midlife when he died of a heart attack. And Alvin and Celeste's son Greg had just emerged from childhood when brain cancer took him.

My three older sisters are gone. Armella died in January 2012, a month after her eighty-ninth birthday. She had a stroke shortly before Christmas, but seemed on the way to recovery. She was able to speak and laugh with her children and grandchildren, and she enjoyed a CD message I sent her about how beautifully she used to sing. She was learning how to walk again, a few steps at a time with her walker, but the effort wearied her, it became clear in hindsight. When they went to awaken her one morning, they found that she had died gently in her sleep.

Alvina had reached eighty-nine too when she died in 2009, following a stroke. But Alvie's stroke was more damaging than Armie's. Of my three older sisters, Alvie had the most vigorous temperament. So it is troubling now to think of her lying there so helpless, unable even to raise a defending arm, unable to rail against or even to sound a syllable of protest against her helplessness. But I choose now to focus on the soothing sound of Alvie's singing. She sang as mellow an alto as ever I heard. Now I sometimes imagine myself singing, and in truth, the imagined sound is a great improvement over the real one. So I know it can be done, and I like to think that after her stroke, Alvie imagined herself singing softly, ever more softly, until her song reached a final fading note.

For sure, our generation is passing away, but, as it says in Ecclesiastes, whereas "one generation passeth away, another generation cometh." Still, there remains Janice, so our generation is not quite done yet. Not done at all, in fact—just connecting with the next generation. Here is a part of the e-mail Janice sent to everybody—to her children, to mine, to all her siblings' children and grandchildren—after Armella's funeral:

> We went to the Bellevue restaurant [one of the Riccis' restaurants] for testimonials from the grandchildren . . . . The recurring theme was that Armie allowed people to be themselves. She did not interfere or scold or criticize. She praised the children and grandchildren for their accomplishments and never censured them for their mistakes . . . . Throughout these very emotional events, I felt sad but happy at the same time to view my sister's life—a life that had such a positive impact on so many beautiful people, for the Riccis, just like her, are leading lives filled with laughter and love and an abundance of grace.

Well said, Jan. Yes—yes. How blessed we are to be a part of it all.

Part 8

Life Today

Being arrived at that happy age when a man can be idle
with impunity.

—Washington Irving

The Good Old Days

When I was young, we did without just about everything. But you surely do not want to hear more about the deprivations I suffered as a very young child, when droughts and plagues and assorted travails befell us, one atop the other, in Ellis County, Kansas.

That all ended in 1936. Until then, I thought there were only three kinds of weather: dust storms, tornadoes, and blizzards. But then I learned that there is rain too—big round raindrops pattering onto the dirt yard, preceded by a mild gust of wind carrying the fresh, clean smell of rain. To this very day, my first response on awakening to a rainy day is joy. The reaction is only momentary, however. Then the customary suburban association of rain with gloom settles in. But first impressions die hard, and from time to time in my fifty years of teaching, I would tell my students that if they have not seen Gene Kelly perform "Singin' in the Rain," their lives are incomplete. (The other absolutely must-see performance on my list of two is Judy Garland singing "Somewhere over the Rainbow.")

With rain came a wheat crop, and with a wheat crop came the purchase of a radio in 1935 and Dad's putting up a windmill charger to provide the electricity for running it. I would not want to go back to the days when we did without radio, because that's when we did without indoor plumbing too. To be sure, I find that silence is a sweeter sound than talk radio, particularly of the modern, vitriolic variety, and I generally prefer the sight of a printed page to whatever is on TV, but there are good radio and TV programs too, and I would not want to do without them.

Nor would I wish to do without my computer. I was very, very slow to adapt to this new technology when it swept into my world. I clung to my typewriter, a Royal Portable, which had served me so well for several decades (though it was an earlier desk model, the Underwood, on which I taught myself to type). Why should I part with the tried and true in favor of this newfangled thing called word-processing, I wondered.

I could barely stay awake at a seminar on technology and scholar-ship I had to attend in the 1970s. A professor from MIT was brought in to explain how scholars would soon be able to stay in touch with one another via something called electronic mail, or e-mail for short. At home, Mary resisted my cynicism toward e-mail and computer-aided research. She continued to wax enthusiastic about her far-fetched notion that someday we would be able to access library holdings from the comfort of our homes.

Then in the 1980s, my son Mike came home from college, bringing with him a Kaypro and a daisy-wheel printer, not for me but for his mother. Mary was supplementing our meager income by editing a newsletter for Saint Peter's College. I couldn't help but notice her weekly column about using e-mail, especially since she always left an underlined copy next to or in front of wherever I was. She would recall, pleasantly to be sure, how I had laughed at my brother Alvin when he had opined that someday I would be able to phone him in Kansas from our home in New Jersey without the help of an operator.

Saint Peter's let Mary borrow a laptop, an Epson. One evening, right after I finished chatting with Alvin on the phone, Mary man-aged to ease me off my prejudices. Like the character from Dr. Seuss who finally tries eating green eggs and ham, I finally tried writing on her Epson. My appreciation was not as instantaneous as in Dr. Seuss's story. It took me a few tries before I *liked* using Word Perfect (or was it just Word?) but soon enough I saw the enormous advantages of, for example, pressing the Undo key instead of opening a bottle of sludgy Liquid Paper. Then I also came to see the advantages of e-mail over postal mail—and since I am hard of hearing, I soon came to prefer e-mail to the telephone. In fact, e-mail has become my lifeline to my large and far-flung family.

The Internet makes it very easy to retrieve the past, and I enjoy as much as anyone the pictures of life in the 1940s and '50s circulated by fellow senior citizens. In general, these clips, at least the ones I have seen, present the past as a time when life was simpler and therefore happier. What is really attractive about the good old days though, it seems to me, is that we were younger back then, and that's what makes the difference. In any event I would *not* like to return to the times when we did without radio, television, computers, and indoor plumbing. No, not at all.

Fleeting Disappointment

Airline stewardess was once right up there with movie star at the pinnacle of glamorous occupations. Around two thousand women applied for just forty-three positions offered by TWA in December 1935, I just now learned on the Internet. In 1936, the *New York Times* reported that "the girls who qualify for stewardess must be polite, weigh 100 to 118 pounds, be 5' to 5'4" tall, and between twenty and twenty-six years old. They were required to be unmarried," the *Times* continued, "and they were fired if they decided to wed." To me, these restrictive requirements for the job of airline stewardess seemed a little off-putting, and I wondered why so many pretty girls applied for it. Then I read further and was reminded that there were very few job openings for women, the pretty and the plain alike, in fields other than teaching and nursing in those days. In fact, the very first stewardesses were hired as nurses in the days before they had to be young and petite and pretty.

These reflections on life in the sky bring to mind a disappointment I experienced when boarding an airplane just a few years ago. In the full range of disappointments that life can offer, this was a very minor one—trifling, in fact.

In this anecdote I am an unremarkable, elderly male boarding a plane at JFK for Los Angeles in the post-9/11 era. I had flown maybe forty times before this, but never first class. Because of my credit card purchases, I had accumulated an abundance of air miles. So on one of those rare times when the availability of my free miles coincided with the dates when I actually wanted to fly out to California to visit my daughter Mary Frances, I decided to treat myself to first class.

I made it right through everything like the sophisticated, seasoned traveler I now envisioned myself as being. My belt had a leather buckle, so I didn't have to remove it. I would not suffer the ignominy of holding my pants up with one hand, while guiding heaps of outerwear, valuables, and carry-on along the conveyer belt with the other. I wanted, for once, to seat myself comfortably, relaxed, without having worked up a sweat. And then, and then—oh, the joy of it!—and then I would sit there in first class, expressionless, impassively gazing at each cabin passenger as they struggled along the narrow aisle, awkwardly swinging their heavy carry-on to the front of them, there being no room at their sides, passing by my wide seat on their way to their cramped ones far back in the cabin.

I had often wondered, when boarding, what goes through their minds, these one percenters in first class as they watch us ninety-nine percenters lurch by in slow fits and starts. What are they thinking? They don't give a hint, pretending they are not enjoying, relishing, their exclusiveness, sitting there, smug, self-satisfied, facing us. Well, today it would be my turn. I'd be the one seated in soft leather, gazing in snooty nonchalance at the sweaty polloi struggling past me.

I was, of course, among the first to board, using the separate lane set aside for us elite few in first class. Maintaining my studied savoir faire, I handed the attendant my boarding pass and proceeded down the long corridor to the door, already enjoying the pleasure awaiting me. And then—I was too stunned to utter any protest or even to gasp. My high hope of happiness ahead was dashed, utterly, in the instant I saw that the door was a third of the way down the fuselage instead of right behind the cockpit where it had always been before. We first-class passengers would be turning left into our sequestered space in the front of the plane while economy class would turn right and head into the main cabin. The coach-class herd would not file past us. They would not even see us.

The flight attendant's cheerful "welcome" did nothing to relieve my disappointment as I turned left and made my way to the second row back from the cockpit and sank into my heavily upholstered seat. After I was handed my martini some time later, I looked over my shoulder at the five or six rows of fellow one percenters solemnly sipping their drinks behind me. Straining just a bit, I raised my head higher and saw one last ninety-nine percenter—saw his back that is—hastening down the long, narrow isle as the flight attendant drew the curtain that separated us from them for the duration of the flight.

Going My Way
The Life I Could've Had

One of the things I have never done is to apply for a paying job. I did have jobs from early youth on, but doing chores was an unsalaried position on our farm. My first paycheck came from the advertising department of the *Hays Daily News*. I went there in a hands-on journalism course I was taking at Fort Hays State. When the course ended, the newspaper offered to keep me on in the advertising department. Since I would be able to make my own hours, thereby enabling me to finish my coursework and still graduate, I accepted. I stayed at the *Hays Daily News*, getting my AB degree meanwhile, until I was drafted into the Army (no application necessary) at the outbreak of the Korean War in 1950. When I was discharged, I decided to use my G.I. benefits to do some reading and see New York, so I enrolled in a master's program at Fordham University. My thought was that after money from my G.I. Bill ran out, I would then find something to do, probably in advertising.

There was a shortage of professors in the humanities in the 1950s, which explains why I was offered, without my first asking, a temporary position in the English Department at Saint Peter's College. I held on to it as a place from which I would decide what I really wanted to do. After fifty-one years went by, I made a choice: I decided to retire. So I did that, and now here I am.

And life has been good. There have been, as in all lives, inadequacies along with fulfillments, but overall it has been very good. Teaching was easy for me, and sharing life with my wife and children brought joys far beyond the imaginings of my early years (and troubles too, though I feel no urge to tally them here). Would my life have been better, happier, and more meaningful, if I had tried harder to shape it into a pattern of my designing? I just don't know—but I doubt it. I did, however, just once, take charge of my destiny, radically changing its direction. It was way back when I was still a teenager. I did not, like Robert Frost's Traveler, choose between attractive alternatives. I just declined a way of life, a vocation, without having any alternative in mind at all. To clarify this turning point in my life, it might be best to start where the story begins.

That's at the age when one is asked, What do you want to be when you grow up? A stock answer in the pre-Sputnik era was fireman or policeman. But not where I lived. In western Kansas, the answer was more likely to be farmer, there being an insufficiency of other role models in our sparsely populated, treeless prairie. There was no fire department anywhere near one-room Hope Valley School, and there were no policemen either within hailing distance. There was no radio—or more accurately, no electricity yet for powering a radio to put us in daily touch with the range of lives lived outside the farms around us. But we read about them in books that came our way. These introduced us to wide varieties of experience in impossibly faraway places like Chicago, but also included the adventures of sheriffs in real Kansas towns like Dodge City, not far from Hays, our own county seat where Wild Bill Hickok had once been sheriff.

But I never thought of becoming a sheriff.

When I moved on to junior high school in the city, the days of actual lawmen like Hickok were long gone. Hays did have police and fire departments, and much else too. This bustling metropolis opened up for us adolescents an array of opportunities, of pathways to interesting lives—the whole gamut from architect to zoologist. And for the girls, after the publication of the Nancy Drew books in 1930 there was the profession of detective to dream about in addition to the choice of nurse or teacher.

So a whole world of possibilities lay before us, we thought, and we had only to choose a suitable path. We were optimistic seventh graders at Hays Junior-Senior High, but still close enough to the Great Depression to be wary of that wonderful untruth that "You can be whatever you want to be." So for most of us, what we wanted to be remained within the reaches of possibility. As the time for advancing into senior high school approached, we had to choose between registering for the vocational track or the college prep. I'd probably have opted for the college prep, even though none of my five older siblings had yet been able to surmount the financial barrier in the way to college. But I didn't have to make that choice. My mother planted the idea of attending a preparatory seminary way off in Pennsylvania, and I acquiesced. For my part, the excitement of going off to a faraway land was enticement enough to subdue any misgivings I had about the authenticity of my vocation for the priesthood. Then too, the heady experience of being the center of special attention in my large family was not to be lightly relinquished.

I enjoyed my years at St. Fidelis. Yet I left early. I quit, to use the word we used, after five years, one year shy of completing high school and junior college in preparation for major seminary.

So what kind of a life could I have had if I had stayed the course? It dawns on me now that I am absolutely unable to imagine the life I could have had on "my road not taken." A sure indication that I was never serious about preparing for the priesthood is that I never saw myself as a priest—as visiting the sick or comforting the afflicted. I never actually visualized myself in a chasuble. I never even imagined myself wearing a roman collar. Well, maybe once or twice after choir practice I did entertain a vision of myself as Father O'Malley crooning to that knockout of a nun, Ingrid Bergman, the way Bing Crosby did in *The Bells of St. Mary's*. That this beguiling fantasy remains imprinted in my memory surely reveals more about the kind of life I was aching to live when I left St. Fidelis than the life I could have had by continuing on my way there.

All in the Family Circle

A Father of Six Ponders Gay Marriage

The word *wedlock* does not sound as romantic as *marriage* or *matrimony*, perhaps because the suffix—*lock*—vaguely suggests being put in irons. But according to my dictionary, the *lock* in *locksmith* is an altogether different word than *lock* in *wedlock*, where it is an offering or gift, quite like a dowry to seal a deal—a *wed*, which means a *pledge*. So etymologically considered, *wedlock* ought to be as tender sounding a word as *matrimony*. But I don't think that *wedlock* evokes a sense of the sacred the way that *matrimony* does, especially when conjoined with *holy*, as in *holy matrimony*.

My wife and I, both Roman Catholic, were married—were united in holy matrimony—in 1958. A sense of transcending grace touched us then and continued to touch us, however lightly at times, through weal and our small shares of woe till death parted us after forty-seven years. That was nine years ago.

Today I remember a conversation I had long before then, back in the '90s, with my son Paul about marriage. Gay marriage was only a distant possibility back then, and it seemed to me, I told Paul, that in the interest of clarity there ought to be different words for marriages that unite two men or two women instead of the traditional man and woman. There might be less opposition to gay marriages, I pointed out, if they were labeled as such: all the same marriage rights included, but called something else—civil unions, for example. "So we wouldn't call them married," Paul responded, "just 'civilated' or maybe 'unionized,' but definitely not 'married.'" Paul, who is gay, then said that no matter what words we coined for same-sex marriages, such coinages would for years and years connote a different, second-class sort of marriage, not the all-out loving commitment to which getting married bears witness, and that's what most gay couples yearn for.

Great changes have come about in the few years since Paul and I had that conversation. James, the younger of my two gay children, and his partner married in San Francisco during a window of legal opportunity, June 16 to November 24 in 2008, and then flew back to their home in Brooklyn. The wedding reception we had at a nearby restaurant for family and friends was notable only in being absolutely unremarkable. So five of my six children are married now.

We were all together again in May 2011. The children came from as far away as Paris and Los Angeles to celebrate their mother's life on the fifth anniversary of her death. Prior to an evening mass and dinner at a restaurant we, the children and their spouses and the grandchildren, gathered at Union Cemetery in Hackettstown, New Jersey, a stone's throw from the house on Schooley's Mountain where the children grew up. The sky was overcast and there had been heavy showers off and on. But we were prepared with eighteen umbrellas for the eighteen of us, ready to unfurl them. And it looked like we'd have to do that, as the sky darkened ominously while we joined hands.

Then just as we completed a circle and were about to begin the little ceremony we had prepared, the sun shot out as if on cue and shone on us while we said our prayers, exchanged our anecdotes, and read Mary's favorite poems. Then a thunderclap announced a drenching rain, but we were all back in our cars by then. At the restaurant, later, we all marveled at how the sun had appeared as if by magic and stayed the rain until we had concluded our celebration.

On June 24th, a month after that celebration, New York became the sixth state to recognize gay marriages. Opposition on religious grounds was intense, and deeply felt emotions surfaced with the result that some of the arguments seemed less than carefully reasoned. One of them strikes me as especially vacuous: that gay marriages would cheapen traditional marriages. I don't see how my James's marriage can have any negative impact on my other children's marriages: on Mike's, or John's, or Mary Frances's, or Ann's.

All of us have probably said things in anger that we have later come to regret. Such may be the case, I imagine, with the bishop who instructed all pastors in the Brooklyn Diocese "to not invite any state legislator who voted for gay marriage to speak or be present at any parish or school celebration." That announcement took me aback: if voting for gay marriage is bad, then entering into a gay marriage is surely worse. An inescapable implication here, I think, is that anyone in a gay marriage must be shunned.

What would have absolutely diminished—desecrated—our long marriage, Mary's and mine, would have been for any of our children to have refused to join hands with others of our children or their spouses in our family circle on that wonderful day when the sun shone down on us all.

Seeing Isn't Believing

I am trying to retrieve a memory of my earliest experience with water. What comes immediately to mind is not my own experience, but Helen Keller's when water from a pump in the yard washed over her hands, her first step toward uniting herself with the world of sight and sound. My next watery memory is of a baptism, but not my own. I have no recollection of the cup or so of water spilling over my own infant head since I wasn't quite one yet at the time. The baptism that I speak of is a total immersion witnessed by William Jennings Bryan when he was six.

The experience was terrifying, Bryan later said, leaving him with a fear of water so great that it led him to give up his goal of becoming a Baptist preacher. He became a lawyer instead, and served as a member of the prosecution at the Scopes trial in Tennessee in 1925. Yes, that's the famous Monkey Trial where John Scopes was found guilty of the crime of teaching Darwinian evolution in a high school biology class. Bryan, a staunch defender of such fundamentalist religious orthodoxies as the belief that the world is only six thousand years old, was renowned for his oft-quoted observation that he was "more interested in the hymn 'Rock of Ages' than in the age of rocks."

Water—along with rock and William Jennings Bryan—has been on my mind. One of the things I did on a trip to Kansas in 2009 was to join my brothers in a visit to the new Sternberg Museum in Hays. This really fine collection of fossils from millions of years ago made quite an impression on me.

It's hard to believe that the bone-dry plains of my earliest memories were once filled to the brim with water. Wooden posts were hard to come by on the treeless prairie, so farmers used stone posts to support the barbed wire fences that enclosed their herds of cattle. Quarrying and setting these posts was extremely heavy work. They were typically quarried from a layer of limestone about a foot wide that one can see where the earth is exposed at the edges of gullies or at the banks of the Smoky Hill River. The posts on our farm were set over a hundred years ago. I was about to say they would last forever, when fact intruded on fancy, the particular fact here being the visible imprints of fish on the posts that testify to their impermanence. These hard posts were once mushy sediment into which dying fish sank, back when the Great Plains area was a great ocean.

These fishy stone posts lead me to wonder why it happens sometimes that seeing is not believing. Stone posts are seen everywhere in northwestern Kansas. You can't really leave your house without seeing these testimonies to a lengthy underwater era, so you'd think that no one in this part of the United States would take seriously the idea that the earth is only six thousand years old. Almost a century has passed since the Scopes trial, but that was in Tennessee, where there may not be any stone posts. Still, stone posts notwithstanding, from time to time a State Board of Education in Kansas decrees against the teaching of evolution in Kansas schools. And then, I hasten to add, the board is voted out of office and the ban is lifted.

"Who you gonna believe, me or your lying eyes?" This quotation, attributed to, among others, Richard Pryor and Chico Marx, seems apt here.

Stone posts figure in my memory in other ways too. I remember once, perhaps I was about eleven or twelve, when we—Dad, Virgil, and I—had just finished the annual spring chore of checking the fence enclosing our pasture. The fence consisted of three strands of barbed wire attached to the stone posts that Dad and his brothers had quarried years earlier from a limestone deposit on Grandfather's farm.

Loose wire had to be reattached to the stone posts and stretched taut. Sagging posts had to be reset upright. In short, the fence needed to be in good repair, not simply to make good neighbors of us, but to keep our cows from wandering into our own neighboring field to feast on the young green sorghum plants there. When mature, sorghum, which is a tall grass but looks like corn plants, would provide our cows with food all winter. But when still in the early growing stage, the young plants contain hydrogen cyanide and are deadly poisonous to cows, who did once break through a poorly mended section of fencing, and we all remember the grief of running, frantically hurrying and shouting our cows off the green sorghum field and back into the pasture. We left behind the two that had broken out first. Little Sonia and Die Weissohr (White Ear) lay there, swollen-bellied. Our frustrated collie kept running from one to the other, still trying to bark them back onto their feet.

So mending fences was a task we took very seriously. We were at the far corner now, half a mile from home, our job completed: every strand of wire tight and secured to a post. Dad didn't get on the tractor, or in the wagon either, for a ride back to the house and supper. Without saying anything, he started to walk. Our wagon had wooden wheels girded with iron hoops, so the ride over our rock-strewn pasture was very bumpy. Riding in it, you got jolted around. After Dad had walked out of earshot, Virgil told me about the accident Dad had years ago, five months before I was born. The internal injuries he suffered still pained him if he was jolted around. I'd probably heard about Dad's accident before then, but without its registering in my memory. I do not remember hearing much about it later on from anyone else, either. Dad himself never talked about it with me, probably because he grew tired of repeating it to my older siblings.

Baseball, Boxing, Opera, Whatever

I never attended any great athletic events. I did go to a baseball game between the Philadelphia Athletics and the New York Giants one time, but it was a mid-season, ordinary affair, and I don't even remember who won. That was in 1954 at the Polo Grounds, the multipurpose stadium near Harlem that has long since been resurfaced as a complex of apartment houses. I never made it at all to Ebbetts Field or Shea Stadium or Yankee Stadium or any of the new arenas that have replaced them.

But, no, I do not have a snooty disdain for popular sports, which is so often misattributed to academic types like me. To prove that the baseball versus opera duality does not apply to me, I need only point out that I have not frequented the Metropolitan Opera House either, having gone to an opera only twice in my life. And once is how often I went to the ballet. So the score on opera versus baseball is a tie—a very low-scoring tie.

So what have I been doing all these years in the very shadow of big-time ballparks and renowned opera houses, but so rarely inside them? For much of my life I toiled in the groves of academe, presenting literature—poems, plays, and novels—to students, who then wrote papers about them. It was my task to comment on, evaluate, and return these papers. So grading papers was what I mostly did over the years. Sunday afternoons, while Phil Simms was throwing footballs to Mark Bavaro in Giants' Stadium, I was grading papers. But every now and then I would look up from a paper I was grading, and to clear my head, I would turn on the radio.

The radio—that's where sports and opera converged. Two memories intertwine. The first is of listening to opera at Saint Fidelis Seminary. Bill Schroeder and I, both of us upperclassmen now in 1946, could use the senior lounge on Saturday afternoons where in winter and early spring we listened a few times to the Texaco-sponsored live broadcasts from the Metropolitan Opera House in New York City.

The other radio-prompted memory is of an even earlier time— all the way back to the farm when we got our first Philco in 1935. We enjoyed listening to boxing matches, and when title fights were broadcast, a couple of uncles and aunts sometimes joined us around the radio. The sports pages of the *Hays Daily News* carried pictures of the fighters, so we could visualize them as we listened to the announcer's blow-by-blow description. So all these years later, these fighters go around and around in my memory, like towels and socks and T-shirts churning in a clothes dryer. Max Baer, James Braddock, and Max Schmeling are a jumble of boxers tumbling around. Tommy Farr, Billy Conn, and Tony Galento are entangled there too. I am sorting them all out now, and yes, Joe Louis is separate, alone. Joe Louis, the Brown Bomber, was our hero. When we played boxing, Virgil and I, one or the other of us always got to be Joe Louis, and got to knock out whoever was playing the role of the "bum of the month."

If you want, you can watch the Joe Louis fights on the Internet, as well as many of the other fights from the past. I think I'll go watch the "long count" fight between Jack Dempsey and Gene Tunney. Or maybe listen to some Mozart. Or just take a nice nap, since I don't have to grade any papers this day.

Slow, Slow, Quick, Quick

There is a picture of me trying to dance with Mary, my bride, at our wedding on August 16, 1958. We were married in St. Gregory the Great Church in Bellerose, New York, and at least a dozen of Mary's students attended. They pooled their resources to buy us a set of impossibly delicate glasses, truly an extravagance in that era. Half a century later, most of those glasses have been broken, yet the few that remain bear witness to this day to Mary's enormous popularity as a teacher.

In this photo of me dancing with my bride, I appear to be immobile—emphatically stationary—as if my shoes were nailed to the floor. I was, at the time, a couple of months shy of thirty, and by the time I limbered up a bit, I was pushing eighty. Mary was an excellent dancer and she tried to teach me a couple of times, but for a variety of reasons that don't make any sense, I was unable to learn. She did not press the issue since, in our forty-seven years together, the matter came up so seldom—only at the handful of weddings we attended. At these, I simply shuffled in whatever direction Mary was guiding me. When the obligatory minutes were up, she would accept someone else's invitation to dance, whereupon I would remove myself to the sidelines, where I alternated between dual roles of wallflower and barfly.

My inability to dance seldom troubled me—only during those wedding dances, in fact. These being few and far between, my dancing problem seemed trifling in comparison with other personal failings—like being unable to pronounce the French phrases that the authors I taught were so fond of sprinkling throughout the prose they wrote.

It turned out that some writers, notably African-Americans, gave me a rationale for stubbornly remaining invincible against instruction in dancing. The fault, these writers implied, lay not in my will, but in my genes. Let me explain. After the Supreme Court ruled in 1967 that the laws against interracial marriage were unconstitutional, Dick Gregory, a black stand-up comic, told an audience that in a few hundred years there will no longer be any racial tensions in America. "We will all just be a little darker—and dance a little better," he opined. But the time when evolution would make dancing easy and natural to all, even me, lay in the very distant future, according to Gregory's prediction. For me, in the here and now, klutziness on the dance floor was my natural state, my default position, as it were. No use to try to budge me from it.

As if to confirm my rigidity, I came across Zora Neale Hurston's description of her dancing. It's in her essay, "How It Feels to Be Colored Me." She describes "walking into a cabaret in Harlem, with a white person. . . . A jazz orchestra plunges into a number . . . I dance wildly; I yell within, I whoop; I shake my assagei above my head, yeeeeooww!" and in this manner Zora dances on for several passages, immersed entirely in the music. Then the music ends and "I creep back slowly to the veneer we call civilization with the last tone and find the white friend sitting motionless in his seat, smoking calmly. 'Good music they have here,' he remarks, drumming the table with his fingertips."

I already knew that in basketball, white men can't jump, and that served as rationalization for my not being able to dunk a basketball. Hurston's experience verified the same excuse for not being able to dance. It just wasn't in my nature. Now I don't mean that I literally believed these strict, racial explanations. They were only fleeting thoughts—comical ways of viewing my dancing disability (and my basketball shortcoming). In reality, I knew better, of course. I did watch Gene Kelly in *Singin' in the Rain* every chance I got. So I did not confuse amusing fictions with actuality. But the belief that I was absolutely incapable of dancing—that was real.

And it remained real until I was about to celebrate my eightieth birthday. A friend e-mailed me a clip of Fred Astaire and Eleanor Powell, along with a note that it's never too late to learn. No, I am not confusing Eleanor Powell with Ginger Rogers. Frank Sinatra comments on Fred and Eleanor's dancing; the song is "Begin the Beguine" and what a joy it is to watch!

A few days later I saw an ad for dancing lessons at a nearby Fred Astaire studio. I went for some lessons and persuaded myself that I actually could learn to foxtrot and waltz—that the only thing that had kept me from learning was the fear that I could not learn. But it also became true that I could not learn at this particular studio. They played the same music even though different students might be learning different dances. For example, on my third and final lesson my instructor was teaching me the waltz but the music being played was a cha cha, which another couple was practicing on the spacious floor. So a friend, Pat Salvesen, and I joined a few other couples for lessons with a professional dancing instructor, Fred Meyer, who charged a mere six dollars per person for a two-hour session. With this instruction and encouragement under my belt, I got up at a New Year's Eve party and danced with Pat and the other women at our table, and what fun it was! But I'm not sure that I should go to the gym tomorrow at the Pascack Senior Center and see if I can finally dunk a basketball.

Why I Am Not Running for President

I am Loren Schmidtberger. I am a natural-born American citizen, originally from Kansas, as was Stanley Ann Dunham, President Obama's mother. I am now a legal resident of Clarkstown, in Rockland County, New York, and I am here to tell you that I have decided not to run for president of the United States in the 2016 election, or any election after that either.

Now you may suppose that my reason for not throwing my hat into the ring is my age. Not so. I am only eighty-six, and Sophocles was in his nineties when he wrote *Oedipus at Colonus*; Senator Robert Byrd was eighty-nine when he was elected to his last term in office. Similarly speaking, Harold Stassen was eighty-five in his last run for the presidency and Ralph Nader may well continue his pursuit of that high office, even after he has turned 102. So age is not the problem.

But what *is* the problem, then? After giving the matter the careful consideration it deserves, I have decided not to run because of difficulties with my birth certificate. Oh, I have one—finally—a delayed birth certificate it is called—and I will release it shortly. Perhaps.

Until I was in my early twenties, though, I had no birth certificate at all. I was in the Army when this personal deficiency first came to my attention. I was in Officer Candidate School at Fort Bliss, Texas, in 1952 when I learned that one of the documents I needed in order to become an officer in the United States Army was a birth certificate. So I wrote to the courthouse in Ellis County, Kansas, requesting my birth certificate.

I received in reply a letter from Isadore Schmidt, informing me that he had forwarded my request to the Office of Vital Statistics in Topeka, and that no certification of my birth was to be found. Underneath the typed note was his handwritten one: "Nothing to worry about, Loren." What I should do, he advised, is supply two documents attesting to my birth, which would enable him to obtain a delayed birth certificate for me. He would supply one of the documents himself, that is, my inclusion in the 1930 census. For the other document, he suggested my baptismal certificate. Once he had that in hand, he would get me a delayed birth certificate. Isadore, or Izzie, as we called him, was a first cousin and was willing to extend himself, always, to help a relative.

St. Boniface Church sent me a copy of my baptismal certificate right after I requested it. Unfortunately, it incorrectly gave my first name as Lawrence. The priest who baptized me may have been hard of hearing or opposed to shortened forms of saints' names—who knows. I sent it to Izzie, who phoned my mother. My sister Alvina was living at home then, so the two of them came to the courthouse two blocks away in Hays. Izzie had them sign an affidavit testifying that Loren was, in fact, the same fellow as the one named Lawrence in the baptismal certificate. So that took care of one document. With the arrival of proof of my inclusion in the 1930 census—the second document—Izzie assured us that my delayed birth certificate would come through in no time at all.

It came through—or, rather it began to come through—almost exactly a year later. A form that represented the final stage in obtaining a delayed birth certificate arrived at headquarters of the 53rd AAA Brigade in Swarthmore, Pennsylvania, where I was already completing my first year as a commissioned officer. Apparently, the requirement of a birth certificate for becoming an officer could be satisfied retroactively. The form listed my full name (correctly), date and place of birth, race, sex, and each parent's place of birth (Russia) for good measure. It called for my signature and the signature of a notary, who in this instance was the adjutant officer of the Intelligence Unit of the brigade. I signed where indicated—thereby swearing an oath to the accuracy of the information therein—and after Col. Loos affixed his seal and signature, I mailed it off to the Office of Vital Statistics in Topeka, Kansas.

When I was discharged from the Army nine months later, waiting for me at home was my delayed birth certificate. "It came just a few days ago," my mother said. "Better late than never," I thought, and filed it along with my discharge papers. In the few times subsequently that I have had to produce the certificate, I gave it only a cursory look, and never gave the manner in which it came into being much thought either until these many years later when questions surfaced about the authenticity of President Obama's birth certificate. I pulled up a copy of *his* certificate on my computer, and after seeing how unremarkable it is, I wondered how acceptable my own birth certificate would be. I dug it out and looked it over—carefully, for once. The upper half is simply a photocopy of the certification of birth that Colonel Loos and I signed in 1953, a solid twenty-five years after my birth. "Not good," I thought. It looks as if I, rather than a doctor or a midwife or a parent, was the chief testifier to the facts of my own birth, the other testimony coming from a colonel then serving in Military Intelligence. Not good.

I looked at the bottom half of my delayed certificate of birth, titled "Abstract of Supporting Evidence." There it is, all of it—the name changing, the alteration of official records, the photocopies of photocopies. Not good at all, I thought.

I am by temperament indecisive, but as I slid my delayed birth certificate back into its folder, I decided there and then, never, ever to run for president of the United States.

Blackberries

I am hoping to resolve a family argument. The matter at issue is trivial. And the argument never became overheated, but it has certainly been long-lasting. It's about blackberries. No, not the electronic kind. The edible kind.

Blackberries, or *schwarzbeere*, as we Volga Germans called them, were the principal ingredient in *maultashen*, pastries that looked like Italian ravioli or Jewish kreplach or Chinese wantons, and were filled with *schwarzbeere*. No one quarreled about the taste of *schwarzbeere maultashen*; one and all found them delicious. But inevitably there would surface the theory, usually voiced in munch-muted German, but sometimes in English too, that these mouthwatering berries were not really blackberries at all.

"*Schwarzbeere*," Uncle Bunny would intone, "Real *schwarzbeere* look like mulberries—just a little bigger." Nodding in agreement, his brother, Uncle George, would stop chewing to explain that the berries squishing in our palates were smaller than mulberries and were actually blueberries. "*Blaubeere*," he would insist, swallowing for emphasis.

Whereupon one of my cousins, not shy about combating the opinions of his elders, would point out that blueberries looked like, well, blueberries, which these berries before us definitely did not. And on and on it went, long after Uncle Bunny opened another bottle of beer, and long after stout Aunt Maggie, sliding her fork carefully under the last of the *maultashen* on the serving tray, had proclaimed, unaware, I am sure, of the Shakespearean overtones, that *schwarzbeere* by any other name are *schwarzbeere* still, and taste the same.

That was seventy-five, maybe eighty years ago. Seated at my computer earlier today, I doubted that modern technology would shed much light on the nomenclature for the berries in a long-forgotten pastry indigenous, I thought, to an isolated Volga German community in Ellis County, Kansas. But I turned on my computer anyway, and while waiting for it to boot up, remembered again those voices from so long ago. I heard multi-talented Uncle Bunny, who sang and played polkas on his accordion with such zest and joy until he succumbed at last to alcohol. I heard Uncle George, hardworking and so mechanically gifted he could fix anything, and did too, until he dropped dead on a street in Wichita of a heart attack. I heard the booming laugh of big-bodied Aunt Maggie, who staved off ailments, grave and mild alike, until she passed her goal of 100, and then passed away peacefully and content.

Then my computer screen lit up. Not really hoping for anything at all, I typed "schwarzbeere Volga German" into a search engine. *Sogger dis!* I couldn't believe it! Seven hits. Okay, only six, because one of the seven was actually for Arnold Schwarzenegger. But each hit led to other hits. There drifted down the screen page after page of information about Volga Germans, recipes for *maultaschen* and theories about what kind of a berry it actually is that the Volga Germans called *schwarzbeere*. I read several explanations that were scholarly and lengthy, but the answer to the question of what exactly to call the berry that went into the making of our *schwarzbeere maultashen* remained elusive. Here is just one brief excerpt from a three and one-half page explanation of what Volga Germans are talking about when they talk about blackberries.

"When we speak of 'blackberries' in North America," this expert begins, "we may be speaking of two different species. . . . To English-speaking Americans, 'blackberries' are the fruits of a bramble . . . of the genus Rubus. In the same subgenus are loganberries, marionberries, dewberries, boysenberries, and youngberries. . . . Now let's consider the other blackberry that Americans of Volga German descent may talk about, the Solanum nigrum. The most common Volga German name for Solanum nigrum is Schwartzbeere." Our expert, at the end of his three and one-half page treatise on the proper word for the berry in *schwarzebeere maultashen* concluded that, "In short, there is no simple answer."

Smoke Detectors on the Debt Ceiling

I feel a certain sense of empathy for President Obama because we share a particular experience: we both quit smoking. To be sure, he dithered about it, taking forever. But I won't cast stones because I took even longer. Still, putting aside the question of who quit faster, I think our shared experience lends me some potential insight into the president's occasional timidity vis-à-vis the Republicans—timidity that is so disappointing to Obama's supporters, including myself. I am thinking, in particular, of Obama's lackluster negotiations with the Republicans when it came to negotiating the debt ceiling. To explore this thesis, I must ask the reader to travel with me back to my high school years at St. Fidelis.

Students over sixteen who had their parents' permission could smoke a pipe during leisure time after supper. Enticed by the fragrance of Sir Walter Raleigh Rum 'n' Maple tobacco smoke, I joined the circle of pipe-smokers. During vacations, my smoking began to include cigarettes. Then, as Easter approached one year, I realized something unsettling about my smoking: I couldn't bring myself to give it up for Lent the way almost everyone else did. I found it difficult to admit that I couldn't quit smoking, so I resolved the problem by denying it. "I can quit any time I want," I told people.

In 1964, the surgeon general published the report that would finally catalog, in stark detail, the catastrophic harm smoking inflicted. By that point, I was teaching full-time in a college in New Jersey, four of my six children had been born, and I was frantically trying to write my PhD dissertation. Needless to say, I still smoked. Heavily.

Still, in light of the surgeon general's report, I decided to quit. But things didn't go well. Instead of giving up cigarettes, I developed a cat burglar's skill at sneaking smokes. I didn't enjoy this clandestine addiction, so I sought the help of various concoctions to ease me through withdrawal. Nicotine-laced gum did not help, nor did patches, and hypnotism was a complete waste of time. In fact, on my way home from my last session of hypnosis, I walked into a 7-Eleven for a pack of gum, but walked out with a pack of Camels. To be sure, I threw the pack away after smoking one cigarette, but a few hours later, I went to a different store and bought another pack. My hypnotist had successfully instilled in me the command to throw away my cigarettes, but not the command to stop buying them, a recipe for financial ruin.

I didn't quit—cold turkey—until 1989. And when I quit, I didn't rely on patches or pills. Instead, my wife's heart faltered, badly, and the doctor told us she needed a quadruple bypass. When she was wheeled into surgery in Lenox Hill Hospital, we were both, technically speaking, still smokers. When she was wheeled out and finally—miraculously—opened her eyes again, we were officially nonsmokers. For me to have waved temptation in front of her by continuing to smoke would have been a form of assisted suicide.

It has now been twenty-five years since my last cigarette. But even after all these years, I can vividly recall how, during those first smoke-free months, I suffered panic attacks the likes of which I can no way describe.

While these intermittent bouts of panic did not leave me completely incapacitated, they did diminish my ability to carry out ordinary responsibilities. Fortunately, my responsibilities were relatively light during that period. True, I spent a lot of time filling out financial-aid forms for my coterie of college-aged children, but at my own college, everything was smooth sailing. By that point, I was a senior member of the faculty (which, in plain English, translates as an "old fart"), so when I strode up to the lectern to face my students, their expectations of lucidity were not high. In short, I got through the agony of cigarette withdrawal relatively unscathed, emerging as a bone fide nonsmoker at last.

Now to get back to President Obama: his circumstances while kicking the habit were vastly different from my own. I dealt with lectures and student loan applications, all set against the joyful backdrop of my wife's return to health. The president, on the other hand, faced our country's deficits, foreclosures, and joblessness. He dealt with earthquakes, floods, and famine. He presided over a bitterly divided nation. And he inherited a courageous military mired in two endless wars not of his own making. Yet President Obama managed to remain calm, cool, collected; in control; on top of it all, publicly laughing off lunacies like the birther blather while privately ordering the end of Osama Bin Laden in a covert operation. That daring raid succeeded, and even the president's detractors were forced to concede—glumly, minimally, and ever so briefly—that Barack Obama had guts.

So why, it is now asked over and over by friend and foe alike, why did this man with nerves of steel suddenly cave in when it came to the showdown over the debt ceiling? When the Republicans still refused to raise the debt ceiling after obtaining just about every concession under the sun, why didn't President Obama invoke the Fourteenth Amendment and raise the ceiling himself? What exactly happened during these negotiations?

I have a sneaking suspicion. Back when I was in the first critical months of giving up smoking, sitting close to someone enjoying a cigarette used to set off panic attacks. Unless I was able to leave the room, I would eventually put an end to my sense of delirium—the conviction that I was being tortured—by bumming one from the smoker.

Now consider this: When we saw the president and his advisors watching the mission to capture or kill Osama Bin Laden, did you notice that no one in that tension-filled room was smoking? Not a curl of smoke appears in that now iconic photo.

I don't know if there are any pictures of the president and former Speaker John Boehner alone together during their private negotiations, but we do know that Boehner was a two-pack-a-day smoker. So here is what I think: I think that a crescendo of craving routed our iron-willed president. He begged Boehner for a cigarette. They may have even made a joke of it, something like, "My kingdom for a Camel." But—wily negotiator that the Speaker is—he dangled the cigarette for the president to see, but withheld it until the president promised not to invoke the Fourteenth Amendment—ever.

Yes, I think it went something like that.

Celebrating Memorial Day

Memorial Day came yesterday, and with it memory of two very different pictures—one that is profoundly sad, and another that couldn't be happier.

The first, of course, is the dreadful events of September 11, 2001, and the loss of life that day and in the two wars that followed. My oldest son actually worked in one of the Twin Towers. On that fateful day, though, he was still on his way to work, not already at work, when the first plane hit. That's when my daughter Ann, home with two small children in New Jersey, telephoned to ask which tower Mike worked in. I didn't remember, and she told me to turn on my television. Both of us thought we were watching an accident unfold until we saw the second plane hit and knew this was no accident. It wasn't very long—how long I just don't know—before Margie, Mike's wife, reached Ann by cell phone to let us all know that Mike was safe. What strikes me now is that I have no memory whatever of my thoughts between seeing the second plane hit and receiving Ann's relayed message that Mike was okay. Also unsettling is my lack of any memory at all of what my wife did during this time or, for that matter, what we did for the rest of the day. A coping mechanism, perhaps.

I prefer to let my thoughts wander back to the happy picture. It's the photo of a sailor giving a great big smooch to a nurse in Times Square on V-J Day, in 1945. I think he nearly sweeps the girl completely off her feet into his embrace. I'm not sure of that detail, but the picture absolutely captures the spontaneous, exuberant happiness we all felt on hearing the news that Japan had surrendered—that World War II was over with at last.

My little sister, Janice, and I were the only ones at home on the farm with our parents that August day. Both of our brothers were on active duty in the Pacific at the time, so it would be impossible to exaggerate the relief we felt at learning the war was over, and that Alvin and Virgil would be coming home—Alvin five years away by that point. I remember too a nagging sense of inadequacy at being unable to think of anything to say or to do that would truly register the depth of our joy that day.

Then five years later, the cold war heated up in Korea. Here in the United States, it was feared that the Russians would try to bomb American cities, so we encircled the major ones with anti-aircraft weaponry. When the war ended in 1953, I was stateside, a 2nd lieutenant with the 53rd Anti-Aircraft Artillery Brigade, whose guns encircled Philadelphia and Pittsburgh. I celebrated the war's end by buying a used car, thinking that I would be discharged soon and drive home to Kansas in it. I still have a picture of that '49 Studebaker Champion. It had a memorable design. From the front it looked a bit like an airplane fuselage.

I wonder if my buying a used car to celebrate the ending of the Korean War might have represented the beginning of a trend. Super-sales at car dealerships have certainly evolved into a Memorial Day tradition. Yesterday, Rockland Chrysler, Jeep, Dodge made the local Channel 7 news with its record-setting sales this weekend of, one supposes, Chryslers, Jeeps, and Dodges. Good news, that. To be sure, using Memorial Day weekend as a merchandising festival is offensive to some, but I am not one to add a voice in protest. Yes, I know—putting a deposit down on a new Buick is not the same as laying a flower on a grave, but visiting a car lot on the way back from a graveyard does not cheapen the earlier commemorative act either.

Rain

When I wake up on a rainy day, my first reaction is happiness. "You are either making this up," my friends tell me, "or maybe you should see a shrink." No, no, no. My skeptical friends are like the people who can't fully appreciate their warmth under covers because their heated bedrooms lack a contrasting cold.

An example of the intermingling of comfort and discomfort is offered by Herman Melville. In *Moby-Dick*, the narrator, Ishmael, snugly comfortable in bed on a cold winter night, explains that "to enjoy bodily warmth, some small part of you must be cold. If, lying under your blanket, the tip of your nose be slightly chilled, why then you feel most delightfully and unmistakably warm. For this reason, a sleeping apartment should never be furnished with a fire."

Living here in the Northeast where the rainfall is generally plentiful, and sometimes way, way too plentiful, my friends and neighbors have not experienced prolonged drought, so they cannot fathom the depth of longing I once had for rain. In short, to really enjoy rain one must have known rainlessness. I do not mean the occasional month or two here in the Hudson Valley when a water shortage is declared and lawn sprinklers are turned off. I mean the everlasting drought of my childhood. And if, perchance, you too have seen waves of heat shimmering across the vast parched plains and have felt the unending, relentless wind sweeping the sky clear of clouds day after day after day, then you too know the withering, helpless anxiety of rainlessness.

I was born in 1928, and "Maybe tomorrow" is among my earliest hopes. "Maybe tomorrow it will rain," I remember praying, my prayer endlessly unanswered as I turned four, then five, then six, then seven, during the years of drought that descended on the Great Plains and stayed there. Rain finally fell in 1936, in abundance, ending the drought and the dust storms that were its by-product. I remember those dust storms as happening mostly in the spring, the grand finale of them all happening on Black Sunday, April 14, 1935. Long before I read T. S. Eliot's famous line, I knew that "April is the cruelest month."

Rain does finally fall in "The Wasteland," Eliot's poem about spiritual drought, just as it eventually fell on our farm in Kansas. My memory's juxtaposition of poetry and prairie, of fancy and fact, evokes another memory of a supplication, one quite like my own childhood prayer for rain. It's a poem written way back in the thirteenth century.

> Western wind, when wilt thou blow
> [So that] the small rain down can rain.

This is how the poem begins. We know nothing about the circumstances that cause this person to wish for rain. Nor do we know the connection between the wish for rain, and the next, more ardently voiced yearning:

> Christ, if my love were in my arms
> And I in my bed again.

I sometimes included this poem—these four lines are all of it—in one of my courses, and students generally liked it, brevity, I suppose, being one of its attractive features. I don't remember anyone's being troubled by the lack of a connection between the anonymous author's desire for rain in the first two lines and then his yearning for hearth and home in the next two lines. But it was fun to imagine plausible contexts that would link together the hope for rain and the desire to embrace one's love in one's own bed.

There is no way of knowing if the western wind that the poem addresses ever did blow, as it eventually did in my real life's long-deferred answer to my childhood prayers. As for me, I don't walk around stoop-shouldered under the weight of worries about rain. Not at all. For over seventy years now, I have lived where water is abundant and soggy basements rather than dry fields are the worry of the day. My Dust Bowl memories lie in the unconscious recesses of my mind, inactive save for those mornings when I am roused into semi-consciousness by the strumming of raindrops on the roof overhead. I breathe deeply then and exhale a long, slow sigh of relief. The drought is over. It's *over*. It is raining now. All is well, and I stretch myself awake.

Part 9

Thoughts, Scattered and Otherwise, on Literature, Verve, and Verse

Ad Astra per Aspera [To the stars through difficulties]

—Kansas state motto

In Praise of Anne Bradstreet, 1612–72

When I was growing up, one of my morning chores was watering the chickens. This meant carrying three gallons of water from the well to a trough in the chicken house. I remember two things I learned from this. The first was that it is easier to carry two pails containing half the water in each than one pail with all three gallons in it. I think I figured this out for myself after lifting, or trying to lift, a three-gallon pail of water.

The other thing I learned was to stay behind the door to the chicken house as I pulled it open to let the chickens out in the morning. Dad cautioned me that by keeping the door as a shield between the chickens and me I wouldn't get knocked over as they came flying out, filling every space in the open doorway in their eager flight into the sunrise.

Once a week Dad took a bottle of Germazone and poured some of it into the water trough to keep the chickens healthy, the equivalent for them of my One A Day Multivitamin/Multimineral Supplement for Men. Chickens are prone to many ailments—a really amazing array of them in addition to chicken pox—and Dad believed that often as not, Germazone could restore the variously afflicted chickens to good health.

His treatments ranged from adding Germazone to the drinking water to stirring Germazone into various food combinations, to rubbing Germazone onto sores. Dad thought that Germazone was a good disinfectant, equal to, but less painful than, hydrogen peroxide, and much less painful than alcohol. His suggestion that we use Germazone as an alternative treatment for our own cuts and abrasions was roundly rejected by my older siblings. My oldest brother went so far as to maintain that Germazone didn't do any good, even to the chickens. "It's nothing more than snake oil," Alvin insisted. My parents usually presented a united front in confrontations with the children, but on this one Mom stayed out of the way. Her abstention apparently counted as a negative, and Germazone went untried on the humans in our household, and on chickens too after Dad retired and Alvin took over the running of our farm.

I gave the matter no thought over the years until I sat down recently and looked up Germazone on the Internet. I wanted to see if it had ever been officially declared worthless. In my research, I came upon instructions for its use for treating chicken pox: "Wash mouth and throat with vinegar and salt, a level teaspoonful in a cup of vinegar." This sounded like instructions for treating a *person* who has chicken pox until I read further and saw the proportions were for adding Germazone to a *trough* of water. The article was published in 1952.

Further research led me back in time to *Mrs. A. Basley's Western Poultry Book*, published in 1910. In it were letters to Mrs. Basley, seeking her help in ministering to sick chickens. I found these pleas for help to be touching mementos of an earlier era before agribusinesses replaced so many of our farms and when there were warm, personal relationships between farmers and the animals they raised. Here is one exchange:

Dear Mrs. Basley,

> Will you kindly tell me what ails my White Leghorn hen? She sits around most of the time and squawks and slings her head and when I hold my ear to her side I can hear a continual rattling. Her comb is red and she eats well. I feed corn, wheat, Kaffir corn and table scraps. They run on plenty of green range. Her nostrils are clean. Age 8 months.

Mrs. Basley replies,

> Your hen seems to have chronic bronchitis or is taking a cold frequently. See that she does not sleep in a draft nor in a house that is too tightly closed. Give her a teaspoonful of honey night and morning for a week and I think she will be well by then. A little red pepper and chopped onions in her food would also help the cure.

The tender loving care prescribed so long ago by Mrs. Basley in her book makes for a nice transition to an even earlier one, the very first book of poems published by an American author, *The Tenth Muse* by Anne Bradstreet, in 1650. One of her poems is a tribute to her children. In it she sees her home as a chicken house. It begins with this couplet:

> I had eight birds hatcht in one nest,
> Four cocks there were, and hens the rest.

The poem goes on to celebrate her four boys and four girls in a separate stanza for each one, and maintains the comparison of children and chickens throughout. I think it marvelous that Anne Bradstreet was able to write a book full of really good poems while raising eight children in very primitive circumstances, long before laundromats, microwaves, or even Germazone came on the scene.

As for our own farm, most of it is gone now. After Dad and Mom retired to a house they built in Hays, Alvin continued to live in the farmhouse alone until he married, then he and Celeste decided to make their home in Victoria. The farmhouse and yard stood on a quarter section that we rented, but thought of as our own, adjoining as it did a half section that we really did own. Alvin continued to farm this half section, but he decided to stop farming the quarter we rented, on which the farmhouse now stood empty. The owner found a new tenant and eventually sold the quarter section.

I saw the farm of my childhood for the last time in 2011. I was back in Kansas for a visit with my brothers. After Sunday mass in Victoria, the three of us and Virgil's son, Gary, had dinner. After dessert and coffee, and while Alvin was having his nap, Virgil and I decided to drive down to show Gary the farm where we had grown up. After a few miles, we passed St. Boniface Church, but by this time of day there were no parked cars and no clusters of people outside it. Then four miles farther south we passed the one-room school where Virgil and I had been the only students one year. But it was gone, as we knew it would be. We turned left, and after half a mile, went down through a gulch and up Der Gayla Barrich. Then half a mile farther on, our old house came into view. But that was all. Gone was everything else. Alvin had forgotten to tell us what the new owner had done. All gone were barn, corral, granary, garage, pigpen, tool shed, machine shed, cook house, henhouse—gone—vanished entirely. Just the house stood there, painted a light, pleasing lemon-yellow as it had always been. But where all the buildings had stood, now was a field of ripening green-gold wheat edged by a few wild sunflowers.

The Long and Short of It

Two obsessions come to mind—both from literature rather than real life. They are Captain Ahab's obsession with a white whale named *Moby-Dick* and Inspector Javert's obsession with Jean Valjean in *Les Miserables*.

Both books are very long. My copy of *Moby-Dick* checks in at 761 pages, and my English translation of *Les Miserables* is even longer. I first read *Les Miz* when I was a freshman at Hays Junior High. Mrs. Binder, the librarian at the municipal library, recommended it. She noticed that I had read all of the Tarzan books by Edgar Rice Burroughs and the westerns by Zane Grey, and now steered me to the stories of Edgar Allan Poe and to the five Leatherstocking Tales by James Fenimore Cooper. Sometime after *Les Miz* came *The Count of Monte Cristo* by Alexandre Dumas. I remember that while checking it out, Mrs. Binder explained what "abridged" meant.

I had plenty of time for reading that school year, 1941/42. This was before anyone had television. Virgil and I had no radio even, and my two-month obsession with a pinball machine at the Cozy Café still lay in the future. Remember too that after school ended at Hays Junior High, I did not have to help with milking the cows and all the other barnyard chores. In Hays, I went straight to the library and the encouragement of Mrs. Binder.

It was at Saint Fidelis that I first read *Moby-Dick*. Not assigned in any class, the novel was recommended by Phil DeCarlo, who generally wasn't that much of a reader, but he raved about *Moby-Dick* to us, his fellow sophomores. "It starts out slow and easy," Phil said, "but then suspense builds and builds until you can't stand it and the final chapters just explode!" I haven't heard a better review since then.

When I began teaching in 1955, long novels were still a common assignment in colleges. A few weeks ago, I came across a reading list for my fall 1956, one-semester course called The Novel. It has eight novels on it, including *Moby-Dick*. (The others were Theodore Dreiser, *Sister Carrie*; Henry Fielding, *Joseph Andrews*;

Fyodor Dostoyevsky, *Crime and Punishment*; Nathaniel Hawthorne, *The Scarlet Letter*; Ernest Hemingway, *The Sun Also Rises*; William Faulkner, *The Sound and the Fury*; and Jane Austen, *Pride and Prejudice*.) Inexpensive paperbacks were becoming available, so students did not have to spend a mint on books. CliffsNotes weren't around yet, so there weren't any time-conserving alternatives to reading these time-consuming novels.

How times have changed! By 2005, when I retired, my list of novels had shrunk to three or four, supplemented by twenty or so short stories. I'm not sure what to make of that, if anything. I don't think that students' minds slowly dimmed as the twentieth century receded into the twenty-first, though their attention spans certainly did seem to shorten. But that may be because they are busier nowadays, occupied and preoccupied in ways I was not, and so, between their taskings they have less leisure for savoring a sentence by Herman Melville.

Lord, keep me from turning into an old grouch, obsessed with the shortcomings of the young. I once planned to reread *Les Miz*, in an unabridged version this time, but the copy I bought for that purpose has long since disappeared from my bookshelves. I still own a heavily dog-eared copy of *Moby-Dick*, a relic from my earlier years of teaching, and may give it another rereading on a plane sometime—unless I decide to give *War and Peace* a long-deferred *first* reading instead. I've owned an abridged translation—unread—for years. *War and Peace*, you see, is one of those novels that English professors are assumed to have read, and I have slithered my way through fifty-one years in the profession with this singular deficiency of mine unnoticed all the while. By nodding thoughtfully when other professors opined about *War and Peace*, by smiling or frowning in timely fashion, I not only let my deficiency go undetected, but I acquired a modest reputation as a perceptive reader too.

Yes, I think I'll give *War and Peace* a try, now that I have the inclination as well as the time. I'd better do that before one of my grandchildren gives me a gift of one of those new phones or pads that I see them fiddling with the whole day through.

"I Could Not See to See"

My eyes—mine eyes—"Mine eyes have seen the glory of the coming of the Lord!" But banish the thought, the song. Today is a quiet, easy, late summer morning here in my study. It's not the right time for anything so rousing, so spine-straightening as "The Battle Hymn of the Republic." So let me back up and start over.

My eyes—my eyes—my mind's eye. I see a line in a poem. "I could not see to see," it says. That line—"I could not see to see"—kept running through my mind when I was in Kansas, visiting Alvin in October 2012 when he was dying at Hays Medical Center. It still runs through my mind every now and then, obviously, as it did just now.

"I could not see to see" is the last line of a poem that begins, "I heard a Fly buzz—when I died"—an attention-grabber of a line, to be sure. The poem is by Emily Dickinson, one of her many poems about death. In this one, she imagines herself to be the person doing the dying. She notices that the people around her bedside appear to have just finished some heavy crying. They are quiet now, but are gathering their breath to cry up a storm when death arrives. In preparation for the awesome event, she recites her will, naming the people to whom she is leaving her possessions. That done, she feels ready for the arrival of death, expecting it to be a great dramatic event, something grand like witnessing "the glory of the coming of the Lord." But then a bluebottle fly interposes—one of those big, blue-green flies, larger than a common housefly.

> With Blue—uncertain—stumbling Buzz—
> [she explains]
> Between the light—and me—
> And then the Windows failed—and then
> I could not see to see—

An older student, a nurse, once explained to me in discussing this poem, that in the process of dying, the sense of hearing is the last to go, so that after this dying person's eyesight failed, she could still hear the fly buzz, but was unable to see so as to *see*—to *comprehend*—the devastating disappointment at hearing a fly buzz as her final, conscious experience.

Was Emily Dickinson's interest in death excessive or morbid? I don't think so. Her bedroom windows overlooked a graveyard, which was frequently in use. Also, people died in their homes back then, so deathbed watching was a more widely shared experience than today.

Does having this poem circulating in my memory indicate that I have an excessive attraction to the morbid? No, I don't think so. My brother Alvin was blind from macular degeneration, so it would have been surprising for me *not* to think of the line, "I could not see to see," when I last saw Alvin.

In case you are dying now to read the entire poem, here it is.

> I heard a Fly buzz—when I died—
> The Stillness in the Room
> Was like the Stillness in the Air—
> Between the Heaves of Storm—
>
>
> The Eyes around—had wrung them dry—
> And Breaths were gathering firm
> For that last Onset—when the King
> Be witnessed—in the Room—
>
>
> I willed my Keepsakes—Signed away
> What portions of me be
> Assignable—and then it was
> There interposed a Fly—
>
>
> With Blue—uncertain—stumbling Buzz—
> Between the light—and me—
> And then the Windows failed—and then
> I could not see to see—

"Honey, It's Time to Leave"

Returning from Oakland, California, I looked at the rain gauge I keep near the front door and saw that it had rained three inches while I was away. I'd been out to California to visit Janice, my sole surviving sibling, and godmother to my youngest son, James.

Those three inches of rain led my thoughts on a rather oblique path to a recent, and merry, gathering in my friend Joan Gussow's living room where a bunch of us searched through her huge dictionary for the etymology of the word "gossip." We did so to settle a dispute: some of us cited certain folk etymologies, whereas I thought that the word "gossip," as a noun, simply meant "woman."

Joan's dictionary verified my position, and gave the additional information that "gossip" is a shortened form of "god's sibling," that is, the person we refer to at a baptism nowadays as the godmother or godfather. In the same way that "sibling" is frequently shortened to "sib" in modern usage, "god sibling" in the Middle Ages shortened into "god sib" and then elided from "god sib" to "gaw sib" to "gossip," while losing its religious meaning entirely. By Shakespeare's time, a gossip was simply a woman or a close relative or friend.

But my own introduction to "gossip" as a word for woman came via Nathaniel Hawthorne's wonderful novel, *The Scarlet Letter*. In an early chapter, a man chides a group of women for their harsh condemnation of the heroine, the gorgeous and illicitly pregnant Hester Prynne. "Hush now, gossips," the man remonstrates.

My recalling this passage constitutes no great feat of memory: in my fifty-one years of teaching, I presented *The Scarlet Letter* at least a hundred times, each time calling attention to the note at the bottom of the page that explained that "gossip" in Puritan times simply meant "woman." As for the verb form, "to gossip" is to engage in the small talk characteristic of groups of women—according to men, that is. Over the years gossiping took on the connotation of being unworthy, of sounding a bit nasty, like, well, gossiping.

But what does all that have to do with three inches of water in my rain gauge, one may wonder? Bear with me, please. In those fifty-one years of teaching literature, I did sometimes venture outside *The Scarlet Letter*. Occasionally I tried to explain how drama got started in England. Toward the end of the Middle Ages—1300 to 1500—guilds would put on little plays depicting events from the Bible: the story of Cain and Abel, of Abraham and Isaac, and the like. A guild would often select a thematically appropriate episode. The boatwrights' guild, for example, would choose the story of Noah and the flood. To make it more interesting, they added, for comic effect, materials not in the Bible at all.

In the Noah play, when the ark is finished, the animals are all on board and rain is beginning to fall, Noah's wife refuses—would you believe it? Just like a woman, she refuses to leave her circle of gossips, with whom she is drinking and yakking. Poor Noah is beside himself. "I am aghast for fear of drowning," Noah yells at her, tugging her arm. But she slaps him away with a stick. (An early instance of slapstick comedy, do you notice?) "My dear gossip," he pleads, but to no avail. According to the stage directions, Noah's wife pushes him away and then keeps on drinking and blabbing until Noah's sons forcibly carry their drunk mother onto the ark.

It goes without saying that Mrs. Noah's wine-sipping gossips are left to perish in the ensuing deluge.

But here in Rockland County, it had only rained three inches.

The End of the
World—for Marvin

The play I am going to play with is *J.B.* by Archibald MacLeish. I
first saw it when it was put on in 1957 at Brooklyn Tech by students
in Mary Heslin's English class. A year later, Mary would become
my wife and the play would open on Broadway. So the play I saw
was really the world premier. Mary had obtained a copy of the acting script from a friend of Archibald MacLeish. Mary's friend also
obtained MacLeish's permission to put on the play as a school exercise.

What brought the play to mind was my friend Marvin Penny's
essay on the nature of nothingness, or the beguiling question of how
nothing can beget something—or something like that. Marvin was
the only out-and-out atheist in our small group of eight wordsmiths
here in Rockland County. A point at issue as I perceived it (probably
incorrectly) is whether there is any need for a prime mover to set
off the big bang. Now I, being no physicist, or any kind of scientist
for that matter, feel absolutely unqualified to speculate, either intel-
ligently or randomly, in this area, but the thought of a prime mover
does raise a related question, one that the play, *J.B.*, is all about.

J.B. is a retelling of the Book of Job in a modern setting. As such, it
asks the question that reverberates down through the ages: Why does
God let bad things happen to good people?

In the biblical account, you may recall, Satan bets God that if Job,
a good, God-fearing man, is subjected to enough misery, he will curse
God. God gives Satan a free hand. Satan sees to it that Job loses everything: land, wealth, children, wife, and health. Job finally asks God,
"Why me?" God explains in a whirlwind, which, I understand, means
we are not let in on the secret. In any event, Job remains steadfast,
Satan loses the bet, and Job gets everything back and more.

The modern J.B. is a millionaire businessman who experiences
the same trials and tribulations that beset ancient Job. Were the play

written today instead of half a century ago, J.B.'s downward spiral would begin with his having to give up a bonus that he had actually earned and deserved. (On second thought, I'd best not tamper with the plot.) A bit of verse recited in the play catches the conundrum around which the play revolves: "If God is God he is not good; if God is good he is not God." To paraphrase: if God is omnipotent, then he is bad for permitting unmerited misery; if God is good, then he must be powerless to stop unmerited misery, so he's not really in charge— not God at all. In the play, as in the biblical account, the conundrum remains unanswered. J.B. accepts the fact that life can be brutally unfair, but his understanding of God's ways to mankind recedes into mystery—beyond human comprehension utterly.

What has this to do with the idea of nothingness? Archibald MacLeish provides the link in one of his best-known poems, "The End of the World," which takes place in a circus. We are in the big top, watching the show. An armless man is lighting a match with his toes; a lion is nuzzling a woman's neck; a tiny girl is waltzing with a monkey when

> Quite unexpectedly the top blew off.

> And there, there overhead, there, there hung over
> Those thousands of white faces, those dazed eyes,
> There in the starless dark, the poise, the hover,
> There with vast wings across the cancelled skies,
> There in the sudden blackness the black pall
> Of nothing, nothing, nothing—nothing at all.

What a terrifying vision of annihilation the poem presents. A pictured nihilism—a reversal of the big bang—an implosion back into nothing.

And yet, in this vision of the world reduced to nothing, something has been created. Indeed, to me this poem wonderfully demonstrates our inexhaustible creative capacity. A poet takes the idea of the end of the world, its uncreation, if you will, and fits it into that most intricate design, the tightly controlled verse form of the sonnet. There it is: three quatrains, then a closed couplet; rhyme scheme *abab cdcd efef gg*.

Talk about bringing order out of chaos—of an artist's making something amazing and beautiful out of nothing! Now, Marvin, isn't that something!

Here is the opening part of the sonnet:

> Quite unexpectedly, as Vasserot
> The armless ambidextrian was lighting
> A match between his great and second toe,
> And Ralph the lion was engaged in biting
> The neck of Madame Sossman while the drum
> Pointed, and Teeny was about to cough
> In waltz-time swinging Jocko by the thumb
> Quite unexpectedly the top blew off.
>
>
> And there, there overhead, there, there hung over
> Those thousands of white faces, those dazed eyes,
> There in the starless dark, the poise, the hover,
> There with vast wings across the cancelled skies,
> There in the sudden blankness the black pall
>
> Of nothing, nothing, nothing—nothing at all.

The Jolly Song

The first song I ever learned has stayed with me over the years. From time to time I have sung it—"The Jolly Boys at School"—not out loud and usually only a few lines. What seems remarkable to me is that I remember its two stanzas and the refrain, though I was not yet of school age when I heard my mother singing it. I think she sang it fairly often—often enough for me to have learned the song by heart. In one of my memories, she is singing to herself, my five older siblings being away for the day at Hope Valley School. I am off to the side of the stove, listening.

> Oh they always seem so jolly, oh!
> So jolly, oh! So jolly, oh!
> Wherever they may be.

My mother is standing at the ironing board, moving the iron back and forth as she sings. She sets the iron down and folds the ironed blouse, singing all the while.

> They sing, they play,
> They laugh, ha, ha; they laugh ha, ha,
> They dance, they sing, what jolly boys are they.

I remember it as clearly as if it were yesterday—this scene from about eighty years ago.

What puzzles me now is that I have never heard anyone else sing this song. My older sisters sang a lot, but this song was not in their repertoire, which, in the pre-radio days, consisted almost entirely of songs from the school songbook, supplemented by our church's Gregorian chants and hymns. So my mother did not learn this happy, bouncy song from her older children. She must have learned it when she was just a little girl in her own school before her stepmother yanked her out of it at the age of eight—a grief to last a lifetime.

But this song my mother learned in her two years in school stayed with her, which brings me back to my puzzlement over never having heard anyone else sing it. So this morning I entered the lines "Song about Jolly Boys" into a search engine and got three hits. The first was a news item about local school activities in *The Brookfield Courier*, Madison County, New York, April 10, 1881. The article said "The younger boys of the school . . . rendered a very happy song entitled 'What Jolly Boys Are We.'" That was all. My second hit yielded a similar reference in a New Zealand newspaper in 1883. The third hit yielded all thirteen lines of the refrain under the heading "Songs Taught in the Public Schools." The newspaper was—I couldn't believe my eyes—the *Rockland County Journal*, Nyack, New York, Saturday, April 1, 1871. A paper from right where I was sitting! And straining credulity even further, the words were exactly as I remembered them:

> And they always seem so jolly, oh!
> So jolly, oh! so jolly, oh!
> Wherever they may be.
> They dance, they sing,
> They laugh, ha, ha! They laugh, ha, ha!
> They dance, they sing, what jolly boys are we.
> Fa la la, Fa la la
> Fal to the ral la la la la la
> Slap, bang, here we go again
> What jolly boys are we.

It wasn't until I had children of my own that I finally made a connection between my mother's singing about jolly schoolchildren and the schooling she was denied. Singing was her way, I have come to think, of dealing with the heartbreak of having the door to the classroom slammed shut in her face. That song, "The Jolly Boys," was something valuable she retrieved, that she held on to, from her brief stay in school. It gave her something to build on.

A song, a ditty, a snippet like that can reverberate in mysterious ways. There is the fact that my older siblings were the very first in our rural district to go to high school. Then all four of my sisters became teachers, as I eventually did too. In suggesting that I go to a Franciscan seminary all the way in Pennsylvania, my mother was nurturing the indefinite possibility of a vocation to the priesthood, but definitely securing for me a better education than was locally available.

I met the woman I married in graduate school when she was already a high school teacher. Mary loved school and teaching. She did all the research and consulting and planning that made it possible for our six children to attend some really good prep schools, securing for them better educations than our local high school offered, and opening the door to their higher educations.

After I found the entire refrain of mother's song in the 1871 issue of the *Rockland County Journal*, I rushed downstairs to share this coincidence with my son Paul, who was home from Paris, and my daughter Mary Frances, home from Los Angeles. They were home because

that evening they would join me and all their other siblings at a gala dinner where Columbia College would award Mike, our oldest, with the 2013 John Jay Award for distinguished professional achievement.

School days. *Left*: Me in front of my one-room, prairie schoolhouse. *Above*: Mary appearing in a *New York Times* photo of a Brooklyn public school (front row, center, with braids).

One purpose of these awards—Mike's was one of five awarded that year—was to fund scholarships, making financial aid available to talented students who would otherwise not be able to attend Columbia College. It was a lavish, black-tie affair with about seven hundred guests, so we were all dressed to the nines, my four sons and I in tuxedos and my two daughters all coiffed and gowned.

While Mike was giving his speech, I experienced a pleasant intermingling of emotions, beginning with a sense that my wife was present too, invisible, as a hovering joy. I looked at my children and their spouses and my grandchildren seated around me and at Mike at the lectern and I was glad beyond words. It felt good to be part of a continuity—remember that earlier in the day I had finally found the school song my mother used to sing. So when the master of ceremonies moved the celebration along to its conclusion, I thought of my mother's singing and for an irrational split second before the glee club began, I anticipated hearing, "They dance, they sing . . ."

But no, the glee club went straight into a resounding rendition of the Columbia school song, "Sans Souci" [No Worries], and that was all right too.

My six children and me in 2013 all spiffed up. *Seated, from left to right*: Ann, Mary Frances. *Standing*: Paul, John, me, Mike, James.

Afterword

The Fine Print, Historically Speaking, and Further Reading

Family lore is, by its nature, subjective. In my case, family stories have traveled through three separate countries in two different languages. Nonetheless, the history of the Volga Germans has benefited from renewed interest and an ever-increasing body of research and scholarship. This essay is thus intended to put my family's experience into broader historical perspective, with suggested reading for those interested in learning more about the Volga Germans.

Their story begins in war-torn Europe, or, more specifically, in the aftermath of the bloody Seven Years' War, which raged from 1756 to 1763. (The North American extension of that conflict is known as the French and Indian War.) Residents of Hesse, in present-day Germany, were deeply affected, suffering from forced conscription, plunder, and the high taxes associated with warfare, not to mention the horror of war itself. Many Hessians and other Germans from adjoining war-ravished areas yearned to seek better lives elsewhere.[1]

---

1. Fred C. Koch, *The Volga Germans: In Russia and the Americas, from 1763 to the Present* (University Park: Pennsylvania State University Press, 1977), 7. On Hessian anguish at a century and a half of strife, exorbitant taxation, and enforced labor to benefit "profligate princelings" and their foreign wars, see also Irina Mukhina, *The Germans of the Soviet Union* (London: Routledge, 2007), 9.

Meanwhile, Catherine the Great, newly crowned Empress of Russia but an ethnic German, was seeking to populate her empire's wild, lawless southeastern frontier along the Volga River with dependable, permanent settlers who would introduce more advanced agricultural methods. Almost immediately after her coronation in 1762, she issued an invitation to potential settlers. It was so vaguely worded, however, that it drew little response. Her second invitation, called the Manifesto of July 22, 1763, set forth the enticing details, most notably freedom from Russian governmental intrusion, as well as a perpetual exemption from military service.[2]

Catherine the Great was offering exactly what the Hessian people, and others from the Rhineland, the Palatinate, and Saxony, longed for—relief from the misery, deprivation, and strife imposed on them. From 1764 to 1769, some eight thousand families emigrated from those regions to the lower Volga River Valley (in today's Russian Federation, near Kazakhstan, roughly between the present-day cities of Kamyšin and Balakovo). They formed 104 distinct colonies, of which 72 were Protestant and 32 Catholic. Then, as quickly as the door had been opened, it was slammed shut again; having exhausted its funds, Catherine the Great's program was summarily ended.[3]

This squares with the earliest history I have of my family. I know that my great-great-great-great-grandfather Johann Georg Schmidtberger was born in 1740 in what I think was Regensburg (present-day Germany) and emigrated in 1767 to the Herzog colony along the Volga River.[4]

Conditions on the desolate, windswept Russian steppe were dreadful. The colonists endured everything from wolf attacks to

2. Koch, *The Volga Germans*, 6 (all dates in Russia prior to 1918 refer to the Julian calendar then still in use).

3. James W. Long, *From Privileged to Dispossessed: The Volga Germans, 1860–1917* (Lincoln: University of Nebraska Press, 1988), 42. See also Koch, *The Volga Germans*, 8.

4. Catherine's Manifesto of July 22, 1763, was translated into German and circulated widely in Regensburg. The city also served as a staging ground for emigrant departures to Russia. George J. Walters, *Wir Wollen Deutsche Bleiben: The Story of the Volga Germans* (Kansas City, MO: Halcyon House Publishers, 1993), 42, 44. That said, other members of my family place our earliest roots in the Alsace region.

marauding Kirghiz tribes.[5] Blizzards, famine, and drought exacerbated their misery. Isolated geographically, linguistically, and in almost every other way imaginable, the colonists struggled mightily—and suffered terribly—before, as the generations started to pass, transforming their allotted land into productive, thriving farms.

Two particular points about Volga German farming bear mention. First, the colonists did not own their own land; a farmer and his heirs had a right to exploit his allocation as long as he did so. Called the *mir* system, which was then common in Russia, a farmer had what is known as a "usurfuctuary tenure" on the land—that is, the right to exploit it—but no title to it. Title to the land belonged to the village council (known as the Gemeinde).[6] Thus, land was allocated by the Russian government to the colonies, who then allocated it among their members; there was no possibility of purchasing land.

A second point was the question of Volga German fertility off the fields: they had enormous families. The population of the original 27,000 settlers dipped to a low of 23,000 in 1775 due to the harsh conditions, but then began to rebound, reaching approximately 55,000 by 1811.[7] These two points—limited farmland with no possibility of purchasing additional land and robust fertility—would eventually come into dire conflict. Before that, about a hundred years of peace and prosperity would pass.

In 1871, as part of Tsar Alexander II's Great Reforms, the Russian government enacted policies with far-reaching consequences for the Volga Germans. As historian James W. Long explains, "In its relations with the colonists, the government changed radically: formerly a special guardian or protector of the settlers, it now became an

5. Alexandria Dinges, "Three Countries, One People: How the Volga Deutsch Survived the West," *Voces Novae: Chapman University Historical Review* 4, no. 1 (2012): 45. See also Koch, *The Volga Germans*, 32.

6. Tony Waters, "Towards a Theory of Ethnic Identity and Migration: The Formation of Ethnic Enclaves by Migrant Germans in Russia and North America," *International Migration Review* 29, no. 2 (Summer 1995): 515–44, esp. 525. See also Koch, *The Volga Germans*, 31, 80.

7. Koch, *The Volga Germans*, 69. A much later study shows that the average family size among Volga Germans was 9.5, compared to 6.5 for former state peasants and 6.1 for former serfs. Long, *From Privileged to Dispossessed*, 68.

unresponsive and insensitive bureaucracy, often hostile to and jealous of what it perceived to be an unintegrated and ungrateful pampered foreign element."[8] Worse, the Russian government revoked Catherine the Great's military exemption—the one granted "in perpetuity"—which was viewed as a profound and fundamental betrayal.

Meanwhile in the United States, President Abraham Lincoln signed the Homestead Act on May 20, 1862, granting untilled land to those willing to farm it. Even more important was the Ameri-

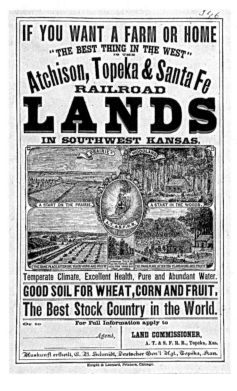

can government's grant of land to promote railroads, upwards of 130 to 155 million acres between 1850 and 1871. Railroads require passengers and freight to survive—and unsettled land provides neither—so the railroads launched advertising campaigns aimed at potential settlers, and sold those settlers the land they'd been granted. Long states, "It is no exaggeration to state that the ... railroads initiated and organized the colonization of Kansas, Nebraska, and the Dakotas from the numerous Germans from Russia."[9]

In 1873, catastrophic crop failure added to the Volga Germans' woes in Russia. In 1874, a meeting was held in the Herzog colony, attended by some three thousand representatives of Catholic com-

8. Long, *From Privileged to Dispossessed*, 16–17. See also Koch, *The Volga Germans*, 198.

9. Long, *From Privileged to Dispossessed*, 120–21.

munities. Five emissaries were selected to travel to the United States and report back. The five Catholic emissaries joined nine Protestant emissaries and traveled to the United States that year, returning with prairie grass, soil samples, and abundant literature from the railroad companies.[10] According to chronicler George Walters, "The Volga Germans who wanted to emigrate did not want to make the same mistake their forebears had made one hundred and ten years earlier, when they blindly accepted the words of Russian agents, and went off to a faraway land they knew nothing about. Before emigrating this time, representatives were chosen to select the new land."[11]

Even before their grievances with the Russian government had reached the boiling point, the Volga German colonists had been made aware of the opportunities in America in general, and the Homestead Act in particular. A certain Reverend Wilhelm Staerkel, a Reformed minister, traveled to Missouri and Kansas as a missionary in the 1860s, returning to the Volga in 1869, much impressed with what he saw: "he told his listeners that if he were a farmer, he would rather move to America than become a soldier in Russia."[12]

In October of 1875, five families left Katharinenstadt, eventually reaching Topeka, Kansas, which would become a hub for Catholic Volga Germans, just as Lincoln, Nebraska, would become a hub for Protestant Volga Germans. By 1876/77, Catholics from the eastern side of the Volga River had founded Liebental, south of Hays, Kansas, and then five additional villages, including Pfeifer and Herzog (Victoria).[13] Of course, the reader will recognize Pfeifer as where my

---

10. Koch, *The Volga Germans*, 204–7.

11. Walters, *Wir Wollen Deutsche Bleiben*, 119.

12. Koch, *The Volga Germans*, 205.

13. Ibid., 212. The immigrant families waited in Topeka while the men scouted land to the west. They took the Atchison, Topeka & Santa Fe to Great Bend, but thought that the price of land there, $5 per acre, was too high. They returned to Topeka and this time, accompanied by agents Adam Roedelheimer and Martin Allen, took the Kansas Pacific railroad to the Hays area, where land cost less—some $2 to $2.50 per acre—and this is where they settled. Norman E. Saul, "The Migration of the Russian-Germans to Kansas," *Kansas Historical Quarterly* 40, no. 1 (Spring 1974): 38–62. See also Reverend Francis S. Laing, *German-Russian Settlements in Ellis County, Kansas* (Topeka: Kansas State Historical Society, 1910), 6–7.

mother's family settled, and Herzog/Victoria, where my father's family settled. All total, between 80,000 and 100,000 Volga Germans left Russia, principally for the Great Plains, between 1874 and 1914.[14]

My father's family left Russia in 1892. This places him far from the avant-garde, and his relatively late arrival explains why the land he eventually purchased was so far from the village—all the other, closer land, was already taken. Still, the timing of his departure is not necessarily surprising, since, as Long explains, "the 1889–92 period was the most dreadful experienced in the Volga German settlements since their founding" due to famine brought on by drought and crop failure.[15]

The economics of the Volga German migration are nuanced. Historian James Long states that "immigration to America was an alternative only for the wealthier and nonindebted." Fred Koch, on the other hand, states that "most Volga Germans entered the New World with little money."[16] Both are probably right. Recall that land in the Volga colonies was owned by the colony itself, not by individual farmers. Thus, if a farmer wished to emigrate, his allotted land was simply returned to the community without payment. Instead, the primary way to raise capital was through the sale of personal possessions.[17] Others had entrepreneurial undertakings, such as my grandfather's shoe business, that generated relative wealth and would have provided the means to immigrate.

To demonstrate the varying distribution of wealth in the colonies along the Volga, Long cites a fascinating 1888 survey of the number of draft animals owned per household. There are striking divergences, with 18.1 percent having no draft animals at all, qualifying

14. Dittmar Dahlmann, "The Russian Germans: A Heterogeneous Minority during the First World War," in *Germans as Minorities during the First World War*, edited by Panikos Panayi (Burlington, VT: Ashgate, 2014), 173.

15. Long, *From Privileged to Dispossessed*, 79. Long includes a description of colonists feeding the thatch from their roofs to their livestock in a desperate—and unsuccessful—attempt to keep them alive.

16. Long, *From Privileged to Dispossessed*, 120n16; Koch, *The Volga Germans*, 3.

17. Long, *From Privileged to Dispossessed*, 120n16; Koch, *The Volga Germans*, 210 (use of household auctions to raise funds to emigrate; community permission—and payment of all taxes and debts—required to leave).

them as "indigent," and 12.6 percent having only one such animal—insufficient to exploit their own allotments—and thus qualifying these families as "not well-off." The report indicates that those with greater than four draft animals were considered as solidly established and in a position to hire labor, and one can see that the majority of households (60.1 percent) owned somewhere between two and ten draft animals. A very small fraction—an oddly prophetic 1.2 percent—owned more than twenty draft animals.[18] Clearly, there were significant variations in wealth among the colonists.

Relative wealth on the Russian steppe, though, did not necessarily translate into wealth and status in the new world. The Volga Germans were largely regarded as occupying the very bottom of the social order in the United States. Sociologist Hattie Plum Williams stated that, "In the west, another nationality denominated 'Russian' occupies the lowest seat in the localities where he has settled."[19]

Newly arrived immigrants typically relied on networks of extended family for support. Thus, while my father's father—Johannes Schmidtberger—had the means to *leave* Russia, the key to his successful *arrival* in America may have had nothing to do with the Schmidtbergers at all, but rather with his wife's family, the Appelhanses. His wife, Catharine Appelhans Schmidtberger, had an older sister, Magdalena, who had emigrated in 1876 to Ellis County, Kansas, with her husband, Martin Riedel, and the newly arrived Schmidtbergers stayed with them until they were in a position to establish themselves independently.[20]

18. Long, *From Privileged to Dispossessed*, 66.

19. Dinges, "Three Countries, One People," 50, citing Hattie Plum Williams, *A Social Study of the Russian German* (Nebraska: University of Nebraska Press, 1916). In addition, great confusion was caused by the fact that the Volga Germans were not the only ethnically German colonists who had been enticed into, and later left, Russia. In fact, the Black Sea Germans—brought by Tsar Alexander I in the early 1800s to farm in what is present-day Ukraine—are much better known. These populations had completely different experiences, and Koch, for example, notes that "the Black Sea Germans often came to the United States with cash and those from the Volga only rarely"; Koch, *The Volga Germans*, 218.

20. Ellis Island records include a passenger manifest from the ship *Italia*, arriving in New York on June 28, 1892, with my father, his younger brother, and their parents aboard. My

After the initial hardships and before the throes of the Dust Bowl, the immigrants largely thrived in their new homes. According to Timothy Kloberdanz, "because of their idealistic attitudes toward hard work and its resulting benefits, many Volga Germans experienced a relatively rapid rise in economic status and eventually left their jobs in the fields to become independent farmers and landowners."[21] Their success, particularly with regard to agriculture, was largely based on their history of communal farming: according to Dinges, "the Russian Germans were successful in their agricultural exploits because of their willingness to work communally.[22]

As a result, "by 1903, Ellis County, Kansas, had one of the highest total crop yields and some of the highest crop yields per acre of farmed land in the state."[23] This is the very same Ellis County that, according to Kloberdanz, contained Volga German Catholic settlements that most closely resembled the former colonies along the Volga.[24] The very same Ellis County that my family called home. With the rise in fortunes would eventually come a concomitant rise in status: according to Koch, "the inflammatory slur 'those damn Rooshians' has been silenced and most of those who uttered it never really knew who those people were."[25]

Finally, our thoughts turn to those left behind on the vast expanse of the Russian steppe. While many left, many others stayed behind. The experience from my own family is instructive: my grandfather Johannes Schmidtberger was the only one of six siblings to leave, and his wife, Catharine Appelhans, was only the second of eight siblings to leave. The rest stayed.

grandfather (and father) are listed on the manifest as "farmers." Directly below their names one sees Martin Appelhans (misspelled as "Abelhans"), accompanying his daughter and son-in-law's family.

21. Timothy J. Kloberdanz, "The Volga Germans in Old Russia and in Western North America: Their Changing World View," *Anthropological Quarterly* 48, no. 4 (1975): 209–22, esp. 216.

22. Dinges, "Three Countries, One People," 53.

23. Ibid., 54, citing A. E. Davisson, "Union Pacific Railway Company Agricultural Bulletin: The Wheat Crops of Kansas and Nebraska," Kansas Historical Foundation, August 15, 1903, Item 210044.

24. Kloberdanz, "Their Changing World View," 215.

25. Koch, *The Volga Germans*, 221.

The Volga Germans remaining in Russia suffered from terrible famines that decimated the population in 1921 to 1922, though the end, when it came, was political. Beginning in 1941, Stalin started deporting the Volga Germans, primarily to Siberia, under appalling conditions.[26] On August 28, 1941, the Presidium of the Supreme Court of the Soviet Union announced that thousands of "spies" had been unmasked among the Volga Germans, and the government had the remaining 380,000 deported to the Altai and to Kazakhstan, but mostly to Siberia. In effect, Long writes, "Stalin erased the Volga Germans from history."[27]

Further Reading

Dahlmann, Dittmar. "The Russian Germans: A Heterogeneous Minority during the First World War." In *Germans as Minorities during the First World War*, edited by Panikos Panayi, 171–88. Burlington, VT: Ashgate, 2014.

Dinges, Alexandria. "Three Countries, One People: How the Volga Deutsch Survived the West." *Voces Novae: Chapman University Historical Review* 4, no. 1 (2012): 43–69.

Egan, Timothy. *The Worst Hard Time: The Untold Story of Those Who Survived the Great American Dust Bowl*. Boston: Houghton Mifflin, 2006.

Height, Joseph. *Paradise on the Steppe: A Cultural History of the Kutschurgan, Beresan, and Liebental Colonists, 1804–1972*. 2nd ed. Bismarck: North Dakota Historical Society of Germans from Russia, 1980. Primary focus on the Black Sea Germans.

Kloberdanz, Timothy J. "The Volga Germans in Old Russia and in Western North America: Their Changing World View." *Anthropological Quarterly* 48, no. 4 (1975): 209–22.

Koch, Fred C. *The Volga Germans: In Russia and the Americas, from 1763 to the Present*. University Park: Pennsylvania State University Press, 1977. A seminal work and, along with James W. Long's *From Privileged to Dispossessed*, provides a comprehensive history. These two works

---

26. Mukhina, *The Germans of the Soviet Union*, 42–45, 90.

27. Long, *From Privileged to Dispossessed*, 252.

should mark the starting point of any search for an understanding of
the Volga Germans.

Laing, Reverend Francis S. *German-Russian Settlements in Ellis County,
Kansas*. Reprinted from *Kansas Historical Collections* 11. Topeka: Kansas State Historical Society, 1910.

Long, James W. *From Privileged to Dispossessed: The Volga Germans, 1860–
1917*. Lincoln: University of Nebraska Press, 1988.

Mukhina, Irina. *The Germans of the Soviet Union*. London: Routledge, 2007.

Pauley, Bruce F. *Pioneering History on Two Continents*. Lincoln, NE: Potomac Books, 2014.

Penner, Mil. *Section 27: A Century on a Family Farm*. Lawrence: University
Press of Kansas, 2002.
    Primary focus on the Mennonite experience.

Riney-Kehrberg, Pamela. *Rooted in Dust: Surviving Drought and Depression
in Southwestern Kansas*. Lawrence: University Press of Kansas, 1994.
    A factual, detailed presentation of the Dust Bowl that includes interviews with many survivors.

Saul, Norman E. "The Migration of the Russian-Germans to Kansas." *Kansas Historical Quarterly* 40, no. 1 (Spring 1974): 38–62.

Shortridge, James R. *Peopling the Plains: Who Settled Where in Frontier
Kansas*. Lawrence: University Press of Kansas, 1995.

Stratton, Joanna. *Pioneer Women: Voices from the Kansas Frontier*. New
York: Touchstone, 1982.
    Includes a brief history of the founding of Victoria, Kansas, by Scottish
    gentry and their subsequent departure not long thereafter.

Stumpp, Karl. *The German-Russians: Two Centuries of Pioneering*. Translated by Joseph Height. Bonn, NY: Atlantic-Forum, 1967. Originally
published as *Die Russlanddeutschen: Zweihundert Jahre Unterwegs*
(Freilassing in Bayern: Pannonia-Verlag, 1965).

Toepfer, Amy Brungardt, and Agnes Dreiling. *Conquering the Wind: An Epic
Migration from the Rhine to the Volga to the Plains of Kansas*. Rev. ed.
Lincoln, NE: American Historical Society of Germans from Russia, 1982.
    A gem with a detailed history of the founding of each of the Volga
    German towns in Ellis County, Kansas.

Walters, George J. *Wir Wollen Deutsche Bleiben: The Story of the Volga
Germans*. Kansas City, MO: Halcyon House Publishers, 1982; reprint
ed., 1993.
    A Volga German himself, Walters provides a valuable insiders' view.

Waters, Tony. "Towards a Theory of Ethnic Identity and Migration: The Formation of Ethnic Enclaves by Migrant Germans in Russia and North America." *International Migration Review* 29, no. 2 (Summer 1995), 515–44.

Weigel, Lawrence. *Volga German Traditions.* Hays, KS: Sunflower Chapter, American Historical Society of Germans from Russia, 2013.
This volume collects the articles written by Mr. Weigel for the *Ellis County Star* from 1972 to 1976, including songs, anecdotes, and daily experiences of Volga Germans. A real treasure for readers interested in the feel of daily life in Volga German towns.

Williams, Hattie Plum. *A Social Study of the Russian German.* Lincoln: University of Nebraska Press, 1916.

Online Resources

Kansas Historical Society/Kansas Historical Foundation: www.kshs.org

The American Historical Society of Germans from Russia, Sunflower Chapter (Hays, Kansas): http://www.sunflowerchapterofahsgr.net

The Center for Volga German Studies at Concordia University: http://cvgs.cu-portland.edu

Germans from Russia Heritage Collection, North Dakota State University Libraries: https://library.ndsu.edu/grhc/

The International Center for German-Russian Studies at Colorado State University: http://engagement.colostate.edu/russian-federation-partnerships-at-csu-russian-federation-partnerships-at-csu/

©Lydia MacLear Photographs

About the Author

Loren Schmidtberger is professor emeritus of English at Saint Peter's University in New Jersey. His writing has appeared in journals such as *American Literature*, *Cross Currents*, *Thought*, *The Mississippi Quarterly*, and *America*.

Born in 1928, Dr. Schmidtberger was raised on a farm near Victoria, Kansas. He attended St. Fidelis Minor Seminary in Herman, Pennsylvania, before obtaining his BA from Fort Hays State University. Following service in the U.S. Army during the Korean War, he obtained his PhD from Fordham University.

Dr. Schmidtberger taught at Saint Peter's University for fifty-one years, specializing in American literature, particularly the works of William Faulkner. He was appointed the Will and Ariel Durant Professor of Humanities in 1991.

CPSIA information can be obtained
at www.ICGtesting.com
Printed in the USA
BVHW041235210222
629674BV00014B/487